The Overseer

THE OVERSEER

Plantation Management in the Old South

William Kauffman Scarborough

The University of Georgia Press

Athens

To Fletcher Melvin Green

Published in 1984 by the University of Georgia Press
Athens, Georgia 30602
© 1966 by Louisiana State University Press
Introduction to this edition © 1984
by the University of Georgia Press

Text design by Jules B. McKee

The paper in this book meets the guidelines for
permanence and durability of the Committee on
Production Guidelines for Book Longevity of the
Council on Library Resources.

Printed in the United States of America
88 87 86 85 84   5 4 3 2 1

Library of Congress Cataloging in Publication Data

Scarborough, William Kauffman.
  The overseer: plantation management in the Old South.

  Reprint. Originally published: Baton Rouge: Louisiana
State University Press, c1966. With new introd.
  Bibliography: p.
  Includes index.
  1. Plantations—Southern States—Management—History.
2. Slavery—Southern States—History. I. Title.
HD1471.U52A137 1984   307.7'2   84-8701
ISBN 0-8203-0732-7 (alk. paper)
ISBN 0-8203-0733-5 (pbk.: alk. paper)

73534

Contents

Illustrations and Tables   vi

Acknowledgments   vii

Preface to the 1984 Edition   ix

Introduction   xix

1 ROLE OF THE OVERSEER
   IN THE PLANTATION ESTABLISHMENT   3

2 CONTRACTUAL AND SOCIAL RELATIONS   20

3 A STATISTICAL VIEW OF THE OVERSEER   51

4 MANAGERIAL DUTIES AND RESPONSIBILITIES   67

5 DISCORD BETWEEN OVERSEER AND PLANTER   102

6 THE OVERSEER DURING THE CIVIL WAR   138

7 THE OVERSEER ELITE   158

8 THE STEWARD   178

9 CONCLUSION   195

   Notes   203

   Bibliography   229

   Index   243

Illustrations

NEGROES AT HOME   15

PICKING COTTON   37

COTTON-GIN—GINNING COTTON   110

HARVESTING THE RICE   151

All illustrations reproduced from *Harper's New Monthly Magazine.*

Tables

ENUMERATION OF OVERSEERS IN LEADING PLANTATION STATES, 1850-1860 / 10

SLAVEHOLDERS AND SLAVES, 1850 / 11

SLAVEHOLDERS AND SLAVES, 1860 / 11

AGRICULTURAL PRODUCTION, BY STAPLE REGIONS, OF SELECTED SOUTHERN COUNTIES, 1860 / 53

STATISTICAL ANALYSIS OF OVERSEERS IN TOBACCO AND GRAIN REGION, 1860 / 55

STATISTICAL ANALYSIS OF OVERSEERS ON RICE COAST, 1860 / 57

STATISTICAL ANALYSIS OF OVERSEERS IN SUGAR PARISHES, 1860 / 59

STATISTICAL ANALYSIS OF OVERSEERS IN COTTON BELT, 1860 / 62

COMPOSITE STATISTICAL ANALYSIS OF SOUTHERN OVERSEERS, 1860 / 64

Acknowledgments

IN a study of this nature, the author necessarily becomes indebted to many persons for their assistance and encouragement during the long period of research and writing. My deepest debt of gratitude is owed to Professor Fletcher M. Green of the University of North Carolina, in whose seminar the foundations for this study were laid, and who, in subsequent years, continued to assist me with his incisive criticism and stimulating guidance. Special thanks are also due to Professor J. Carlyle Sitterson, Professor Cornelius O. Cathey, and Professor Stephen Baxter for their useful comments and suggestions while the initial manuscript was being prepared for submission as a doctoral dissertation at the University of North Carolina.

Professor James C. Bonner of the Woman's College of Georgia read the manuscript in its entirety before the final version was prepared and offered several helpful suggestions based upon his many years of research in the field of southern agricultural history. I wish to thank the editor of *Agricultural History*, James H. Shideler of the University of California at Davis, for permission to quote portions of my article on the plantation overseer, which appeared in the January, 1964, issue of that journal.

Perhaps no aspect of this project has been more enjoyable to me than the perusal of original manuscript sources in various archival repositories throughout the South. I gratefully acknowledge the cheerful and knowledgeable assistance rendered by the staffs of the Alabama Department of Archives and History (especially Mrs. Virginia Jones, Librarian); the Mississippi Department of Archives and History (especially Miss Charlotte Capers, Director, and Laura D. S. Harrell, Research Assistant); the Louisiana State University Department of Archives (especially V. L. Bedsole, Archivist, and Miss Marcelle F. Schertz, Reference Archivist); and the Southern Historical Collection of the University of North Carolina (especially Mrs. Wesley Wallace and Miss Brooke Allan). It is a distinct pleasure to acknowledge the splendid cooperation and invaluable aid offered by the editorial staff of the Louisiana State University Press, particularly Charles East, Assistant Director, and Mrs. Theodore Hubert, Editor. Finally, my wife and children have displayed exemplary patience and sympathetic understanding during the long (to them, it must have seemed interminable) period in which this volume was growing to maturity.

WILLIAM K. SCARBOROUGH

Hattiesburg, Mississippi
October 24, 1965

Preface to the 1984 Edition

IN the two decades which have elapsed since this book first appeared in 1966, there has been a remarkable proliferation of writings on slavery and the plantation system. Characterized for the most part by scholarship of high quality, these works have utilized new sources, innovative methodology, and the comparative approach to offer fresh insights into the institutions and inhabitants of the slave South. For example, such scholars as John W. Blassingame and Eugene D. Genovese have mined the hitherto virtually untapped slave autobiographies and narratives to view the South's "peculiar institution" from the perspective of those who endured its iniquities, thereby clarifying slave attitudes and personality types. Less successful have been the efforts of the so-called econometricians to apply quantitative methods to the economics of American Negro slavery.

The principal focus in this galaxy of recent works has been on the slaves and their masters, with only incidental attention to other functionaries in the plantation-slave regime. With one notable exception, there have been few substantive challenges to the interpretation of plantation management which I advanced nearly twenty years ago. Consequently, there is little in recent southern historiography or in my own subsequent research to induce me to modify substantially the conclusions reached at that time. However, the treatment of overseers in two major studies published in the mid-1970s—Genovese's magisterial *Roll, Jordan, Roll* and the pioneering cliometric work by Robert Fogel and Stanley Engerman, *Time on the Cross*—does warrant a response.

In his brief discussion of overseers, Genovese quite properly criticized me for failing to give sufficient weight to the role of slaves in exploiting the natural antipathy between overseer and planter which I discuss at length in chapter 5.[1] I am now persuaded that blacks played a much more active part in defining the limits of the slave system than was apparent to me when I wrote this book. In light of recent scholarship, it is clear that slaves deliberately sought to promote disharmony among personnel in the managerial hierarchy—for example, between driver and overseer, overseer and proprietor—in order to ameliorate the material and psychological conditions of their daily lives. There is ample evidence of such tactics in this book, but my original analysis was not sufficiently explicit.

Whenever a new overseer was employed, there was invariably a period of testing as the slaves sought to determine the disciplinary parameters of the new regime. If, after the initial period of testing, the slaves were satisfied with their new manager, affairs usually proceeded smoothly and there were few disciplinary problems. In the contrary event, the disgruntled slaves might seek to oust the overseer by acts of massive disobedience or, if circumstances did not warrant such extreme action, to undermine his authority and mitigate the harshness of his administration by carrying complaints directly to the owner.

Most planters were well aware of the divisive techniques employed by their cunning black wards. Nevertheless, much to the consternation of plantation managers throughout the South, most slaveholders permitted—and some explicitly directed—their slaves to carry complaints over the head of the overseer to the master. To comprehend why they did so, it is only necessary to understand the antithetical roles played by owner and manager under the slave system. The overseer represented the most odious features of slavery. It was he "who had to absorb the bitterness of bondage" felt by those whose labor he directed and upon whom he inflicted punishment.[2] The planter, on the other hand, precisely because of the presence of a hired intermediary who administered the most distasteful elements of the system, was enabled to assume the role of benevolent protector to the members of his black family.

In essence, then, the practice of affording southern slaves a direct avenue of appeal to their masters, or the latter's agents, served as a safety valve, imparting flexibility to the system and alleviating frustrations which were potentially explosive. In my judgment, this safety-valve concept explains, at least in part, why the vast majority of large slaveholders elected to retain the overseer system despite all its deficiencies and why insensitive planters, like Bennet H. Barrow of Louisiana, who dispensed with white overseers had so many disciplinary problems. Thus, as Genovese has so perceptively observed, "both masters and slaves in effect used the overseers to detach themselves from the harsher side of the regime."[3]

The most direct challenge to my analysis of plantation management in the Old South was mounted by Fogel and Engerman in their controversial, and now largely discredited, study entitled *Time on the Cross*. In support of their central theme of black achievement under adversity, these two cliometricians professed to find evidence that blacks served in top managerial positions "on a majority of the large plantations" in the antebellum South.[4] More specifically, basing their conclusions exclusively on data from the 1860 census, they contended that fewer than one-sixth of the proprietors of moderate-sized units (sixteen to fifty slaves) employed a white overseer, only one-fourth of the large planters (more than fifty slaves) did so, and only 30 percent of those owning slave parcels in excess of one hundred utilized white managers.[5]

Their estimate concerning moderate-sized holdings is scarecely surprising since presumably those units at the lower end of the scale were substantially more numerous than those at the upper end. No one has ever contended that the employment of hired overseers was common on units of less than thirty slaves. Indeed, I have argued that a distinction should be made between the total number of slaves and the number of working field hands, and that utilization of white overseers increased significantly as the number of field hands entered the range between twenty and thirty (pp. 8–9). However, the Fogel-Engerman assertions concerning managerial personnel on large plantations were truly astonishing and utterly at variance with the great mass of evidence which can be adduced from plantation records, agricultural periodicals, travel accounts, legal stipulations, and the philosophical disposition of the planters.

Accordingly, I scrutinized the procedures by which Fogel and Engerman had formulated their conclusions about overseers, detected three major flaws in their methodology which collectively imparted an overwhelmingly downward bias to their estimate of white overseers on large units, and presented my findings at a conference entitled *"Time on the Cross:* A First Appraisal," held at the University of Rochester in October 1974. Other scholars in attendance at that conference were equally incredulous about the alleged discovery of large numbers of black overseers. Among these was Kenneth Stampp, who remarked that "procedures which cannot find white overseers on large plantations but discover black overseers instead, are not likely to win new converts among conventional historians."[6] Unfortunately, a projected symposium volume of papers presented at the Rochester conference was aborted, and my dissection of the Fogel-Engerman thesis regarding overseers was never disseminated beyond those who attended the meeting. In consequence, some later writers, most notably the distinguished southern historian Clement Eaton, have accepted without question the validity of the Fogel-Engerman data and have continued to propagate the misinformation initially unveiled in *Time on the Cross*.[7] I am pleased, therefore, to be afforded this opportunity to set the record straight.

The authors' conclusions about overseers were derived exclusively from the Parker-Gallman sample of 5,229 farms in 382 cotton-producing counties, drawn from the manuscript census schedules of 1860.[8] Data were compiled from Schedules 1, 2, and 4, which provide information concerning free inhabitants, slaves, and agricultural operations respectively. A sampling procedure was devised in which five-farm block samples were selected at random from every fourteenth page of Schedule 4, the agricultural census. Then the name of each farm operator in the sample was matched with the head of household in Schedule 1 and the slaveowner in Schedule 2 to obtain a profile of labor, management, and production on each farm. The five-farm blocks were extracted from the middle of larger blocks of nine farms, and, in the event that data for any of the middle five proved unreasonable or incomplete (for example, failure to obtain a match with Schedules 1 or 2), one of the outer four farms was substituted.[9]

Unfortunately, there are at least three serious problems with the methodology outlined above. To begin with, the sample from which

Fogel and Engerman drew their conclusions is unrepresentative of the entire plantation South.[10] Since the Parker-Gallman data base is limited to *cotton* counties, those units which, because of the size and complexity of their operations, were most likely to employ white overseers—namely, the rice and sugar plantations—were excluded from the sample. Even seasonal employees, such as sugar makers and engineers, were usually white on Louisiana sugar plantations. It strains credulity to infer that blacks were managing either these units or the huge rice estates in South Carolina, whose owners were commonly absent throughout the entire growing season. Since approximately one-third of the 1,980 plantation units counting one hundred or more slaves were rice or sugar plantations, the magnitude of their omission from the sample is readily apparent. Second, since the names of absentee owners normally do not appear in Schedule 1 of the county in which their agricultural property was located, it is likely that they too were excluded from the sample because of the failure to obtain a match with names on Schedules 2 and 4. Once again, for reasons so obvious they do not require elaboration, absentee plantations were more likely to be under the management of white overseers than resident units of comparable size.

After adopting a data base which excluded the managers of all rice and sugar plantations and a sampling technique which eliminated most overseers of absentee estates, Fogel and Engerman proceeded to commit yet another blunder—perhaps the most serious of all. By starting with the agricultural census and matching the names of farm operators with heads of household in Schedule 1, the data-gatherers *missed all overseers not actually listed in the households of farm operators*. The fact is, however, that a great many overseers were *not* listed in the household of the proprietor for whom they were overseeing. Some appear as heads of separate households adjacent to large plantations, which it is reasonable to assume they were managing. Others listed separately on the returns, such as managers of absentee properties, do not appear in close proximity to any agricultural unit. Still others are listed in clusters with several planters, and it is impossible to determine for whom each was overseeing.

In order to estimate the magnitude of the possible error resulting from the methodological procedures of Fogel and Engerman, I have scrutinized more closely my own census data on overseers. In the course of my research for this book, I compiled statistical information on *all* overseers listed in Schedule 1 of the 1860 census in seventeen sample counties throughout the South (see chapter 3). I have subsequently divided the overseers in each of these counties into three categories: those positively overseeing for a specific proprietor, those presumed to be managing for a specific planter, and those who could not be matched with a particular agricultural operator. Those in the last group are the most significant, for, presumably, they would *all* have been missed in the Parker-Gallman sample. The results show that the percentage of overseers which could not be matched with a specific farm unit ranged from a low of 18 percent in Hinds County, Mississippi, to a high of 71 percent in Northampton County, North Carolina. Other percentages, computed for random counties, include: Yazoo County, Mississippi (cotton), 34 percent; Terrebonne Parish, Louisiana (sugar), 43 percent; Lowndes County, Mississippi (cotton), 52 percent; Prince George County, Virginia (grain), 59 percent; and Colleton District, South Carolina (rice), 67 percent.[11]

It does not require a cliometrician to discern that, on the basis of these figures alone, the number of white overseers excluded by the Fogel-Engerman sampling technique was substantial indeed. Moreover, once again those most likely to have been managing large units were overlooked. On small holdings the overseer was frequently a relative of the farm operator or resided within his household. In either case, he would be listed as a member of the proprietor's household and, consequently, would be included in the Parker-Gallman sample. By contrast, those managing large units usually occupied a separate dwelling and were therefore listed separately on the census returns. These would not appear in the Parker-Gallman sample.

In their supplementary volume on evidence and methods, the authors of *Time on the Cross* applied percentages derived from the Parker-Gallman sample to the size distribution of slaveholdings in 1850 and deduced that no more than 40 percent of plantations with fifty or more slaves could have been using white overseers.[12] In the first place, it seems a questionable procedure to compare percentages obtained from 1860 data to total numbers derived from the 1850 census. But no matter. Since numbers is the name of the game, I will play it. And since Fogel and Engerman chose to make their estimate as a residual, I shall follow the like procedure—though doubtless in a less sophisticated manner than that to which econometricians are accustomed.

According to the census of 1860, there were a total of 26,000 overseers in the seven leading plantation states (see p. 10). In the same year, the number of upper-class planters (those owning fifty or more slaves) in the entire South was about 11,000, and the number of middle-class planters (those owning between fifteen and fifty slaves) approximated 100,000.[13] If we assume the accuracy of the Fogel-Engerman estimate that 14.5 percent of the middle-class planters had white overseers,[14] then the total number managing units of this size was about 14,500. Analyzing these figures, it becomes readily apparent that there were more than enough overseers in just the leading plantation states to provide a white manager for every one of the large plantations in the region plus the 14,500 medium units assumed by Fogel and Engerman to have had such an operative. Of course, not *all* large plantations had white managers, and, contrary to the impression conveyed in *Time on the Cross*, no reputable scholar has ever contended that they did. Thus, if we subtract those which did not employ such a functionary from the total of 11,000 and add that figure to the number of overseers enumerated in such other slave states as Tennessee and Arkansas, we can place several thousand overseers on units with fewer than ten slaves and still emerge with the conclusion that the white overseer was indeed a ubiquitous figure on large plantations of the slave South.

Thus, the Fogel-Engerman thesis that blacks played a major role in the top-level management of large southern plantations falls on all counts. Such an interpretation is inconsistent with virtually all evidence afforded by traditional sources, and the authors' inept use of census data invalidates the conclusions they have drawn from that source. For those obsessed with statistics, my best conjecture is that 90 percent of those units with one hundred or more slaves employed white managers and probably 75 percent of those with fifty or more slaves followed the same practice. In other words, the actual proportion of white overseers on large plantations in the antebellum South was three times the figure postulated by the authors of *Time on the Cross*.

Apart from its significance for this book, the failure of Fogel and Engerman to sustain their position on overseers calls into serious question their contention that blacks enjoyed considerable occupational mobility within the slave system—an interpretation which, in turn, is indispensable to their central theme of black achievement under adversity. But, more than this, their mishandling of the overseer question is symptomatic of one of the fundamental weaknesses of *Time on the Cross* and, indeed, of the "new economic history" generally. When faced with an apparent discrepancy between quantitative data and evidence from traditional sources, the cliometricians almost invariably accept the former as somehow more scientific and thus more valid than the latter. Instead of dismissing in such cavalier fashion the findings of traditional historians, they might render a greater service to the cause of truth by subjecting their own methods to intensive scrutiny when evidence adduced by those methods clashes sharply with well-established viewpoints.

I am indebted to Charles East, who, as assistant director of the Louisiana State University Press, was instrumental in bringing to fruition the original edition of this book and who, more recently, while serving in a like capacity with the University of Georgia Press, initiated the proposal for this paperback edition. I am particularly grateful to his successor, Malcolm Call, and the staff of the University of Georgia Press for their support in making my study of overseers once again available to students of the plantation South.

WILLIAM K. SCARBOROUGH

University of Southern Mississippi
June, 1984

Notes

1   Eugene D. Genovese, *Roll, Jordan, Roll: The World the Slaves Made* (New York: Pantheon Books, 1974), 682n32.

2   William D. Postell, *The Health of Slaves on Southern Plantations* (Baton Rouge: Louisiana State University Press, 1951), 24–25.

3   Genovese, *Roll, Jordan, Roll,* 21.

4   Robert W. Fogel and Stanley L. Engerman, *Time on the Cross: The Economics of American Negro Slavery* (Boston: Little, Brown and Company, 1974), I, 212.

5   *Ibid.,* I, 200.

6   Transcript of session, "A New Direction for Southern History?" October 24, 1974, p. A-77.

7   Clement Eaton, *A History of the Old South: The Emergence of a Reluctant Nation,* 3rd ed. (New York: Macmillan Company, 1975), 255, 391; Eaton, *Jefferson Davis* (New York: The Free Press, 1977), 38–39.

8   Letter from Stanley L. Engerman, August 5, 1974; Robert E. Gallman, "Self-Sufficiency in the Cotton Economy of the Antebellum South," *Agricultural History,* XLIV (January, 1970), 6; James D. Foust and Dale E. Swan, "Productivity and Profitability of Antebellum Slave Labor: A Micro-Approach," *ibid.,* 40n.

9   Foust and Swan, "Antebellum Slave Labor," 58–59; Gavin Wright, "Note on the Manuscript Samples Used in These Studies," *Agricultural History,* XLIV (January, 1970), 95–98.

10   Not only is the sample unrepresentative, but it is very small with respect to large plantation units. Materials provided to participants in the Rochester conference reveal that half of the 5,229 farm units in the Parker-Gallman sample had no slaves at all, only 651 had between sixteen and fifty slaves, and a mere 144 had slave parcels in excess of fifty.

11 It should be noted that these percentages have a substantial downward bias. Some of the overseers whom I have positively correlated with specific units were not listed in the household of the farm operator in Schedule 1. They were matched on the basis of information obtained from Schedule 2 or from sources outside the census.

12 Fogel and Engerman, *Time on the Cross*, II, 151–52.

13 Lewis C. Gray, *History of Agriculture in the Southern United States to 1860* (Washington: Carnegie Institution, 1933), I, 483.

14 Fogel and Engerman define medium-sized plantations as those with sixteen to fifty slaves, while Gray employs the range ten to fifty. Since few overseers were utilized on units of ten to fifteen slaves, any discrepancy arising from the difference in definition is negligible.

Introduction

NO figure occupied a position of greater importance
in the managerial hierarchy of the southern plantation system
than did the overseer. It was this agent who, in great measure,
determined the success or failure of planting operations on the
larger estates devoted to the production of staple agricultural
products. To the overseer were entrusted the welfare and supervision of the Negroes; the care of the land, stock, and farm
implements; the planting, cultivation, and harvesting of both
staple and subsistence crops; and many other responsibilities
associated with the management of a commercial agricultural
enterprise.

The key position of the plantation overseer has been conceded by most historians familiar with agricultural operations in the Old South. John Spencer Bassett described the overseer as the essential center of industrial operations in the plantation system.[1] Terming him a "neglected figure" in southern history, James Benson Sellers asserted that "no one played a more important role than he in the plantation regime." [2] Another authority on slavery and plantation agriculture, Kenneth M. Stampp, has observed that, despite their dissatisfaction with the performance of the overseer class, most planters "looked upon the overseer, with all his faults, as an indispensable cog in the plantation machinery." [3]

A contemporary traveler, Captain Basil Hall of the British Royal Navy, following a journey through the United States in 1827–28, characterized the overseer as "a very important personage . . . since much of the success of an estate, as well as the happiness or misery of the negroes—which appears to be nearly the same thing—depend upon his character." [4] Even members of the planter class, who were not usually blessed with the faculty of registering an objective appraisal of their managers, were compelled to acknowledge the utility, and even the indispensability, of the overseeing profession. Thus, Martin W. Philips, one of the foremost agricultural reformers in the Old South, regarded the position occupied by the overseer in temporal affairs to be "equal, if not superior to any class of men." [5]

Despite this recognition of his key importance, many secondary writers have created a stereotyped image of the overseer which, in this writer's judgment, does not accord with the facts. The overseer has frequently been pictured as a rough individual of humble background and dense ignorance who took delight in abusing the Negroes placed under his care and in thwarting the wishes of his employer. In one of two brief references to the managerial class, Carl Bridenbaugh charged that overseers were "brutal and unscrupulous." [6] George Dangerfield described the lot of slaves left to the mercy of an overseer as "sometimes intolerable," and characterized overseers as "a harsh and disillusioned set of men, who believed themselves to be the victims of the system that employed them, and whose abilities were measured solely by the amount of their production." [7]

Scholars of the present generation are deeply indebted to

such pioneer specialists in southern history as Lewis Cecil Gray, Ulrich Bonnell Phillips, Ralph Betts Flanders, and John Spencer Bassett, for without the labors of these truly great historians, studies such as this could never have been written. However, these writers have inadvertently contributed to the myth, created by the planter class and by superficial travel accounts, of the general ineptness of the overseer group. Thus, Gray characterized overseers as "hired subordinates, who at best were men of little education, with narrow vision and sympathies; at worst cruel, licentious tyrants." [8] Moreover, declared Gray, "in numerous instances overseers were unreliable and dishonest." [9] Remarking that "competent overseers did not crowd the profession," Flanders ascribed to the majority of managerial subordinates such uncomplimentary traits as cruelty, ignorance, intemperance, and immorality. [10] Phillips, whose contributions to an understanding of life in the Old South remain unsurpassed, described plantation overseers as "crude in manner, barely literate, commonplace in capacity, capable only of ruling slaves by severity in a rule-of-thumb routine, and needing fairly constant oversight by their employers." [11]

This image of the overseer contains an element of truth, particularly with regard to the character of a large floating population of incompetent and ill-paid slave managers in the Lower South, but does not accurately portray the condition of the managerial profession as a whole. It is the purpose of this book to ascertain the degree of competence which marked the general performance of the overseer class, and to rediscover the overseer so that he may be accorded his proper recognition as a vital figure in the plantation-slavery regime. It is also hoped that this study will provide a fresh interpretation of one of the many groups which comprised the white middle class in the Old South—a class which has received too little attention from scholars attracted by the more exciting prospect of discoursing upon the occupants of white-columned mansions or upon the humble status of their less fortunate charges.

The most complete secondary treatment of the overseer to appear thus far is John Spencer Bassett's excellent work, *The Southern Plantation Overseer as Revealed in his Letters*, published in 1925. However, this pioneering study was limited to a consideration of the overseers on James Knox Polk's absentee cotton plantation in Yalobusha County, Mississippi. With the collection of formerly inaccessible plantation manuscripts in state archives throughout the South and with the publication of countless articles and monographs relating to the agricultural system of the Old South, it is now possible to undertake a more comprehensive study of the position occupied by the overseer throughout the entire South.

The writer has sought to achieve that goal. However, in a work of this type, the relentless consideration of time, combined with the overwhelming mass of material, has necessarily dictated certain limitations. Primary emphasis will be upon the period 1775–1865, although a brief sketch of the introduction of the overseer system into colonial America will be presented at the outset of the study, and occasional examples from the pre-Revolutionary period will be cited where appropriate. The overseer system manifestly experienced its greatest development in the nineteenth century with the rapid spread of slavery into the fertile cotton and sugar regions of the Southwest. Hence, the bulk of the data in this study concerns plantation management during that century. No attempt has been made to organize material chronologically, as there was little tendency for variations in the overseer system to appear with the passage of time.

It has seemed advisable instead to concentrate on variations in plantation management among the four principal staple crop areas of the Old South—the tobacco and grain region of Virginia and North Carolina, the rice coast of South Carolina and Georgia, the Louisiana sugar parishes, and the cotton belt of the Lower South. It was felt that such a procedure would make possible the formulation of conclusions which would be applicable for the entire South. Accordingly, primary attention in compiling research data has been focused upon Virginia, South Carolina, Louisiana, and Mississippi, and, to a lesser degree, on North Carolina, Georgia, and Alabama.

Although the overseer occupies a central position in this monograph, two other members of the Old South managerial structure fall within its scope and are discussed briefly. The steward, who occupied a supervisory post just above that of the overseer in the plantation organization, will be discussed at some length in Chapter VIII. The post of assistant overseer, or suboverseer, will be considered briefly in the initial chapter.

Reliance has been placed upon three principal types of primary sources in the preparation of this study. More than seventy manuscript collections, located in the libraries of the University of North Carolina and Louisiana State University and in the state archives of Alabama and Mississippi, have been examined with extreme care and attention to detail. Such collections of journals, diaries, and correspondence relating to plantation management have proved to be of incalculable value in determining the precise function of the overseer in the management of the plantation and its labor force.

Second, the manuscript census returns for the several states have provided statistics regarding the age, background, education, family, and personal estate of the overseer which could not be derived from any other source. Census data on more than fifteen hundred overseers in seventeen sample counties have been compiled from Schedule 1, Free Inhabitants, and Schedule 2, Slave Inhabitants, of the Census of 1860. The original manuscript returns for all states are located in the National Archives, Washington, D.C. The sampling method has been utilized because the study of all overseers would be unending and, as Professor Frank Lawrence Owsley sagely observed, this procedure has "seemed to be one that takes into consideration the finite nature of man's life and the finite quality of the reader's patience with and interest in statistics." [12] The results of an exhaustive analysis of the census returns from sample counties in Virginia, North Carolina, South Carolina, Georgia, Louisiana, and Mississippi are presented in Chapter III.

Finally, contemporary agricultural periodicals have provided the best expression of the views of articulate spokesmen for the overseer class, and have sharply defined the conflict between overseer and planter regarding managerial policies. A perusal of such agricultural papers as the *Farmers' Register,* the *Southern Cultivator,* and the *American Cotton Planter* renders painfully apparent the general estimation in which the professional overseer was held by his employer.

The Overseer

1

Role of the Overseer
in the
Plantation Establishment

THE overseer system was introduced into America by the Virginia Company and was derived from the English practice of utilizing bailiffs to manage the great landed estates in the island kingdom. Indeed, in the early colonial period southern overseers were sometimes known as "bailiffs." Many overseers in the English colonies during this period were indentured servants whose terms of service had expired.[1] The first Negroes were brought to Louisiana from the French sugar islands in the West Indies during the first decade of the eighteenth century, and the overseer system was introduced into that colony shortly thereafter. An extant overseer agreement of 1744 indicates that the system was then functioning in Louisiana in

3

substantially the same form that it later assumed throughout the South.[2]

Widespread use of overseers in colonial America, especially after 1700, is credited by one writer with providing the planter aristocracy with the necessary leisure to indulge an increasing interest in the arts and other cultural pursuits.[3] This was undoubtedly a factor in promoting planter leadership in cultural affairs throughout the entire antebellum period.

One unique feature of the overseer system during the colonial period was the practice of leasing developed plantations, with slaves and stock, to overseers for a share of the crop. Under this arrangement—not to be confused with the practice of paying farm managers by crop shares—the overseer assumed responsibility for maintenance of the slave force and, in return for his services, received one-third of the net proceeds from sale of the crops. Long-term leases of seven or twenty-one years, or even longer, were common.[4] However, the practice of renting plantations to overseers had largely disappeared by the end of the colonial period, primarily because it encouraged methods resulting in soil exhaustion.[5]

With the exception of a few practices, such as the leasing arrangement and the payment of overseers by crop shares rather than cash wages, the managerial system in the pre-Revolutionary period differed in no important respect from that employed in the nineteenth century. Of course, the vast expansion of staple crop agriculture into the Southwest, the increase in slave population, and the consolidation of existing land and slave units resulted in more widespread utilization of the overseer and magnified the problems of the managerial class. Nevertheless, the broad outlines of the system of management remained essentially the same.

The plantation overseer occupied a position second in authority only to that of the planter, but his power varied greatly with his ability, the disposition of his employer, and the type of plantation on which he was situated. On absentee estates he was frequently given almost complete control of plantation operations. However, on plantations where the owner was in residence during the greater portion of the year his authority might be severely limited. He was often little more than a glorified driver, charged with carrying out routine duties under the watchful eye of his employer. It was in instances of the latter type that friction most frequently developed between planter and overseer.

Springing largely from the yeoman farmer class of society, the overseer was not noted for his erudite comprehension of principles of scientific agriculture. Despite his lack of formal education, however, the successful overseer necessarily possessed a good measure of practical intelligence. Without this, he would have been helpless in the face of the manifold problems inherent in the production of a large staple crop and in the management of an ignorant, and often hostile, labor force.

Those who followed the overseeing profession may be divided into three categories—the sons of planters, a floating population of amateur overseers, and the general body of professional managers. The first group included the young sons of planters who pursued, for a time, the business of overseeing in preparation for later careers as independent agricultural proprietors. Many of these persons managed for their planter fathers and received an annual salary for their services. Others preferred to undergo their period of training on plantations owned by individuals outside their own families. The general reputation of this group was superior to that of the other two categories within the overseeing profession. The most outstanding overseer ever employed on Hugh Davis' "Beaver Bend" plantation in the Alabama Black Belt was John White, the son of a neighboring planter. White, who received a much higher salary than did any of his predecessors, took charge in 1860 during the absence of the proprietor and performed his duties in commendable fashion on a plantation whose previous managers had been conspicuous failures.[6]

The second classification of overseers encompassed within its bounds a fluid population of young men of little competence who found employment by offering their services at a lower rate than the more skilled overseers within their region. Woefully deficient in formal education, possessing little knowledge of agricultural techniques, and incapable of managing a slave force, these overseers failed to satisfy those who employed them and moved from one plantation to another, rarely staying longer than two or three years. It was this group—quite large in the cotton and sugar regions of the Southwest—that gave the entire overseeing profession a bad reputation.

The third class of overseers was composed of men who energetically and conscientiously pursued their profession and, within the limitations imposed by their own background and their huge burden of responsibilities, performed their function as competently and efficiently as they knew how. Many of these overseers accumulated sufficient capital or secured the credit necessary to purchase a few slaves and enough land to establish themselves as small, independent farmers. A few of the more ambitious and more fortunate were able to rise to the position of planter. Evidence presented herein indicates that this group of overseers was more numerous and more typical of the profession than the class of nominal overseers of little competence mentioned above.

No member of the plantation establishment was the target of greater abuse and vilification than the overseer. Even agricultural reformers, who should have known better, berated him for a variety of evils—the one-crop system, the perpetuation of absentee ownership, and inept management of Negroes, livestock, and soil. With each surge of enthusiasm for southern agricultural reform, a corresponding chorus of criticism was directed toward the overseer system. Few paused to observe that soil wastage and unscientific managerial practices occurred on agricultural units of all sizes, although overseers were utilized only on plantations of considerable size. Planters, for their part, relentlessly castigated the overseers as a group for dishonesty, inefficiency, incapacity, and self-indulgence. There was an almost universal demand for new and better ones. Yet, few critics offered any alternative to the overseer system or did anything to correct the evils about which they loved to complain.[7]

One characteristic common to all critics of the overseeing profession was their failure to appreciate the difficult station occupied by the plantation superintendent. Accorded maximum responsibility with minimum authority, the overseer found himself in an anomalous position. His principal function involved the management of his employer's most valuable asset, the slaves. In return for this vital service, however, he was rewarded with niggardly pay and uncertain tenure. Held responsible for crop results at the end of the year, he was obliged, in many instances, blindly to follow instructions relating to crop management, which were imposed upon him by his employer. Moreover, his authority over the slaves was often diminished by the intervention of the planter. In short, the compensations afforded by his job were not commensurate with his duties, nor were they comparable to those offered by other occupations and professions of the time. It is little wonder, considering the magnitude of his difficulties, that the plantation overseer frequently failed to satisfy his employer.[8]

Travelers venturing into the antebellum South published conflicting reports concerning the character of overseers, although the majority supported the critical appraisal of the planter group with whom they passed the greatest portion of their time. An English traveler, Fortescue Cuming, who visited the Mississippi Territory during the first decade of the nineteenth century, described the overseers in that region as "for the most part a rough, unpolished, uncouth class of people." Terming their "roughness and abruptness" in manners "extremely disagreeable and disgusting," he attributed such traits to the fact that they personally administered discipline to the slaves, rather than appointing a Negro driver for that purpose.[9] Frederick Law Olmsted, in his journeys through the South during the 1850's, found that the general character of overseers was considered to be exceedingly bad: "They were almost universally drunken and dissolute, and constantly liable to neglect their duties. Their families, when they had them, were generally unhappy. They were excessively extravagant; and but a few ever saved anything year by year from their wages." [10]

On the other hand, Basil Hall was pleasantly surprised by his encounters with members of the overseer class. Recording his observations on a trip through the South during the 1820's, Hall declared:

It is the popular fashion in America, and I think elsewhere, to abuse these overseers as a class. But none of my enquiries led me to think so ill of them by any means as I had heard them reported. Their interest, as well as that of the planters, in the long run, is, unquestionably, to use the slaves well. An overseer who acquires a character for undue severity, is much scouted, and sooner or later discovers that his services are not valued or sought after, merely because he produces less effective work than a more judicious person would do.[11]

A. De Puy Van Buren, a native of Michigan, traveled through the Yazoo Valley of Mississippi in 1854–55 and emerged with a generally favorable view of the overseers he met. He remarked, apparently with some surprise, that "you often meet intelligent young men among them." [12]

According to Van Buren and other travelers, the overseer could always be distinguished by his badge of office, a whip, "which is ever in his hand." [13] He could usually be seen riding back and forth through the fields, whip in hand, inspecting the work of the Negroes. The presence of an overseer in the field had a pronounced effect upon the exertions of slaves working under his watchful eye. One observer, on his departure from a medium-sized plantation in the interior cotton districts of the Lower South, noted the following scene: "I passed the hoe-gang at work in the cotton-field, the overseer lounging among them carrying a whip; there were ten or twelve of them; none looked up at me. Within ten minutes I passed five who were plowing, with no overseer or driver in sight, and every one stopped their plows to gaze at me." [14] A visitor to a Louisiana sugar house during the grinding season found the overseer holding "a short-handled whip, loaded in the butt, which had a lash four or five times the length of the staff." The overseer took no notice of his visitors but eyed the slaves, "quickening the steps of a loiterer by a word, or threatening with his whip, those who, tempted by curiosity, turned to gaze after us." [15]

The most colorful descriptions of the southern overseer were those painted by William Howard Russell, a correspondent for the London *Times* who visited several of the great sugar estates in Ascension Parish, Louisiana, in June, 1861. On a visit to the estate of Governor Alfred Roman, Russell ventured into the cane fields and saw several gangs of Negroes at work, superintended by the overseer— "a sharp-looking creole, on a lanky pony, whip in hand." [16] Overseer Gibbs of "Orange Grove" planta-tion, one of the units comprising John Burnside's vast Ascension Parish sugar estate, was described by Russell as "a man grim in beard and eye, and silent withal, with a big whip in his hand and a large knife stuck in his belt." [17] Such a figure must have made an awesome impression upon the slaves working under his supervision.

The number of slaves controlled by each overseer varied with the type of farming. In general, it is likely that in the rice, sugar, and cotton regions most planters employed an overseer when their total number of working field hands ap-proached thirty. [18] The figure in the tobacco and grain area, where slaves were utilized on small farms, was probably closer to twenty. In making generalizations upon this point, it is important to distinguish between the total number of *slaves* and the total number of *field hands*—a distinction usually not made by earlier authorities. Many planters who owned more than thirty slaves, a large proportion of whom were small children, did not employ an overseer. The South Carolina planter and agricultural reformer James H. Hammond considered a ratio of thirty slaves to one overseer too high. "For any thing but corn & cotton," said Hammond, "10 to 20 workers are as many as any common white man can attend to." [19]

Notwithstanding the views of Hammond and others who held a low opinion of the general competence of professional overseers, a ratio of fifty slaves to one overseer was considered the most efficient plantation unit in the Lower South.[20] One hundred was thought to be the maximum number of Negroes who could be managed effectively by a single overseer, although this number was sometimes exceeded in the rice and sugar regions. Frequently estates with large slave parcels were divided into several units, each managed by a separate overseer. Olmsted visited one such plantation, a large absentee cotton estate located on a tributary of the Mississippi River. The property consisted of four adjoining plantations, each under the management of a white overseer and each counting a slave population in excess of one hundred.[21] Similarly, Levin Marshall, a wealthy Mississippi planter, divided his estate into plantation units of approximately a thousand acres and a hundred slaves, with each unit entrusted to a separate overseer.[22]

Employment of overseers on small, marginal plantations fluctuated considerably with the prosperity of the times. Many owners, whose operations were barely large enough to justify the employment of overseers, hired such operatives only in prosperous years. During periods of agricultural depression overseers on these marginal establishments frequently found themselves without employment. Overseers were sometimes hired to supervise affairs on submarginal farms during periods of extended absence by the owner. For example, Julian C. Ruffin was obliged to employ an overseer on his small Virginia farm on two occasions during the 1840's when circumstances compelled him to be away for periods of several months' duration. The slave force on Ruffin's farm, "Ruthven," did not exceed ten at that time.[23]

The total number of overseers in the United States doubled

during the decade of the 1850's. This increase was produced in
great measure by continued expansion of the plantation system
into the Southwest and by consolidation of existing holdings
into larger units in the older agricultural regions. Table 1,
indicates the number of persons listing themselves as overseers
in the leading plantation states in 1850 and 1860. ²⁴ The relatively large number of overseers in Virginia may be attributed
to the division of agricultural property within that state into
small farming units.

Table 1

ENUMERATION OF OVERSEERS IN LEADING
PLANTATION STATES, 1850–60

State	Total Overseers 1850	Total Overseers 1860
Alabama	1,849	4,141
Georgia	2,166	4,909
Louisiana	1,808	2,989
Mississippi	2,324	3,941
North Carolina	989	1,782
South Carolina	1,823	2,737
Virginia	3,747	5,459
Total	14,706	25,958
Total (United States)	18,859	37,883

It is apparent that the greatest numbers of overseers in the
period immediately preceding the Civil War were engaged in
the management of cotton plantations. In 1850 there were in
the South 74,031 plantations producing five or more bales of
cotton, but only 2,681 sugar plantations, and a mere 551 rice
plantations of substantial size.²⁵ The incidence of overseer
employment was higher in the rice and sugar regions because
of the larger size of the plantation units in those areas. Historian Lewis Gray concluded that the majority of overseers were
employed by upper-class planters—those owning fifty or more
slaves. Assuming that each of these upper-class planters had
at least one overseer in 1850, only 11 percent of the 84,328
middle-class planters—those owning from ten to fifty slaves—
could have been utilizing overseers.²⁶ If this assumption is
correct, it is likely that most of the latter group of planters
were situated in the tobacco and grain region.

The following tables show the areas of greatest concentration of slaves in large units and, consequently, the areas in which the incidence of overseer employment was highest, in the decade 1850–60. The largest slaveholdings in 1850 were clearly in South Carolina, with Louisiana a rather distant second. Those planters owning a hundred or more slaves each were distributed among the leading planting states in 1850 as follows: South Carolina (484), Louisiana (320), Alabama (234), Missisippi (216), Georgia (175), Virginia (116), and North Carolina (91).

Table 2

SLAVEHOLDERS AND SLAVES, 1850 [27]

State	Number of Slaves					Total
	100–200	200–300	300–500	500–1,000	Over 1,000	Slaveholders
Alabama	216	16	2	–	–	29,295
Georgia	147	22	4	2	–	38,456
Louisiana	274	36	6	4	–	20,670
Missisippi	189	18	8	1	–	23,116
North Carolina	76	12	3	–	–	28,303
South Carolina	382	69	29	2	2	25,596
Virginia	107	8	1	–	–	55,063
Total (United States)	1,479	187	56	9	2	347,525

Table 3

SLAVEHOLDERS AND SLAVES, 1860 [28]

State	Number of Slaves					Total
	100–200	200–300	300–500	500–1,000	Over 1,000	Slaveholders
Alabama	312	24	10	–	–	33,730
Georgia	181	23	7	1	–	41,084
Louisiana	460	63	20	4	–	22,033
Mississippi	279	28	8	1	–	30,943
North Carolina	118	11	4	–	–	34,658
South Carolina	363	56	22	7	1	26,701
Virginia	105	8	1	–	–	52,128
Total (United States)	1,980	224	74	13	1	384,884

The figures in Table 3 indicate that by 1860, as a result of the consolidation of plantation units in the sugar parishes, Louisiana had taken the lead from South Carolina in the total number of planters owning a hundred or more slaves. The distribution of slaveholdings in excess of a hundred was as follows: Louisiana (547), South Carolina (449), Alabama (346), Mississippi (316), Georgia (212), North Carolina (133), and Virginia (114). However, holders of the very largest numbers of slaves still resided on the South Carolina rice coast. Of the 14 planters who owned slave parcels of five hundred or more each, 8 were South Carolina rice planters.

One good estimate of the size of slaveholdings in a given area was the median number of slaves held.[29] Median holdings in the tobacco region ranged from 14 in portions of Kentucky to 28 in south-central Virginia. The median figure in the South Carolina rice districts was a lofty 70, with a peak of 135 in Georgetown District. In the Louisiana sugar parishes the median slaveholding was 81, with Ascension Parish recording a spectacular 175. Finally, the median figure in the broad cotton belt ranged from 10 in northwestern Alabama to 55 in the Yazoo-Mississippi Delta. Cotton counties with particularly high median slaveholdings included Rapides Parish, Louisiana (125); Issaquena County, Mississippi (118); and Concordia Parish, Louisiana (117).[30] From the foregoing figures it is apparent that the utilization of overseers was nearly universal in the rice and sugar regions, and almost as essential in much of the cotton belt. The use of an overseer was not as common in the Upper South, where individual farms tended to be small, but the large number of these farms made it possible for many overseers to secure managerial positions.

It was not uncommon in some areas, particularly in the rice districts where the supply of qualified overseers was limited, for a single overseer to undertake the management of several different plantations simultaneously. For example, in 1856 Thomas A. Ham supervised agricultural operations on five separate rice plantations in Colleton District, South Carolina.[31] Such an ambitious undertaking was certainly not typical, although there were not infrequent instances in which a single overseer managed two or three plantations located in the same neighborhood but owned by different planters. In 1838 Gabriel L. Ellis managed three separate plantations for the Allston family in Georgetown District, South Carolina, and received a total salary of $1500.[32] Similarly, overseer A. M. Sanford managed three Bryan County, Georgia, rice plantations during the year 1828.[33] These overseers were obviously men who possessed extraordinary managerial abilities.

In the tobacco and grain region, where agricultural holdings were frequently divided into a number of small farms, it was not unusual for a single overseer to manage a number of farms owned by the same planter. On the Potomac River estate of James Mercer, one overseer managed four plantation units. He acted as resident overseer of Mercer's home plantation, "Marlborough," and inspected the three smaller units as conditions warranted.[34]

On some large plantations a suboverseer, or assistant overseer, might be employed to aid the chief overseer in the execution of his duties. The suboverseer was usually a young man in the process of acquiring sufficient training to pursue an overseeing or farming career on his own. An assistant overseer might be employed in instances where the head overseer of an absentee plantation was obliged to be absent for an extended period of time. Cornelius Geiger served as suboverseer on George Jones Kollock's Ossabaw Island, Georgia, plantation for at least six years. He managed the plantation during absences of the head overseer and frequently corresponded with his employer regarding the progress of plantation operations.[35] On Effingham Lawrence's "Magnolia" plantation in Plaquemines Parish, Louisiana, assistant overseers were employed from time to time at the rate of $40 per month, but retained their positions for only brief periods. Their chief function appears to have been to assume the management of "Magnolia" during extended periods of absence by Lawrence's outstanding head overseer, Joseph Acquilla Randall.[36]

The wage scale of assistant overseers was understandably lower than that of head overseers. William H. Haynes received only $25 per month to assist in the management of Maunsel White's "Deer Range" sugar plantation in Plaquemines Parish.[37] The salaries of head overseers on Charles Manigault's "Gowrie" plantation during the period 1833–48 ranged from $200 to $500, while annual wages paid to suboverseers during the same period fluctuated between $150 and $250.[38]

The suboverseer was subjected to as much criticism by his

employer as was the overseer. Writing to "Gowrie" overseer
G. T. Cooper in July, 1848, Charles Manigault commented:

. . . I have had many young men as sub-overseers on the place, & never
yet found one who gave entire satisfaction, for all of them shewed a
jealous disposition being always anxious to put a wrong meaning to their
instructions, or following them in so lose [sic] a manner as shew'd clearly
that they were secretly in opposition to the manager. And if I should
ever have another on my place I have made it a rule to avoid every one
who comes from the Georgia or Carolina shore, or whose family resides
anywhere on or near the Savannah River—for in this case while on the
place their friends & acquaintances are constantly coming to see them—
or they take my Negroes & slip off in a boat to visit their friends. I
could say much more on this subject, but you seem to know it as well
as I do . . . .[39]

This letter provides a key to the puzzle of why assistant overseers were not utilized more frequently than they were. In
many instances where suboverseers were employed friction soon
developed between the chief overseer and his assistant. There
was usually enough conflict between planter and overseer without adding a third agent to magnify the difficulty of making
policy decisions. James H. Hammond observed, in a letter to
Edmund Ruffin, that "two or more managers will not pull
together on one place." [40] The lack of harmony between overseer and assistant overseer often resulted in the untimely
discharge of one of the principals. Such an instance was tersely
recorded in the plantation journal of Louisiana sugar magnate
R. R. Barrow: "Dutton & Ford canot agree and Dutton dismissed   time 1 mo 27 days." [41] As a result, assistant overseers were not ordinarily utilized in the Old South except
under the exigency of special circumstances.

Some southern states had statutory provisions requiring the
employment of overseers on plantations. These requirements
became more stringent with increased agitation over the slavery
question near the end of the antebellum period. A Louisiana
code of 1806 made mandatory the presence of a white or free
colored overseer on every plantation. Following an abortive
slave revolt in St. John the Baptist Parish, the Louisiana
legislature in 1815 specified that there should be one white
person in residence on a plantation for every thirty slaves.
Parish officials were instructed to enforce this statute, and a
fine of up to $500 was to be levied against offenders. Finally,

NEGROES AT HOME

an act of 1855 rendered compulsory the utilization of a white overseer."² South Carolina likewise made the employment of a white overseer mandatory. A South Carolina rice planter visited by Olmsted in the 1850's remarked to the latter that he would not employ a white overseer, even during the summer months when he was absent, if the law did not require it.⁴³

Despite legal requirements such as those cited, the distaste with which some planters viewed professional overseers was so intense that they refused to employ them under any conditions. Thomas Spalding, one of the largest Sea Island cotton planters on the Georgia coast, often boasted of running his Sapelo Island plantations "without the intervention of any white man." ⁴⁴ The proprietor of a James River grain plantation, visited by Olmsted during the winter of 1852–53, refused to employ a white overseer, terming such men "the curse of this country. . . . the worst men in the community." ⁴⁵

Occasionally, planters who had relied upon white overseers for years gave up in disgust and dispensed with them altogether. Declaring that "I have been imposed upon by Overseers more than I ever will be again," an irate Alabama proprietor discharged his overseer one January morning and thereafter managed his property with the assistance of his son.⁴⁶ After several years marked by unfortunate experiences with overseers, Bennet H. Barrow, a Louisiana cotton and sugar planter, also elected to dispense entirely with white overseers. The following entries in Barrow's diary indicate the course of events which exhausted his patience with hired subordinates:

[April 17, 1837.]   Cotten in great danger   Finished planting 3 acres of cotten neglected by my overseer—
[April 26, 1837.]   My overseer so good he is good for nothing—
[October 2, 1837.]   More whiping to do this Fall than all together in three years owing to my D mean Overseer—never will have another unless I should be compelled to leave—they are a perfect nuisance
[October 4, 1837.]   picking finely   200 average—Verry trashy cotten under the eyes of my D. fool Overseer⁴⁷

James H. Hammond, whose planting operations were annually characterized by great expectations and disappointing results, attempted on several occasions to get along without overseers, but found it impossible to do so.⁴⁸

Negro drivers or slave foremen were generally used to direct

the work routine on plantations operated without a white overseer. For example, Alexander James Lawton, a Beaufort District, South Carolina, rice planter, employed no overseer despite
the fact that the combined slaveholdings of Lawton and his
mother rose to almost one hundred by 1833. The number of
full field hands employed by Lawton on his plantation ranged
from about twenty in 1820 to forty in 1840. Apparently Lawton managed his enterprise with the aid of Negro drivers.[49]
Eli J. Capell, proprietor of "Pleasant Hill" plantation in Amite
County, Mississippi, managed his slave force of about eighty
with the aid of a mulatto slave foreman named Tone. The
latter rendered faithful service to his master for many years
and after the Civil War was rewarded by Capell with the
gift of a tract of land, upon which he resided until his death.[50]
The demise of Leven, the Negro foreman of a Louisiana plantation, left the proprietress heartbroken. Lamenting his loss in a
letter to her sister-in-law, she described him as "without a fault
that I ever discovered. He has overseed the plantation nearly
three years and done much better than any white man ever done
here. . . . No pen can tell you the Distress I feel." [51]

For obvious reasons, the utilization of Negro foremen in place
of white overseers was most common on the small farming units
of the Upper South. A unique arrangement was devised by J. H.
Bernard of Port Royal, Virginia. Bernard replaced his overseer with a slave foreman and distributed to his Negroes, as
an annual premium, a sum equivalent to the former overseer's
salary.[52] After trying this experiment for six months, he enthusiastically reported that he had never in his life "had so much
work, so well done, nor with equal cheerfulness and satisfaction." His relationship with his force of about twenty effective
slaves had been so strengthened by the new system, contended
Bernard, "that they could scarcely be pursuaded to change it by
Arthur Tappan and his minions." [53]

One of the most competent slave foremen in Virginia was
Jem Sykes, who was given charge of the routine work on Edmund Ruffin's "Marlbourne" plantation in 1847 and who served
ably in that capacity for some years thereafter. In August, 1848,
Ruffin went to the Springs with two of his daughters and did
not return until the end of September. During his absence at
this crucial period in the farm year the management of affairs
at "Marlbourne" was left entirely in the hands of Sykes, with

the exception of biweekly visits from Ruffin's son, Julian, to give the foreman general directions. The capable Negro discharged his responsibilities in exemplary fashion, completing the latter half of the thrashing and delivering all of Ruffin's bountiful wheat crop to outgoing vessels. Several years later Ruffin penned an account of the above incident which he concluded with the following observation: "The facts of this crop being left to be thrashed & delivered, under the sole care & charge of my negro overseer, & that I could leave the farm without other superintendence for a visit to the Springs, caused nearly as much remark as did the amount of the crop of wheat then made." [54]

There was considerable difference of opinion among members of the planting community regarding the wisdom of utilizing Negro foremen in lieu of white overseers. At the heart of this dispute was a conflict of opinion concerning the capacity of the Negro for self-government. Negro foremen were given vast responsibilities, extending to every phase of plantation management, on the plantations of Jefferson Davis and John McDonogh.[55] On the other hand, drivers on Bennet H. Barrow's "Highland" plantation were allowed little discretion or authority. Barrow, in his diary entry of August 6, 1839, expressed the view that "it is wrong to allow a driver to use any authority." Negroes, he said, "are not Capable of self government" because of "want of discretion—judgment &c." [56] A writer in the *Southern Agriculturist* censured the practice of leaving plantations solely in the care of Negro drivers. "It is a well-known fact," he declared, "that a driver, when left to himself, will not keep up his authority, and *more particularly so of late years than formerly.*" [57] He urged that experienced overseers be hired and paid wages that fully compensated them for their services. It is likely that the practice of replacing overseers with drivers or Negro foremen was not followed extensively except in the tobacco and grain region of the Upper South, where the average slaveholding was small.

Occasionally planters, whose general policy was to employ white overseers, utilized slave foremen for brief periods. This was most likely to occur in situations where the proprietor owned several relatively small farming units. Thus, the "Forkland" unit of W. H. Tayloe's Mount Airy estate, located in Richmond County, Virginia, was entrusted to the care of a

Negro foreman during the years 1851–53. [58] In North Carolina a slave foreman was given complete charge of Ebenezer Pettigrew's "Belgrade" plantation during an interim period of one year when Pettigrew failed to secure the services of a satisfactory white overseer. [59]

Louisiana was apparently the only state in which free Negro overseers (as distinguished from Negro foremen) were ever employed. Eleven free colored overseers were listed in New Orleans in 1850. [60] Four years later the number had risen to twenty-five, of whom twenty-two were mulattoes. [61] It is probable that the free colored overseer was a phenomenon peculiar to the area around New Orleans, where the number of mulattoes in the population was unusually large.

2

Contractual
and Social Relations

OVERSEERS were normally engaged at the beginning of each year for a term of one year. Contract negotiations between planter and overseer were usually carried on in the late fall except in the Upper South, where they were initiated during the summer preceding the term of employment. The potential opportunities afforded to overseers in the older planting regions by the opening of the West enabled them to secure more favorable concessions from their employers than could their counterparts in the newer slave states. Consequently, Virginia and North Carolina proprietors adopted the custom of giving their overseers notice as early as June as to whether they were to be retained for another year.[1]

The practice of engaging overseers during the period from May to July was severely criticized in 1836 by a Buckingham County, Virginia, planter. Writing in the *Farmers' Register*, Edmund W. Hubard raised the following objections to such a system:

This custom of making bargains with overseers in the months of May, June, and July, holds out as can be easily proven sundry inducements for rash and injudicious management in the commencement of the year, and but too frequently gives room for neglect, waste, and general bad management for the remainder of the year. It puts it in the power of indifferent managers to compete more successfully with the really good, in obtaining business. It has the tendency to induce people to form their estimates of the management of men, by their spring and winter's work mainly. It furnishes pretexts for neglect of business at the most important season of the year. It prevents the employer from forming a correct opinion of the qualifications of the overseer previously to renewing the contract for the second year, because that cannot well be determined till the crop is quite or nearly finished.[2]

Notwithstanding the logic of Hubard's argument, the custom of bargaining with farm managers during the summer months prevailed in the Upper South until the close of the antebellum period.

It was desirable for a planter to exercise caution in the employment of a new overseer, for a poor manager could do irreparable harm to the interests of his employer. Many planters required letters of recommendation from prospective overseers, and most proprietors personally interviewed applicants before hiring them. One of the most common methods of engaging a new overseer was through correspondence among planters. A Louisiana planter, plagued by the scarcity of competent managers in his state, wrote to Lewis Thompson seeking the recommendation of a North Carolina overseer. Moore Rawls, a native Carolinian and the manager of Thompson's absentee sugar plantation in Rapides Parish, had suggested the name of a North Carolina overseer. The following request was then communicated to Thompson:

I write these few lines for the purpose of asking of you a favor. Mr Rawls has spoken to me of a young man a—Mr John H. Curry who he thinks would suit me as a manager if he would come out to this country. Should you meet with him or if you know the man and think he would answer you can offer him $500. Or if you know of any young man who is sober and industrious and whom you could recommend please send him out, as I am in want of a manager for the coming year.[3]

A planter considering the application of a prospective overseer frequently checked with the latter's previous employer to ascertain his managerial capabilities. A Mississippi cotton planter received such a request for information from a neighboring proprietor, and responded with an unfavorable evaluation, as the following diary entry reveals:

> Rec'd a letter from Wm. Hall making enquiry about Mr. Robinson's qualifications as an overseer. In reply I gave Mr. R. credit for honesty, sobriety, & agreeableness; for great industry & close attention to business, but objected to his want of authority among the negroes, & the reckless manner in which he permitted them to do their work—alledging [sic] that, owing to these causes, he had never succeeded in retaining a good stand of Cotton or in gathering the crop in good order. I expressed the opinion that he would probably succeed very well with a set of well-trained hands, accustomed to stand in fear of their overseer, & execute their work well, but thought with my hands, *who knew him*, he never could.[4]

It is scarcely surprising that the inquiring planter failed to engage Robinson. Indeed, the unfortunate overseer was discharged from his current post within two weeks of the above notation. A more favorable evaluation was given by Robert F. W. Allston in reply to an inquiry concerning the capabilities of overseer Harman Pitman. Allston declared that he deemed Pitman "a good agent and Should be sorry to part with him." [5]

When it became generally known that a planter was seeking a new overseer, he would often receive applications from aspirants to the position. Thus, John Mitchell sought a post on one of Lewis Thompson's North Carolina farms for the year 1861. Mitchell may have been a competent farm manager, but his knowledge of the English language left something to be desired, as the following letter indicates:

> I under Stand that you are in want of a overseer on your farm   I am working at the carpenters trade at this time tho I can Be hiered an woold like to live with you again not with Stanting I have live with you an somewhat disagreed. I do yet think that I can give satisfaction as I am willing to give your Bizness my Strictestattention   You will excuse me for my Bad Spelling & righting as I am know Scollar[6]

Another North Carolina overseer sought to secure a situation in Louisiana, where he hoped to make his fortune. "I am anxious," he wrote Thompson, "to go to the South and get on a large rich farm." [7]

Infrequently, a planter in need of a new overseer inserted an advertisement in the newspaper. For example, in 1767 James Mercer placed the following notice in the *Virginia Gazette*: "Wanted soon . . . a farmer who will undertake the management of about 80 slaves, all settled within six miles of each other, to be employed in making of grain." [8] This method was seldom used, possibly because many overseers did not have access to newspapers. Most overseers were secured through correspondence among proprietors and through direct application by overseers to prospective employers.

The contract between planter and overseer could usually be terminated by either party at any time. Upon his departure the overseer normally received a proportion of his annual salary equivalent to the time he had served. The following portion of a contract, dated December 11, 1862, between Ruth Stovall Hairston and overseer Jackson Carrol is illustrative of the usual procedure governing the termination of contracts:

The said Hairston is to have liberty to dismiss the said Carrol at any time She the said Hairston may think proper so to do & the said Carrol is to be at liberty to quit the employmt of the said Hairston at any time the said Carrol may think proper so to do   In the event the said Carrol shall be dismissed or quit the employment of the said Hairston the said Carrol is to rec^{ve} in proportion of the above Sum of one hundred & Twenty Dollars as may be in proportion to the time during which the said Carrol remained upon the said plantation. [9]

There were, of course, a few exceptions to the procedure outlined above. George Washington advised the steward of his Mount Vernon estate to discharge without pay, "at any season of the year without scruple or hesitation," any overseer found "inattentive to the duties which by the articles of agreement they are found to perform." [10] In like manner, John Ewing Colhoun, wealthy South Carolina rice and indigo planter, provided, in an agreement with overseer Thomas Gravestock, that "in Case he the said Thomas Gravestock should misbehave or neglect his Business during said Term, the said John E Colhoun is at liberty to turn him away without allowing any Compensation-" [11] Another variation was recorded in an agreement, en-

tered into in the 1830's, between Nathaniel Friend and John
Berry, overseer of Friend's "White Hill" plantation in Prince
George County, Virginia. Under the terms of this agreement
either party could dissolve the contract by giving three months'
notice, but "in case of immediate seperation [sic], the one that
causes the dissolution shall pay the other Thirty dollars—" [12]

The practice of engaging overseers on a trial basis, usually
for a period of one month, was prevalent in some parts of the
Lower South—particularly on Louisiana sugar plantations. This
is indicative of the difficulty experienced by planters in that
area of obtaining competent managers. In some instances the
overseer received no pay during the trial period; in others, his
wages were raised at the conclusion of his initial month of
service if he proved to be an efficient manager.

Typical of the trial arrangements entered into upon Louisiana
sugar estates is the following agreement between R. R. Barrov
and overseer N. B. Holland, as outlined in the pages of Barrow's
"Residence" plantation journal: "Mr Barrow proposed to Mr
N.B. Holland to Set in on the Res to oversee that Both Parties
Might ascertain how they liked each other, after which if Mr
Holland suited as overseer he was to take charge   no compensation was named for Mr Holland during the time Mr H
was on trial." [13] Holland lasted only two weeks, his departure
being occasioned by friction with Barrow's steward, E. A.
Knowlton. Maunsel White, proprietor of "Deer Range" plantation in Plaquemines Parish, was another sugar planter who
occasionally employed overseers on a trial basis. White engaged
Raymond Loussade in mid-December, 1860, for a trial period
of one month. At the end of the month White made the following
notation in his "Deer Range" journal: "This day Raymond
Loussade, was dischar[g]ed in consequence of inability & paid
$50—& allowed to *depart in peace.*" [14] Robert B. Daley, a car-
penter by trade, was engaged by Andrew McCollam to do the
carpentry work and learn the business of overseeing on the
latter's small Bayou Lafourche sugar plantation. During his
trial period Daley was paid nothing for his overseeing services.
He proved satisfactory in his new occupation and, within a
month, was engaged to oversee the property on a permanent
basis. [15]

The mutual obligations governing the relationship between
planter and overseer were usually formalized in a written

contract, signed at the outset of the overseer's term. This contract outlined the salary, provisions allowance, and fringe benefits accorded the overseer in compensation for his services. The proprietor frequently included a series of plantation rules and instructions for the new overseer's inspection and signature.

In addition to a stipulated monetary consideration, it was a general practice to furnish plantation overseers with lodging, provisions, and often a servant and other privileges. Francis Terry Leak employed George Townsend to oversee his absentee cotton plantation in Arkansas during the year 1857 on the following terms: "I am to pay him wages of $400.00 pr year, & am to find him bread for his family, also 600 lbs. flour, 150 lbs. sugar, 75 lbs. Coffee & his meat, with the exception of 500 lbs. pork which he is to furnish & put in the Smoke house. I am also to feed his horse. He is to bring no stock on the plantation, and is to keep but one horse." [16] A notation of November 12, 1861, in Leak's diary reveals that generous terms were offered to James Sergeant. The latter was to be provided with "all his bread, including 300 to 400 lbs flour; 50 lbs sugar, 5 to 10 gall[ons] molasses; a negro boy to cut his wood, make his fires, feed his horse, & draw a bucket of water, night & morning; a negro woman to cook & wash for him whenever his wife is sick; and $350.00 wages."

A contract between Charles Manigault and Stephen F. Clark, calling for the latter to manage Manigault's "Gowrie" and "East Hermitage" rice plantations during the year 1853, contained the following provisions:

I [Clark] engage to keep neither Horse, Hog or Poultry of any kind on Mr. Manigault's Plantation. I am to be supplied (solely for myself and family) with Plantation provisions consisting only of Corn and small Rice, all other provision and supplies for myself I am to procure at my own expense. I am to have a woman exclusively devoted to washing and cooking for me, she being the only person belonging to the Plantation that I am to give any call or occupation to whatever for any of my household affairs, she never to be a field hand. I am also to be provided with a boy to wait on me and to go to the new Ground to cut wood from any logs or stumps for my fire wood.

Clark was to receive a salary of $500 per year. [17]

The following agreement between Peter Hairston and overseer Owen Walker is noteworthy for the comprehensive manner in which it delineates the precise obligations of both employer and overseer. It also illustrates the practice, at one time common in the tobacco region, of paying overseers by crop shares. The contract reads as follows:

Articles of an agreement made and entered into This Sixteenth day of Jany. one thousand Eight Hundred and twenty two Between Peter Hairston of the one part and Owen Walker of the other part both of the County of Stokes and State of North Carolina—Towitt the said Owen Walker hath this day agreed to Oversee the said Hairstons Hands and plantation on Muddy Creek—the Hands are thus   Sam, Cato, Jack, Jinny, Willcox Fanny—Dolly—Dorcas, Aron, Alcey, Mary—Mukey—Betsey, Alcey—Rose and four work horses—a Cart and two stears with all necessary tools to carry on the said buisiness—and to find him the said Walker three Hundred weight of pork which he now Receives and four Barrels Corn to be delivered next fall—also the milk of one Cow—the summer season the Calf to be taken good Care of—The Said Walker to draw the thirteenth part of the Merchantable Corn, Cotton, flax and all small grain   But first the Grain that is now Sow^d to be deducted before divided, and Sow^d in good order between the first of September and fifteenth of October   He the said Owen Walker doth obblidge him self to fully discharge the duty of an Overseer to work duly and truly with the said Hands not to suffer the Horses to be Rode only on said Hairstons Buisiness—He is not to be absent himself at any time from said buisiness   to be particular to take care of all the Stock of every description belonging to said place   to take Care of the fodder and straw so that none Receives damage by neglect —to Keep the fences and Houses in good order as a Good farmer ought to do—to finally finish the Crop before he quits—to all times to give him the said Hairston a full and just account of everything Respecting the buisiness of place—stock &c—and further to go by the said Hairstons directions and for the true performance to perform   Stand to perform and abide by they Both doth by these presents bind them selves to each other to perform every part thereoff—or to make all damages good   As Witness they Hath Hereunto Sett there Hands and Seals the day and date above mentioned.[18]

Not all planters were as generous in their dispensation of fringe benefits as might be indicated by the agreements cited above. The absence of such advantages was striking in a contract of 1836 between Robert Hairston and overseer Creed T. Rowland. Under the articles of this agreement, Rowland was dispatched from North Carolina to Lowndes County, Mississippi, to undertake the management of Hairston's business in that locality. Rowland received an annual salary of $600 and was provided with meat and corn bread "for his white family." However, all other provisions were to be furnished at his own expense. In addition, Rowland was obliged to pay most of the expenses which he incurred in moving to Mississippi, the charges of any guests he entertained, and the hire of any hand he utilized as a personal or family servant.[19] It is a matter of some wonderment that Rowland accepted such a hard bargain.

A number of variable factors influenced the pay scale of overseers. Among these factors were the size of the plantation, number of slaves managed, type of plantation (absentee or resident), economic condition of the planter, length of tenure, experience of the overseer, and the geographic area in which the plantation was situated.

The number of laborers supervised was a vital consideration in determining the salaries of plantation overseers. The management of a large slave force clearly involved weightier responsibilities and called for a man of greater ability than did the control of smaller forces. In like manner, the broader duties entailed in the management of absentee estates generally dictated the payment of higher financial rewards than those received by the overseers of resident plantations of similar size and location. The wage differential induced by this criterion was often of considerable magnitude. Francis Terry Leak, who operated a resident plantation in Mississippi and an absentee unit in Arkansas during the two decades preceding the Civil War, paid his Mississippi overseers annual wages ranging from $135 to $425, while the overseers of his absentee plantation received wages varying from $400 to $800.[20]

If an overseer performed satisfactorily, he could usually look forward to a pay increase. One authority, who confined his study primarily to the sugar plantations of Louisiana, noted the propensity for the wages of an overseer remaining in the employ of a single planter for a term of several years to rise a total of $100 per year for as many as three to five years.[21] A similar tendency was manifested in other regions, although the amount of increase was not so great in areas where the initial salary was lower.

Such a trend prevailed on the Georgia plantations of James Hamilton Couper. The annual salary of Thomas Oden, overseer of Couper's "Hopeton" plantation, advanced from $600 in 1831 to $1,000 in 1836. An identical increase from $600 to $1,000 was registered during the overseership of William Audley Couper on "Hamilton" plantation, although the increase was not so rapid, being consummated during the period 1841–54.[22] The same tendency was displayed on the Ascension Parish, Louisiana, sugar estate of Henry McCall during the 1820's and 1830's. The initial salary of $1,000 was usually increased to $1,200 after a year of satisfactory service.[23] Of course, not all proprietors adhered to the general rule of raising their managers' salaries as tenure lengthened. Grief G. Mason received a compensation of $250 throughout his term of seventeen and one-half years as manager of Peter Wilson Hairston's "Cooleemee Hill" plantation in Davie County, North Carolina. Another Hairston overseer, Johnson G. Giles, received an annual wage of $200 during the entire period from 1843 to 1865. Modest raises of $50 each were accorded two other overseers by the tightfisted Hairston after they had served consecutive terms of five and six years respectively.[24]

There was no perceptible tendency toward a general increase in overseer wages during the nineteenth century. If such an increase did occur, it by no means kept pace with the advance in slave prices which characterized this period. On those plantations whose extant records cover an appreciable period of time the usual starting salary for overseers of similar ability remained nearly constant despite the passage of time. For example, the normal overseer salary on Pierre Phanor Prudhomme's "Bermuda" plantation in Natchitoches Parish, Louisiana, was $800 throughout the period 1838–63.[25]

The usual time for payment of overseer wages was at the end of the calendar year. However, most overseers received advances from their employers for articles needed during the year and then drew the balance at the conclusion of their term. Some of the more frugal preferred to leave the balance in account with the planter, thus insuring the creation of a substantial capital reserve during their term of service. Lewis Thompson's excellent absentee overseer Moore Rawls was one who elected to leave his money in account with his employer, as the following letter from Thompson's son reveals: "Mr. Rawls Said he did not want any money except enough to settle his store accounts. So I got Mr. Robenson [Thompson's factor] to include them in yours and gave him a draft for the whole. and got a receipt for the amount of Mr. Rawls's from him, Rawls which is to be deducted from his yearly wages." [26] During his five years as overseer of Thompson's Rapides Parish, Louisiana, plantation, Rawls was able to save $4,185.70 from an annual salary of

$1,000. [27] Overseer John Griffin accumulated a cash balance of more than $850 during sixteen years of service on John Hartwell Cocke's Bremo estate in Fluvanna County, Virginia.[28] Griffin's annual income was between $200 and $250. By this procedure many overseers accumulated sufficient capital to leave the overseeing profession and embark upon an independent farming career.

The many variable factors affecting the wages of an overseer make broad generalizations concerning the figure received by the average plantation overseer in the Old South extremely hazardous. It is safe to say that wages, in general, ranged from between $100 to $2,000 per year, exclusive of fringe benefits. More precise estimates may be postulated for each of the four major staple regions.

In the tobacco and grain area the maximum overseer salary was about $400, regardless of the size of the farming unit or number of slaves managed. The average in this region was between $200 and $250. Historian John Hebron Moore, basing his estimate on data in various plantation books in the Mississippi Department of Archives and History, has expressed the view that during the period from 1830 to 1860 Mississippi overseers received only $350–$500 per year, with a few exceptional managers earning as much as $600. [29] Possibly a more accurate estimate of overseer salaries in the cotton region is a range of $200–$1,000, with an average figure of about $450.

Peak salaries were commanded by managers of the large rice and sugar estates of South Carolina and Louisiana. Joseph Carlyle Sitterson, who has made an intensive study of plantation operations in the sugar parishes, has estimated that in the 1820's overseers in that region were receiving $500–$700 on moderate-sized units of fewer than a hundred slaves, and as much as $1,200 on a few of the largest estates. By the 1850's the salary scale had risen to $500–$700 on small plantations of fifty slaves or less, and to about $1,000 on moderate-sized units with fewer than two hundred Negroes. On the eve of the Civil War, according to Professor Sitterson, overseers on the largest plantations were commanding salaries of $1,500 to $2,000 per year.[30] Average salaries on the rice coast were slightly lower than those paid in the sugar parishes. However, the financial remuneration earned by managers of the largest South Carolina and Georgia rice estates, such as Governor William Aiken's vast

Jehossee Island plantation, equaled the salaries paid to overseers of the largest sugar plantations.

Bonus provisions were occasionally incorporated into agreements between planters and their overseers as an added inducement to spur the latter toward a supreme effort. Such a provision enabled the overseer to earn a higher salary if an unusually large crop were harvested. The bonus stipulation was opposed by many planters and agricultural reformers, who argued with considerable justification that it encouraged the overseer to overwork the slaves. A variation of the bonus contract was the payment of a straight cash bonus at the end of the year as a reward for good management, rather than as part of a specific production agreement.

The bonus arrangement appears to have been utilized most widely in the newer cotton areas of the Southwest, where owners sought quick returns on their investments. It was frequently charged that in this region the reputation of an overseer depended solely on the number of bales of cotton he produced. Cotton producers normally offered bonuses of from $1 to $5 for each bale above a specified minimum, or a higher salary if the overseer produced a fixed quota.

Dr. Walter Wade, proprietor of "Ross Wood" plantation near Natchez, agreed to give overseer Hiram Reeves $350 as "standing wages" for the year 1847. But if the plantation produced 150 bales of cotton his compensation would be increased to $375, and Reeves could earn an additional bonus of $25 if he made 175 bales. The energetic Reeves responded by producing a crop of 197 bales, thus earning the full $400. In the hope of inspiring his resourceful overseer to an even higher level of production, Dr. Wade altered the arrangement slightly the following year. The contract for 1848 again stipulated standing wages of $350, but now Reeves was "to receive in addition $1 pr. Bale for every Bale after 150." In another year the Mississippi proprietor, who seemingly had an endless variety of compensatory provisions, contracted with overseer John W. Page to manage "Ross Wood" at the rate of $1 for each load of corn, $1 for each stack of fodder, and $3 for each bale of cotton produced.[31]

Mississippi planter Francis Terry Leak often rewarded his overseer with an additional $50 at the end of the year if the latter had given satisfactory service.[32] In the fall of 1860 Leak departed from his policy of paying a fixed bonus to graduate the salary of his overseer in direct proportion to the size of the crop. The following terms were offered J. C. Smith, overseer of Leak's absentee property in Arkansas: "Wrote to J C Smith offering him for his services the next year a salary of $600.00 & one dollar per bale for every bale over 300 in number, averaging 500 lbs per bale; & $5.00 per thousand for all the pork raised, provided we raise more than 5,000 lbs." [33]

Planters in other areas occasionally rewarded their overseers for efficient managerial performances by the payment of premiums or bonuses. John Berkley Grimball, a wealthy South Carolina rice planter, offered his operatives a wide variety of bonus arrangements. His usual method was to offer a reward of four to six cents per bushel on all rice produced in excess of a specified average crop. [34] In 1841, however, one Tyler was engaged to manage Grimball's "Slann's Island" plantation at a salary of $150 plus one-tenth of the net proceeds from the crop in excess of $2,000. [35] Johnson G. Giles, overseer of Peter Wilson Hairston's "Camp Branch" tract in Henry County, Virginia, after having served in Hairston's employ for fifteen years, received annual premiums based on tobacco production in the late 1850's. [36] Thus, although the utilization of some form of bonus agreement was not confined to any specific region, it was employed extensively only in the lower cotton belt.

Another method of compensating overseers was the crop-share system, which prevailed widely along the Atlantic seaboard during the colonial period but which had largely disappeared by the beginning of the nineteenth century. Under this plan an overseer worked with a small number of Negroes owned by his employer and received a share of the crop proportionate to the amount of labor expended upon it by him—the amount of his share varied directly with the number of slaves worked. Shares on the North Carolina farms of Peter Hairston ranged all the way from one-seventh to one-thirteenth during the period 1784–1832. Overseers of Virginia aristrocrat Robert Carter received a crop share of one-ninth as their annual compensation. [37] The monetary reward of overseers engaged on crop shares varied considerably from year to year, but it usually approximated the wage scale instituted in the Upper South following the abandonment of the crop-share system of payment. For example, John Griffin received an annual income of about $200 from his shares, while serving as an overseer on John Hartwell Cocke's Bremo estate during the period 1828–42. [38]

Typical of the crop-share arrangements was an agreement of 1794 between overseer Robert R. Reid and his South Carolina employer John Ewing Colhoun. Reid was engaged to manage the latter's "Twelve Mile Run" plantation upon the following terms: "Mr. Colhoun is to put seven Workers with me, & is to allow me one share out of Eight of all the Corn & Indigo made on sd. Plantatn.—I am to conduct the whole Business of the Plantn. & take care of all Stock of Horses, Cattle, Hogs & c." [39] A unique feature was included in an agreement between Robert Hairston and William Wilson. The latter contracted to manage "Shoe Buckle" plantation in Stokes County, North Carolina, during the year 1834. Wilson was to receive as compensation "the Seventh part of the good grain, tobacco, cotten & flax, that is made on the place—But if he should during the year use spirituous liquor of any kind he is only to have eighth part of what is made." [40]

Ulrich Bonnell Phillips observed that the crop-share system was generally replaced in the nineteenth century by payment of fixed salaries in order "to diminish the inducement for over-driving." [41] This did not solve the problem entirely, for the practice of scaling salaries according to the size of the crop—which also encouraged overdriving—was not abolished in the nineteenth century. Nor did the crop-share stipulation disappear everywhere after 1800. Payment by this method was continued well into the nineteenth century by some of the older planting families in the coastal areas. Members of the Hairston family were still engaging overseers on shares as late as the 1830's, and the same mode of payment was utilized to compensate John Griffin for his services on the Bremo estate as late as 1843. [42]

Variations of the standard crop-share system were sometimes employed in the nineteenth century. Overseer Farran was engaged to manage John Grimball's "Slann's Island" plantation in 1835, for which service he was to receive one-tenth of the net proceeds from the cotton and rice crops. If discharged before the end of the year, he was to receive payment at the rate of $300 per annum. [43] C. Croxton, veteran manager of W. H. Tayloe's "Forkland" plantation in Richmond County, Virginia, received a salary of $50 plus one-twelfth of the grain and peas raised on the place during the years 1840–1842. [44] Croxton was the only one of Tayloe's numerous overseers to be employed on such a basis.

There was some difference of opinion within the planter group regarding the relative merits and demerits of the crop-share system of payment. John Taylor of Caroline was vociferous in his denunciation of the system. Overseers, charged Taylor, were

bribed by agriculturists, not to improve, but to impoverish their land, by a share of the crop for one year; an ingenious contrivance for placing the land in these states, under an annual rack rent, and a removing tenant. The farm, from several gradations to an unlimited extent, is surrendered to the transient overseer, whose salary is increased in proportion as he can impoverish the land. The greatest annual crop, and not the most judicious culture, advances his interest, and establishes his character; and the fees of these land doctors are much higher for killing than for curing. It is common for an industrious overseer, after a very few years, to quit a farm on account of the barrenness, occasioned by his own industry; and frequent changes of these itinerant managers of agriculture, each striving to extract the remnant of fertility left by his predecessor, combines with our agricultural ignorance, to form the completest system of impoverishment, of which any other country can boast.[45]

Taylor urged the payment of monetary wages, which would encourage the gradual improvement of agricultural property, thereby benefiting both proprietor and overseer. A writer in the Columbia *South Carolinian* echoed the sentiments expressed by Taylor. "There are . . . some proprietors of considerable property and pretension to being planters," said he, "who give their overseer a proportion of the crop for his wages; thus bribing him by the strongest inducements of self-interest, to overstrain and work down every thing committed to his charge." [46]

An additional charge leveled at the crop-share system was that it tended to promote dissension between planter and overseer. The interest of the overseer was to draw from the land as much as possible during his year of engagement. On the other hand, the planter was often interested in long-range results, which could best be obtained by a judicious utilization of land and slaves. Moreover, declared C. T. Botts, editor of the *Southern Planter*, "to give a share in the crop, necessarily implies some authority in the management by which it is to be made." Two masters, said Botts, were objectionable and created an intolerable situation for the proprietor, whose superior knowledge and education entitled him to be the sole possessor of authority on the plantation.[47]

Not all observers opposed the crop-share plan. A contributor to the *Farmers' Register* in 1836 lamented the passing of the old crop-share system. Reasoning from the assumption that only ownership of the soil can inspire any lively concern in its improvement, the correspondent contended that the change from crop shares to fixed salaries had destroyed the interest of the overseer in the fruits of his year's work.[48] In similar fashion, a writer in the *Southern Planter* argued that an overseer should be given an interest in the crop. He could not then say, "as when he received stipulated wages, 'Soul, take thy rest,' but eternal vigilance is his interest, the effects of which will be good enclosures, enriched lands, good teams, and increased crops."[49] Notwithstanding these pleas for its preservation, the crop-share system had passed out of existence nearly everywhere by about 1840. Because its demise occurred before the expansion of the plantation system into the Lower South, it apparently never gained a foothold in the cotton and sugar regions.

Slaveholding overseers, whose numbers were greater than most earlier secondary writers have indicated, frequently augmented their income by hiring out Negroes to their employers. For example, in 1798 Michael Boineau, manager of John E. Colhoun's "Bonneau's Ferry" and "Pimlico" plantations, leased seven working Negroes to his employer for the duration of that year. Colhoun agreed to pay his overseer £16 for each slave and, in addition, contracted to furnish them with clothing and provisions.[50] By hiring out his own Negroes and by saving his substantial salary, Jordan Bailey, a Mississippi overseer, managed to acquire a small cotton plantation of his own in the early 1840's. His average salary as manager of "Killona" plantation over an 8-year span was $720, but his average annual income during the same period was increased by the hire of as many as four slaves per year to almost $1,000.[51]

The rates of Negro hire varied widely with time and geographic area. The age, sex, skill, and physical condition of each Negro also influenced the leasing cost. In general the average rate of hired slaves was one-seventh of their sale value per year, although the figure would be proportionately less for younger Negroes and higher for still productive older slaves.[52] Consequently the rates of slave hire advanced appreciably during the nineteenth century as slave prices increased.

In 1802 Arad Welton, overseer for John L. Wilkins in Greenville County, Virginia, hired a Negro to a neighboring planter for a sum equivalent to $17 for the year.[53] During the 1820's and 1830's slaves were hired out by overseers to two of the largest planters in the tobacco region at the rate of $25–$30 per annum.[54] Of course, prime field hands brought a substantially higher recompense. Doctrine W. Davenport, overseer for North Carolina proprietor Ebenezer Pettigrew, hired two such laborers to his employer in 1833 for a total of $150. The following year he received $180 for the hire of three prime Negroes. These rates represented a sum greater than one-half of Davenport's regular salary during each of the years.[55] Payments for the hire of Negroes were higher in the Lower South because of the greater demand for slave labor in that area. In 1845 Negroes were being hired out in Plaquemines Parish, Louisiana, at the rate of $120 per year for men and $100 for women.[56] Five years later prime field hands in the Alabama Black Belt were being hired at an annual rate of about $125. [57]

One difficulty which might confront an overseer who hired slaves to his employer was encountered by J. B. Grace, manager of Charles Tait's "Springfield" plantation in Wilcox County, Alabama. In the fall of 1834 Grace purchased a male slave, whose wife he already owned. He was apprehensive about adding the two Negroes and their children to the "Springfield" slave force for fear that Tait's Negroes would accuse him of giving his own wards favored treatment. Grace resolved the dilemma by hiring his slaves to a neighboring planter.[58] Most slave-owning overseers, nevertheless, found it more convenient to hire out their slaves to the proprietor for whom they worked.

In order to ascertain the relative level of overseer wages, it is necessary to compare the salaries received by overseers with those paid to other white plantation operatives. Because more white laborers were employed on sugar plantations than on any other type of agricultural unit, that region has been selected for the comparison. Aside from the overseer, the most important white employees utilized on sugar plantations were the sugar maker and the engineer. These posts were filled only during the grinding season, which normally lasted four to five months, and each required an individual of considerable skill and experience.

Sugar makers were commonly paid according to the number of hogsheads of sugar produced. During the 1840's and 1850's Louisiana sugar makers received from 75¢ to $1.25 per hogshead up to a maximum salary of $400–$500. An engineer who doubled as sugar boiler and machinist could earn as much as $125–$150 per month during the rolling season.[59]

In addition to a sugar maker and engineer, a number of skilled white artisans—carpenters, bricklayers, coopers—were employed periodically on most sugar estates. Their wages were more modest than those of the sugar maker and engineer, but were still quite substantial. At the close of the antebellum period a carpenter on Maunsell White, Jr.'s "Velasco" plantation received $60 per month plus provisions. A bricklayer on the same plantation was paid at the rate of $2.25 per day.[60] Morris Londerbough, who worked as a carpenter on "Magnolia" plantation at frequent intervals during the 1850's, also received a daily wage of $2.25 plus a house and two meals a day while working.[61] Coopers were usually paid a fixed sum for each hogshead made. During the 1850's they received from 75¢ to $1.00 for each hogshead.[62]

It is difficult to estimate the annual earnings of those laborers discussed above because their employment was not continuous, and they were not paid on a yearly basis. But it seems safe to conclude that only the sugar maker and engineer received an annual income comparable to that enjoyed by most overseers in the sugar region. Undoubtedly some of the most skilled carpenters and bricklayers commanded wages that, in the short run, exceeded those earned by many overseers, although the continuity of employment and the fringe benefits accorded the overseer placed him in a more secure financial position. Still, for the multitudinous duties and heavy responsibilities which he bore, the overseer remained grossly underpaid.

In addition to a stipulated salary and food allowance, all overseers were accorded free housing. They might be lodged in a portion of the plantation house or in a separate dwelling, usually located near the slave quarters. Bachelors were more likely to be housed in the same dwelling occupied by the proprietor and his family. However, separate overseer houses were available on a great number of plantations, including many of the smaller units. References to the construction of new overseer houses are common in extant plantation diaries and letters.

PICKING COTTON

The overseer dwelling on Pierce Butler's absentee rice estate near Darien, Georgia, was described by the critical Fanny Kemble as consisting of "three small rooms, and three still smaller, which would be more appropriately designated as closets, a wooden recess by way of pantry, and a kitchen detached from the dwelling." [63] During the unhappy sojourn of Butler and his actress wife on Butler's Island during the winter of 1838–39, the overseer was relegated to two of the smallest rooms in the house just described. He utilized one room as his bedroom and the other as his office. Somewhat more commodious quarters were afforded the overseer of Dr. John Carmichael Jenkins' "River Place," located below Natchez. The house, erected in December, 1848, had a brick chimney, a gallery, 3-foot cypress weatherboarding, glass windows on the inside and shutters with hooks on the outside, and was whitewashed "thoroughly . . . both inside & out." Upon its completion, a white paling fence was constructed around this pleasant domicile. Furnishings supplied by Jenkins included a bed with curtains and mosquito bar, a table, several chairs, knives, forks, and cooking utensils.[64] It is likely that the structures housing most overseers were somewhat less pretentious than the dwelling erected by Dr. Jenkins. The average domicile of southern overseers could, perhaps, be most accurately described as modest but adequate.

The length of time during which an overseer remained in the service of a single employer was notoriously short in many areas of the Old South. Countless examples could be cited to illustrate the rapid turnover of southern overseers, but two of the most extreme will suffice. On few plantations did an overseer experience greater difficulties than on "Clermont" plantation, located near Natchez, Mississippi. It is probable that the proprietor of this property, Captain John Nevitt, was very exacting in his demands upon subordinates, for he was constantly hiring and firing overseers, millwrights, wheelwrights, carpenters, and other plantation employees. Nevitt changed overseers a total of nineteen times during the 7-year period from 1826 to 1832, and discharged seven different managers in the course of a single year—1827. One overseer lasted only three days, and the one who enjoyed the longest period of employment under Nevitt served for less than a year.[65] Conditions were little better on the Alabama cotton plantation of Hugh Davis, where eighteen different overseers were employed during an 18-year span. The longest term of service was slightly over three years, but the average was about ten months.[66] Despite such examples as the above, it is erroneous to infer that such brief terms typified conditions of overseer employment throughout the South; nor is it correct to conclude that brevity of tenure was necessarily an indication of a lack of overseer competence. It was the general practice on some plantations in the Lower South to change overseers every year no matter how satisfactorily they performed.[67]

Heretofore there has been no attempt to distinguish between different staple areas in assessing the time southern overseers remained in the service of a single planter. As a result, the abbreviated terms which characterized overseer employment in the cotton and sugar regions have been extended to embrace the older, more stable, Atlantic coastal areas. The truth is that overseers in the tobacco and rice regions enjoyed a significantly longer average tenure than did their counterparts in the Southwest. A survey of nearly one hundred managers on the South Carolina rice coast, for which sufficient data was available, reveals that they enjoyed an average tenure of 3.6 years. Continuous terms of ten, fifteen, and even twenty years were not uncommon in Virginia and the Carolinas. This subject will be discussed more fully in later chapters. It will suffice to say, for the present, that the general impression that overseers did not remain in one place longer than a year or two[68] does not accurately describe conditions in many parts of the South.

Managerial terms on absentee estates tended to be longer than those enjoyed by the overseers of resident plantations. Absentee managers were accorded greater independence, and the opportunity for friction to develop between planter and overseer was more remote if the owner resided at some distance. In addition, the greater responsibilities entailed in the management of absentee units required the employment of a more capable group of overseers—a group that was less likely to prove unsatisfactory and thus to require removal. Only four overseers were employed during the period from 1837 to 1861 on Lewis Thompson's absentee sugar plantation in Rapides Parish, Louisiana. The 6-year average term of these overseers was exceptionally high for the sugar region. The average term of overseers on Maunsel White's absentee plantations was almost three times as long as the average at "Deer Range," where White maintained his residence.

Another aspect of the subject of tenure concerns the liability of overseers to discharge on very short notice. One writer has concluded that "this insecurity of tenure undoubtedly contributed to the perpetuation of an incapable group of overseers and frequently resulted in undesirable relations between planter and overseer." [69] The fact is, however, that clauses permitting the termination of contracts upon little or no notice were common in most occupations during the antebellum period. Unless an overseer was particularly unlucky in his choice of an employer, he had little to fear on this point if he behaved himself and conducted his business in an efficient manner. Most overseers who found themselves seeking a new position before the end of their previous term had given their employers sufficient cause to make a change.

There is evidence that some large planters, whose holdings consisted of a number of separate units, rotated their overseers from one unit to another at periodic intervals. On no estate, however, did this appear to be a systematic procedure. Still, the number of instances in which overseers were shifted is sufficiently large to justify the assumption that such transfers were part of a deliberate policy pursued by the proprietor. Such a policy may have been prompted by the belief that a rotation of overseers would result in a more efficient utilization of slave labor. Some owners felt that on plantations where the same overseer remained in control for a number of years, the slaves often took advantage of their knowledge of the overlooker's managerial shortcomings to work at a pace considerably short of their full capacity without being subjected to punishment.

The practice of rotating overseers was particularly striking on W. H. Tayloe's Mount Airy estate and on the North Carolina plantations of Ruth S. Hairston. J. D. Reynolds managed no less than five different farms at various times during his fifteen years of service on Mount Airy estate.[70] An amazing 31 percent of the identifiable overseers on Ruth Hairston's vast holdings in Stokes County, North Carolina, served terms on two or more of the Hairston plantations during the period 1842–66. [71]

Before concluding this chapter, it seems appropriate to ex-

amine the position occupied by the overseer in the social structure of the time. The majority of overseers came from the
yeoman farmer element of southern society. According to
one writer, the overseeing profession was one of only two
escapes open to the poor whites and was therefore "a cherished
ambition." Suffering from competition with slave labor and
lacking the means to acquire the necessary capital to become
planters, the poor whites could aspire only to be overseers
or to become small commercial farmers in areas where cheap
land was available.[72] The overseeing occupation also offered
to "young, landless, moneyless men moving west" the opportunity to achieve a fresh start in life by saving money and ul-
timately becoming farmers or even planters themselves.[73]

The composition of the group comprising the overseer class
varied somewhat among the different staple regions. Lewis
Gray estimated that about 60 percent of the overseers in Virginia in the mid-1840's were former mechanics who had turned
to overseeing "as a supposedly easy way of making a living." [74]
An authority on planting operations in the South Carolina rice
districts noted that the overseers in that region "were generally
young men, some of them of good family, who took this method
of gaining experience and getting a start in the world. A
great many accomplished this and in after years became planters
themselves and made fortunes as landed proprietors." [75] It is
more likely, however, that the typical rice plantation overseer
came from a background similar to that which characterized the
managers of Robert F. W. Allston. The latter drew his overseers from the poorer class who had settled in the pinelands of
Georgetown District, in which the Allston plantations were
situated. Most of the surnames of Allston's managers were to
be found in Georgetown District as early as 1790. [76]

Similarly, overseers in the cotton and sugar states were
usually the sons of yeoman slaveholders or poor farmers. One
feature peculiar to the sugar parishes was the employment
of some sugar makers as overseers during their off season.
Thus, R. Bachemin, who had served as sugar maker on Lewis
Thompson's Rapides Parish plantation during the years 1857–
59, and on Maunsel White's "Deer Range" plantation in the
fall of 1860, was engaged by White in January, 1861, to oversee "Deer Range." Bachemin did not distinguish himself in
the new position and was discharged at the end of March.[77]

Although native Southerners predominated in the overseeing profession, some outstanding managers were foreign immigrants or persons of northern birth. Martin W. Philips was one planter who preferred southern overseers, declaring that "they feel near to us and we to them." [78] On the other hand, Benjamin Talbot, a native of Boston, drew praise from Georgia rice planter Hugh Fraser Grant for his management of the latter's "Elizafield" plantation during the 1840's. At Talbot's death in 1846, Grant remarked that his overseer had been a very efficient man and that his demise represented "a great loss to me." [79] A German traveler, on a voyage down the Mississippi River in 1817, encountered a fellow countryman serving as overseer for one of the wealthiest cotton planters on the Fausse River [False River] in Pointe Coupee Parish, Louisiana. [80] Of course, the overwhelming majority of Louisiana overseers of foreign extraction were French.

Despite exceptions such as those noted above, nearly all overseers were native Southerners. In Virginia and the Carolinas, most were natives of the state in which they were employed. Many who pursued the overseeing occupation in the Southwest, however, had migrated there from the older plantation states. Indeed, this was characteristic of the population at large in the Lower South. This southward migration of overseers will be examined more closely in the next chapter.

Many persons entered the overseeing profession from other occupations. Carpenters and coopers were probably most numerous among those who transferred their talents to the business of managing agricultural units. A former railroad overseer was employed to manage Lewis Thompson's Louisiana plantation in 1856. [81] His lack of farming knowledge apparently proved a severe handicap, because he stayed only one year on a plantation noteworthy for the long tenure of its overseers. Those entering the overseer profession usually had worked on plantations in some other capacity and were familiar with agricultural matters.

Although the customary inclination was in the opposite direction, some independent farmers abandoned their agricultural pursuits temporarily to serve as overseers. This was true only of very small operators, who presumably entered the overseeing business with the hope of acquiring enough capital to expand their operations. One such farmer was William H. Hollwell of Rich Square, North Carolina, who wrote to Lewis Thompson in 1860 requesting a "situation for next year" on one of Thompson's North Carolina farms. Hollwell explained that he could not "take holt" until the end of the year as he was presently engaged in "farming for my self." [82] Another North Carolinian, Archibald Stubbs, was a local yeoman farmer when he assumed direction of Ebenezer Pettigrew's "Belgrade" plantation in 1825. [83]

Some overseers who quit their occupation to farm for themselves experienced difficulty in earning a livelihood and soon resumed the business of overseeing to augment their income. Thus, John W. Page, who had enjoyed a successful 4-year term as manager of "Ross Wood" plantation in Jefferson County, Mississippi, left the employment of Dr. Walter Wade in February, 1846, to commence his own agricultural enterprise. The new business did not prove lucrative and he was soon overseeing again, entering the service of a neighboring proprietor in the summer of the same year. [84] It is likely that few independent farmers undertook overseeing engagements with the intention of pursuing that profession as a permanent occupation.

The entrance of planters' sons into the overseeing profession as a means of preparing themselves for later planting careers has been noted previously and needs little elaboration here. [85] Prominent North Carolina planters Thomas Ruffin and Ebenezer Pettigrew employed their sons as overseers on their own plantations with this purpose in mind. Pettigrew's sons, Charles and William, assumed the management of "Bonarva" and "Belgrade" plantations in 1839 at an annual salary of $200 each. By 1841 William Pettigrew had been assigned complete responsibility for the operation of "Belgrade," and his salary had risen to $350 plus subsistence. William and Charles Pettigrew continued to operate their respective units for many years after the death of their father in 1848. [86] The overseeing career of Holden Evans, Jr., second son of a Rankin County, Mississippi, cotton producer, was an abbreviated one. The 20-year-old Evans began his agricultural career in 1858 as overseer for a proprietor in neighboring Hinds County, but the following year he "bought out" his older brother and commenced farming "on his own account." [87]

The overseer calling was held in social disesteem by a large segment of the planting community. This was undoubtedly an important factor in lessening the attractiveness of the profession in the eyes of many competent young men with managerial inclinations. According to a writer in the *Carolina Planter*, most overseers were "regarded by their employers merely as dependents; who are to be kept at a distance . . . as hirelings, who are hardly worthy the wages of their daily labour. The planter looks down upon his overseer, as one of an inferior and degraded caste." [88] In an address delivered at the first anniversary meeting of the United Agricultural Society of South Carolina in December, 1827, Whitemarsh B. Seabrook referred to the "degrading function" which overseers exercised "in public esteem." [89] The most that can be said for the majority of proprietors is that they treated their subordinates politely but with condescension.

The typical planter view of the social status of overseers was exemplified by Lewis Thompson in a letter to his son Thomas. The elder Thompson, on one of his infrequent visits to his Louisiana plantation, was seeking a plantation upon which his son might locate, and had enjoyed little success in finding a suitable place. Regarding the locale of Meredith Place, from which he had just returned, Thompson observed: "As to Society there was but one or two *neighbors* at all: one of them, I thought very *well off*, the others were cast-off overseers who could not get any employment, and were forced to settle on such cheap places as they could find:" [90] An Alabama overseer was incensed because he could get no introduction to "a nice young lady," who was a guest in the home of his employer. "Was at the table with her today twice & in the Parlor tonight & received no introduction to her," he fumed. [91]

Of course there were exceptions to such snobbish behavior by planters toward their managerial hirelings. As might be anticipated, overseer and employer were most nearly on a plane of social equality on the smallest agricultural units. It was not unusual for the two to take their meals together on such establishments. Francis Taylor, who was intimate with the Madisons, Pendletons, Catletts, and other prominent western Virginia families, frequently dined with the overseers of his small "Midland" plantation during the immediate post-Revolutionary War period. [92] David Gavin, who conducted a small planting operation in Colleton District, South Carolina, sometimes dined with the overseers of adjoining plantations. [93] Occasionally, larger proprietors treated their subordinates with genuine warmth and hospitality. Unlike many of his colleagues, Dr. John Carmichael Jenkins enjoyed harmonious relations with his overseers and frequently praised their professional exertions in his behalf. On one occasion he wrote Samuel Grier, overseer of one of his plantations below Natchez, and invited him "to come up to our party on Monday Evening next." Grier, however, failed to make his appearance on the festive occasion— a fact duly noted by Dr. Jenkins in his diary.[94]

Female proprietors, too, seemed to get along well with their managers, perhaps because they had genuine respect for the agricultural knowledge of the latter. Mississippi manager John Ireland enjoyed a social position almost equivalent to that of a planter during the decade of his overseership of "Locust Grove," a cotton plantation owned by Olivia Dunbar. Indeed, the Irelands and their four children were accepted almost as members of the Dunbar household. The two families visited one another almost daily, attended church together, and assisted one another during troubled times.[95] A Louisiana proprietress was not averse to playing backgammon with her overseer in the evenings. This delightful relationship apparently cooled on one such evening, however, for the overseer was jailed on suspicion of assaulting his employer and murdering her child.[96]

Whatever may have been the view of the planter class regarding the rung on the social ladder occupied by slave managers, the overseer himself had no feeling of class inferiority and showed little resentment toward the proprietary group.[97] He found himself entirely in accord with the equalitarian sentiment which permeated many parts of the country near the end of the antebellum period. Of course, like most other Southerners, he did not include the Negro in his conception of equality. But, despite his lack of property and education, the overseer believed that he was just as worthy as his employer and entitled to just as much respect.

Notwithstanding the exceptional instances of agreeable social relations between planter and overseer cited in the preceding paragraphs, it is a melancholy fact that most southern overseers were obliged to live in relative isolation. Ostracized by most members of the planter class, forbidden to associate with the slaves, discouraged from entertaining company, and prohibited from leaving the plantation except for brief periods,

the average overseer lived in almost a social vacuum. The con-
fining nature of the overseer post is illustrated by an agreement
of 1842 between William Lewis Sharkey, a distinguished Mississippi jurist, and his overseer, Noah A. Ward. The latter,
according to the agreement, was not to leave the plantation
"except on pressing private business or for the benefit of the
plantation, nor is he to have company with him on the plantation." ⁹⁸ The overseers of Louisiana proprietor William J. Minor
were placed under the following restriction: "He must not leave
the plantation except on business of his Employer—He must
never remain off the place at night under any circumstances
without the consent or knowledge of his Employer—" ⁹⁹ Such
restrictions were general on plantations throughout the South.

The isolated position of the plantation overseer is illustrated
vividly by the following passage, contained in a letter of May,
1858, from overseer Moore Rawls to his employer, Lewis Thompson:

for my own part I dont get time Scarcely to eat or Sleep. I have not
been off of the plantation since the 3ʳᵈ of oct   I went to Alexandria
to get the winter Clothing & Co, except once I rode down to Lecompt to
get a watch key. So you Can judge that I Cannot know much about the
crops in our vicinity. The truth is no man can begain to attend to such
a business with any set of negros, without the strictest vigilance on his
part.¹⁰⁰

In the neighboring state of Mississippi, overseer William B.
Farrar took pen in hand one bright Sunday in April, 1861,
and inscribed this plaintive message in the pages of his plantation book: "I am very Lonesome to Day   I think I shall Have
to get me a wife & where shall I find hir   Ladies seem to
Be as scarce as chicken Teeth In This vacinity." 101

With most overseers doomed to lead lonely lives among their
ignorant black charges, it is little wonder that the managerial
profession held so little attraction for ambitious young men in the
Old South.

Most southern overseers entertained fairly modest aspirations
with regard to advancing their social and economic position.
Few had any compulsive desire to acquire great wealth or to
move into the large planter class. Like other simple folk in the
Old South, "their ambition was to acquire land and other property sufficient to give them and their children a sense of security

and well-being, to be 'good livers' and 'have something saved for a rainy day' as they would have put it." [102] It is likely that opportunities for advancement in status were more numerous in the fluid society of the Southwest than in the seaboard slave states where class lines tended to be more rigid. Traveling from Natchez to Tuscaloosa through the interior cotton districts, one observer encountered a number of small proprietors who had commenced their agricultural careers as overseers. He characterized these men in the following terms:

> It is frequently the case . . . that the planter has started as a poor, and entirely self-dependent young man, the basis of whose present fortune consisted of his savings from the wages earned by him as overseer—these are commonly as illiterate as the very poorest of our northern agricultural laborers. Yet again there are those who, beginning in the same way, have acquired, while so employed, not only a capital with which to purchase land and slaves, but a valuable stock of experience and practical information, and somewhat of gentlemanly bearing from intercourse with their employers.[103]

It is extremely difficult to document the movement of individuals from the overseeing profession to small agricultural proprietorships. If one had the patience and stamina to trace, by name, a large sampling of overseers listed in the 1850 census[104] by checking their occupations in later census returns, such documentation would be possible. Nevertheless, there is sufficient evidence from other sources to justify the conclusion that the transition from overseeing to farming was achieved by a great number of southern overseers. A few examples will suffice to illustrate this point.

It required fifteen years for John G. Traylor, an ambitious Alabama overseer, to establish himself as a small, independent, slaveholding farmer. Traylor, a man deficient in formal schooling but devoutly religious, began his overseeing career in 1827 at the age of eighteen. Earning an annual compensation ranging from $200 to $600, the energetic Traylor pursued the business of overseeing on various cotton plantations in central Alabama until the summer of 1842 when he elected to retire from the occupation "on . . . account of my helth not being good." On July 9 he wrote: "This is the end of my over seeing. I have been at it this is 15 years." [105]

About 1840, even before he left the overseeing profession,

Traylor became associated with his brother James in the operation of a small farm near Benton, Alabama. In the twilight of his managerial career the veteran overseer turned his attention to the acquisition of land and slaves. He acquired two hundred fifty-five acres of land for a price in excess of $1,000 and by January, 1842, had purchased a total of six slaves, one of whom was valued at $725. Shortly after he relinquished his last overseeing position, "Brother James and mee divided out things"—as Traylor phrased it—and the former overseer entered upon a period of modest prosperity as an independent cotton farmer. During the next five years he cleared new ground and constructed Negro houses, a stable, a wagon shelter, a corn crib, a smoke house, and a residence for himself. His average corn yield during this time span was five hundred fifty bushels per year, and he marketed about fifteen bales of cotton annually. By 1846 he was sufficiently prosperous to spend several months with his family at Butler Springs, an Alabama summer resort.

The career of Virginia overseer Major W. Cumbea provides another illustration of an able and ambitious overseer who accumulated capital, purchased a farm, and left the managerial profession. Following thirteen years of continuous service on Charles Friend's "White Hill" plantation, Cumbea left in 1858 to operate a small farm which he had just purchased.[106] This purchase was consummated despite the fact that his annual salary as "White Hill" overseer never exceeded $250.[107] It should be noted, however, that Cumbea had few expenses during his tenure with Friend, being supplied with food, housing, firewood, a servant, and other essential items. By 1860 Cumbea owned five slaves, valued at $4,000, and possessed real estate worth $3,000.[108] Others repeated this process time after time throughout the South.

Exceptional individuals might achieve even greater earthly rewards and social respectability than the overseers mentioned above. Although it was much more common for an overseer to rise to a position as an independent farmer, a few gifted and fortunate managers became sufficiently affluent to be classified as plantation owners. Joseph P. Kearney served from 1861 to 1874 as the overseer of Daniel Dudley Avery's sugar plantation, located at Petite Anse Island in St. Mary Parish, Louisiana. Kearney later left the overseeing profession and died in New Orleans in 1909 at the age of eighty-two, "having acquired a

plantation of his own & a fine property." [109]   The rise to prosperity of two former Alabama overseers was recounted by James
A. Tait in these words:

> My father had about 25 years ago, two men who were overseers for
> him, Grace and McNeal. Grace at that time had about 10 negroes, but
> no land. McNeal, when he quit my Father, had about $4,000. He is now a
> rich river planter. Grace is a rich planter in the prairies near Allenton.
> Industry, economy and good management, is the way to fortune; say I.
> says all. [110]

Thomas Hall, Mississippi agricultural reformer and importer
of thoroughbred livestock, began his agricultural career as an
overseer for the prominent Minor family of Natchez. After
managing the Minor interests for eighteen years, he left the
overseeing profession and established himself as a slaveowning
planter. By 1852 he was producing eight hundred bales of cotton
annually and was one of the most respected men in his community. According to one authority, Hall "did more than any
other man to develop an interest in fine livestock of all kinds
among planters of the Natchez trade area." [111]

Georgia overseer Elijah Cook chose an easier route to fortune
and social prominence. He had the good fortune to fall in love
with his employer's daughter and proposed marriage—a prospect viewed without enthusiasm by the young lady's parents.
Following their marriage the bride's mother refused to associate
with her daughter's family for seven years, but in the end
they were reconciled and Cook inherited the plantation upon
the death of his mother-in-law. On the eve of the Civil War,
following the death of his wife and children, Cook sold the
plantation and moved to the Midwest. [112]

Occasionally, former overseers were installed in important
political and administrative positions in the communities where
they resided. M. W. Clement, for twelve years the overseer of
John B. Grimball's "Slann's Island" plantation, served as tax
collector of St. Paul Parish and, in 1853, was elected treasurer
to the Commissioners of the Poor for that parish. [113]   L. W.
McCants, another former South Carolina overseer, was elected
sheriff of Colleton District in 1858. [114]   Two former overseers
for J. Hamilton Couper served respectively as tax collector and
surveyor of Glynn County, Georgia, during the 1850's. [115]   One
of these men, James Myers, who acted as assistant overseer of

Couper's "Hamilton" plantation in the late 1820's, had by 1860 accumulated a considerable estate which included twenty-six slaves.[116] Preston Brown, an intelligent and well-educated Alabama manager, wrote his employer in 1859 that "solicitations of the most urgent character and from citizens of the highest respectability, have been urged upon me to become a candidate for the legislature."[117] Apparently he did not choose to enter the contest, for he was still at his managerial post the following year.

The most spectacular rise to prominence of a former overseer is illustrated by the career of John Henninger Reagan, although in all candor it must be admitted that Reagan's overseeing career was a brief one. Reagan was the son of a farmer of modest circumstances in Sevier County, Tennessee. Seeking money to finish his education at Marysville Seminary, the youthful Reagan journeyed southward during the winter of 1838 in search of employment. Although he had no previous experience as an overseer, he secured such a position on a plantation near Natchez, Mississippi, at a salary of $500 per year.[118] Reagan's brief overseeing career ended abruptly in April, 1839, under the following circumstances, as recounted by Reagan in his *Memoirs:* "During the following April . . . the men complained of not having meat enough; whereupon I called Mr. Jackson's [the proprietor] attention to their wants. He declined to satisfy them, and I refused to continue in his service."[119] Reagan later served as a member of the Texas Secession Convention, as a member of the Provisional Congress of the Confederacy, as Postmaster-General of the Confederacy, and as a member of the United States House of Representatives from 1857 to 1861 and again from 1875 to 1891.[120] Such were the heights to which an humble overseer could ascend!

3

A Statistical View
of the
Overseer

IN order to complete the representation of the plantation overseer which has been projected in the preceding
chapters, it is necessary to provide the reader with a
statistical analysis based on the manuscript returns of the
Federal Census of 1860. Although the background and salient
characteristics of individual overseers may be revealed in the
pages of plantation manuscripts and contemporary farm journals, it is only through a painstaking examination of census
data that a composite picture of the southern plantation superintendent may be formulated. Accordingly, information has
been compiled on more than fifteen hundred overseers in
seventeen sample counties in the South; this is presented here in

tabular form for each major staple area, synthesizing the whole so as to permit expression of general conclusions.

In selecting sample counties every effort has been made to secure a representative cross section of southern overseers. Four counties were chosen from each major staple crop region. Within each region selections were made on the basis of geographic location, volume of staple production, and average size of agricultural units. In instances where several choices were possible, the selection was governed by the number of overseers within each county upon whom data had been secured previously from manuscript sources.

A few examples will serve to illustrate the criteria used in selecting counties within each region. Little difficulty was experienced in choosing the rice districts to be analyzed. Rice production in South Carolina was confined almost exclusively to four districts on the Atlantic coast during the antebellum period. Statistical information was also compiled on overseers in Glynn County, Georgia, but the small number listed in that county rendered impossible the computation of any meaningful averages. Therefore, Glynn County will be omitted from the tabular analysis of overseers in the rice belt. The selection of sugar parishes was governed by several factors. The vast median size of the plantation units and slave parcels in Ascension Parish, Louisiana, dictated its inclusion. St. Mary Parish was chosen because of its uniformly high production record during the two decades before the Civil War. Plaquemines and Terrebonne parishes were selected largely because considerable data from other sources had already been accumulated on specific overseers within each one. In the cotton belt geographic dispersion was achieved by the inclusion of one county in eastern Mississippi, two counties in the western part of the same state, and one Louisiana cotton parish. Table 4 indicates the relative standing of the sample counties within each staple region, in volume of agricultural production for 1860. [1]

Before proceeding to a statistical analysis of the overseers in each region, a word of caution should be offered regarding the reliability of the census data upon which this analysis is based. Manifestly there are numerous errors and inaccuracies in all census returns, especially in those compiled during the nineteenth century. The degree of accuracy varies considerably from county to county and depends in large measure upon the care exercised by those who actually compiled the data in each area.

Table 4

AGRICULTURAL PRODUCTION, BY STAPLE REGIONS,
OF SELECTED SOUTHERN COUNTIES, 1860

County	Leading Crop	1860 Production	Rank Within State
(1) Tobacco and Grain Region			
Prince George Co., Va.	grain	–	–
Richmond Co., Va.	grain	–	–
Northampton Co., N.C.	cotton	6,632 bales	7
Stokes Co., N.C.	tobacco	1,513,040 lbs.	7
(2) Rice Coast			
Beaufort Dist., S.C.	rice	18,790,918 lbs.	4
Charleston Dist., S.C.	rice	18,899,512 lbs.	3
Colleton Dist., S.C.	rice	22,838,984 lbs.	2
Georgetown Dist., S.C.	rice	55,805,385 lbs.	1
Glynn Co., Ga.	rice	4,842,755 lbs.	4
(3) Sugar Parishes			
Ascension Parish, La.	sugar	16,087 hhds.	4
Plaquemines Parish, La.	sugar	12,607 hhds.	7
St. Mary Parish, La.	sugar	30,731 hhds.	1
Terrebonne Parish, La.	sugar	17,022 hhds.	3
(4) Cotton Belt			
Hinds Co., Miss.	cotton	54,685 bales	2
Lowndes Co., Miss.	cotton	51,234 bales	4
Yazoo Co., Miss.	cotton	64,075 bales	1
Natchitoches Parish, La.	cotton	36,887 bales	7

In all cases, figures concerning age and property valuation must be considered approximate. The number of illiterates is probably too low in some counties, possibly reflecting the reluctance of many persons to admit their educational deficiencies. No illiterates whatever were listed in the three Mississippi counties for which tabulations were made. It should be noted, however, that literacy was almost essential for effective service in the overseeing profession. Finally, the difficulty experienced in identifying slaveowning overseers has rendered those figures liable to some distortion. Since the occupations of individual slaveowners are not listed in Schedule 2 (Slave Inhabitants), it was possible to isolate the overseer slaveholders only by constant reference to the names of overseers previously compiled from Schedule 1 (Free Inhabitants). It is apparent that some slaveowning overseers were overlooked in the course of this laborious process. Notwithstanding the above limitations, the general picture conveyed by an analysis of the census returns is reasonably accurate.

In the following tables substantial property holdings have been defined arbitrarily as those with a minimum valuation of $5,000 for personal property and $1,000 for real property. Since it was impossible to estimate the number of overseers listed separately, who had families living elsewhere or who had previously been married, all overseers above the age of forty were assumed to be married or to have been married in the past. A slight distortion may have been introduced in some counties by the incorporation into the tabulations of professional stewards and known former overseers. The number of those so included was small, however, and the effect of their inclusion was insignificant in most instances. In the following analysis other distortions will be noted as they appear.

Statistical data on overseers in the Upper South is presented in Table 5. The characteristics of overseers in this region were most strongly influenced by two factors: (1) the social stability produced by the long-continued existence of a relatively homogeneous, agriculturally-oriented population; and (2) the predominance of small farms and small slaveholdings as the basic units of agricultural enterprise in this area. The stable society of the tobacco and grain region was reflected in the large percentage of married overseers. The number of illiterate farm managers, although higher in this region than in any other staple area, was still surprisingly low—about one-tenth of those listed. In accord with the general proclivity of the agricultural population in this region, individual property holdings were small, but more than one-half of the overseers surveyed owned some personal property and about one-tenth were landowners. The proportion of slaveholding overseers, as might be anticipated, was considerably lower than in the other major staple areas. The low salaries received by overseers in this region undoubtedly constituted an important factor in preventing the accumulation of substantial property holdings.

Table 5

STATISTICAL ANALYSIS OF OVERSEERS IN
TOBACCO AND GRAIN REGION, 1860 [2]

	Prince Geo. Co., Va. 35 Overseers	Rich- mond Co., Va. 19 Overseers	North- ampton Co., N.C. 86 Overseers	Stokes Co., N.C. 26 Overseers	Com- posite Re- gional Aver- age[3]
Average Age	33.8	34.2	32.0	36.2	34.0
Per Cent over Age 40	26	21	21	27	24
Per Cent Married	57	58	60	92	67
Per Cent Illiterate	11	10	13	4	10
Per Cent Owning Personal Prop.	31	63	63	69	56
Per Cent Owning Substantial Personal Prop.	3	0	2	12	4
Average Age, Owners of Substantial Personal Prop.	42.0	–	45.0	36.0	41.0
Per Cent Owning Real Property	9	11	6	15	10
Per Cent Owning Substantial Real Property	6	0	1	12	5
Average Age, Owners of Substantial Real Property	42.0	–	30.0	42.3	38.1
Per Cent Owning Slaves	6	5	8	8	7
Avg. No. Owned	4.5	3.0	3.0	5.0	3.9
Average Age, Overseer Slaveholders	43.5	38.0	37.0	41.5	40.0

Some distortion was introduced into the figures for Stokes County, North Carolina, by the inclusion of one steward, three overseer-agents, and three former overseers. This accounts in part for the disproportionately high average age and for the larger property holdings of overseers in that county. Of the former overseers included, one was listed as a day laborer, one as a farm renter, and the other as a miller.

Most of the overseers listed whose family background could be ascertained were the sons of small farmers. It is interesting to note that the wife of one Northampton County, North Carolina, overseer was listed as a tailoress, and the wives of two others in the same county were employed as seamstresses. With few exceptions, all the overseers listed in the two Virginia counties were natives of that state. About 70 percent of those listed in North Carolina were born in that state and the remainder were from Virginia.

Richmond County, Virginia, was the only one of the sixteen southern counties surveyed which did not have a single overseer with substantial real or personal property holdings. The lowest percentage of slaveholding overseers was recorded in the same county. The owner of the most property among those included in the tabulations for this region was Sterling Adams, steward of the Ruth Hairston interests in Stokes County, North Carolina. Adams listed a personal estate of $18,200, which included five slaves.

Table 6 gives the computed averages for almost 350 overseers in the South Carolina rice districts. On the rice coast, with its large plantation and slave units and the exacting demands imposed by the tide-flow system of rice culture, the group of overseers was superior in ability and character to that of any other region. The stable character of rice belt society was reflected in a high percentage of married overseers, as in the tobacco and grain region. The number of those listed as illiterate was an insignificant 4 percent. The relatively high degree of prosperity enjoyed by rice plantation managers is clearly revealed by the figures relating to the ownership of property. No fewer than two-thirds of those listed owned some personal property, and one-fourth possessed real estate. Moreover, 19 percent of those included in the survey were slaveowners, with seven being the average number owned by each slaveholding overseer. The proportion of rice belt overseers listing substantial real and personal estates exceeded the number listing such property in any of the other staple areas.

Fourteen of twenty-three managers whose family background could reasonably be deduced were the sons of farmers. Of the remainder, three each were the sons of small planters and

Table 6

STATISTICAL ANALYSIS OF OVERSEERS
ON RICE COAST, 1860 [4]

	Beaufort Dist., S.C. 106 Overseers	Charleston Dist., S.C. 54 Overseers	Colleton Dist., S.C. 99 Overseers	Georgetown Dist., S.C. 83 Overseers	Composite Regional Average
Average Age	34.3	33.5	37.0	30.4	33.8
Per Cent over Age 40	19	15	36	12	20
Per Cent Married	72	61	74	58	66
Per Cent Illiterate	7	4	3	0	4
Per Cent Owning Personal Prop.	95	39	77	52	66
Per Cent Owning Substantial Personal Prop.	14	2	17	18	13
Average Age, Owners of Substantial Personal Prop.	39.3	37.0	41.0	41.0	39.6
Per Cent Owning Real Property	30	15	20	30	24
Per Cent Owning Substantial Real Property	23	9	12	22	16
Average Age, Owners of Substantial Real Property	39.2	40.4	42.0	39.0	40.2
Per Cent Owning Slaves	18	13	23	22	19
Avg. No. Owned	8.2	3.0	9.1	8.6	7.2
Average Age, Overseer Slaveholders	36.8	37.7	41.4	39.8	38.9

other overseers, two were the sons of a surveyor, and one overseer in Charleston District was the son of a clergyman. An overwhelming 92 percent of the overseers listed were natives of South Carolina. Most of the remainder were from either North Carolina or Ireland.

An examination of Table 6 reveals that the overseers in Charleston District were somewhat less prosperous than their counterparts in the other three rice districts. This was chiefly due to the smaller average size of the plantation units in that district. The greatest concentration of overseers with substantial property holdings was encountered in St. Luke Parish, Beaufort District. Of the first fourteen overseers listed in that parish, eleven were more than forty years of age, all were married or presumably had been married, and ten had a personal estate of at least $1,000. The average personal estate of the fourteen managers was $2,571 and the highest was $10,000. It is probable that large plantation units predominated in this portion of St. Luke Parish.

In some districts there was considerable evidence to support a logical conclusion that the most affluent overseers were working for the largest planters. This correlation was particularly apparent in Colleton District, where nine of the managers with the largest property holdings were definitely associated with wealthy proprietors. The estates of two of these managers, Alexander J. Anderson and Nathaniel B. Adams, were astonishingly large. Anderson, the manager for A. R. Chisolm, owned thirty-one slaves and listed $10,000 in real property and $35,000 in personal property. The combined land and slave property of Adams, who was overseer for James King, was valued at $40,000, and his slaves numbered forty-two. Spectacular as were these holdings, they did not quite match those of John J. Anderson of Prince George Parish in Georgetown District. John Anderson owned forty-seven slaves, and the total value of his estate was estimated at $45,000. Such holdings, of course, were exceptional, but they do demonstrate the amount of property which could be amassed by topflight overseers on the rice coast. Since the average age of the three men was forty-six years, it is probable that all were professional managers rather than planters' sons who had inherited their property.

The overseers in four selected Louisiana sugar parishes are analyzed in Table 7. Because of the more fluid nature of society in this region, the percentage of married overseers was somewhat lower than it was in the older slave states. The number of illiterate overseers again was almost negligible. Contrary to what might be anticipated, the figures indicate that sugar

Table 7

STATISTICAL ANALYSIS OF OVERSEERS IN
SUGAR PARISHES, 1860 [5]

	Ascension Parish, La. 41 Overseers	Plaquemines Parish, La. 41 Overseers	St. Mary Parish, La. 72 Overseers	Terrebonne Parish, La. 74 Overseers	Composite Regional Average
Average Age	32.8	34.9	30.2	37.1	33.8
Per Cent over Age 40	17	17	8	34	19
Per Cent Married	58	50	46	73	57
Per Cent Illiterate	2	5	0	5	3
Per Cent Owning Personal Prop.	37	29	49	46	40
Per Cent Owning Substantial Personal Prop.	12	5	12	18	12
Average Age, Owners of Substantial Personal Prop.	46.6	37.5	35.1	39.2	39.6
Per Cent Owning Real Property	10	29	11	10	15
Per Cent Owning Substantial Real Property	7	5	10	7	7
Average Age, Owners of Substantial Real Property	46.0	37.5	35.1	41.4	40.0
Per Cent Owning Slaves	20	7	12	23	16
Avg. No. Owned	7.0	5.9	4.2	4.2	5.3
Average Age, Overseer Slaveholders	39.2	46.3	34.0	38.4	39.5

plantation managers were not as prosperous as their counterparts on the rice coast. The sugar parishes were, in varying degrees, characterized by the division of agricultural proprietors into two general groups—a small number of large planters and a greater number of small operators. Overseers in the region apparently fell into similar categories. Thus, fewer than half of those listed owned any property whatever, and only about fifteen per cent were landowners. On the other hand, the number of those with substantial amounts of personal property was comparable to that in the rice districts.

It is probable that the figures relating to overseer ownership of property in Plaquemines Parish are too low. Of the forty-one persons surveyed in that parish, three were identified as assistant overseers and eleven as agents. In the case of the latter, it was impossible to differentiate their property from that of their employers. Therefore, it has been assumed that all these agents possessed some real and personal property, but they have not been classified as substantial property-holders or as slaveowners except where it could reasonably be inferred that the property listed was their own. As a result, it is difficult to draw definite conclusions regarding the size of overseer holdings in the parish.

A significantly large number of plantation overseers in the sugar region were the sons of small planters—that is, those with total property holdings of at least $25,000. Of course, the number of proprietors falling within that classification was much greater in the sugar parishes than in the two regions discussed previously. In sharp contrast with findings in the older slave states, only half of the overseers listed were natives of Louisiana. The population movement from Upper South to Lower South is graphically illustrated by the figures for Terrebonne Parish, where only 36 percent of the enumerated overseers were born in Louisiana. The remainder came from the following states and foreign countries in the numbers indicated: seven from Tennessee; six from South Carolina; five each from Georgia and New York; three each from Alabama, Kentucky, and Scotland; two each from Mississippi, North Carolina, Virginia, Maryland, and Ireland; and one apiece from five other states.

More overseers with substantial amounts of personal property were found in Terrebonne Parish than in the other parishes surveyed. Nearly one-fifth of the managers listed in Terrebonne possessed a personal estate of at least $5,000, and 23 percent owned slave property. The explanation is to be found in the high average age of Terrebonne overseers and in the fact that at least twelve of those listed were managing absentee sugar estates of considerable size. The average number of slaves on each of the latter units was approximately eighty.

As in South Carolina, there was considerable evidence that the most prosperous managers tended to find employment with the largest proprietors. For example, in Ascension Parish at least three of the five owners of substantial property were overseers for large sugar planters. Alexander Turner, whose personal estate included two slaves and was valued at $5,000, managed William J. Minor's "Waterloo" plantation. H. M. Seale, with six slaves and a total personal estate of $9,000, was listed as the agent of John Burnside's enormous Houmas estate. Finally, W. W. Bateman, overseer for Colonel J. L. Manning, listed personal assets of $25,000 and twenty-five slaves. Bateman, who also possessed real property valued at $5,600, was the largest overseer property-holder encountered in the four parishes surveyed.

An analysis of more than eight hundred overseers in four selected cotton belt counties is presented in Table 8. Note that the number of overseers surveyed is much greater than that in any of the previous tabulations, although the number of counties included is identical. This is clearly a reflection of the greater number of overseers utilized in the management of cotton plantations. One of the most striking facts about the overseers in this region was their comparative youthfulness. This factor, in turn, had a pronounced effect upon the number of married overseers and on the number owning property. Fewer than half of those surveyed owned personal property, and only one-tenth possessed real estate. Nevertheless, the percentage of slaveholding overseers was twice as high in this region as in the Upper South. Since no data on illiteracy appeared in the Mississippi counties surveyed, it was impossible to compute a regional average. However, only 7 percent of the overseers in Natchitoches Parish, Louisiana, were listed as illiterate, despite the fact that numerous persons in other occupations were so listed.

As in the sugar parishes, many cotton plantation superintendents came from small planter families. A smaller number of those whose backgrounds could be identified were the offspring of farmers. One young Yazoo County, Mississippi, overseer, John D. Fayer, was the son of a physician. The heavy white

Table 8

STATISTICAL ANALYSIS OF OVERSEERS IN
COTTON BELT, 1860 [6]

	Hinds Co., Miss. 220 Overseers	Lowndes Co., Miss. 181 Overseers	Yazoo Co., Miss. 268 Overseers	Natchitoches Parish, La. 139 Overseers	Composite Regional Average
Average Age	29.1	32.4	29.5	31.3	30.6
Per Cent over Age 40	10	17	10	17	14
Per Cent Married	32	58	33	60	46
Per Cent Illiterate	–	–	–	7	–
Per Cent Owning Personal Prop.	23	60	20	73	44
Per Cent Owning Substantial Personal Prop.	7	12	3	8	8
Average Age, Owners of Substantial Personal Prop.	33.5	42.5	32.7	32.6	35.3
Per Cent Owning Real Property	9	12	3	18	10
Per Cent Owning Substantial Real Property	3	10	3	14	8
Average Age, Owners of Substantial Real Property	30.6	38.6	33.4	34.4	34.2
Per Cent Owning Slaves	10	22	9	15	14
Avg. No. Owned	3.0	3.0	4.3	4.3	3.6
Average Age, Overseer Slaveholders	33.4	37.8	34.2	35.0	35.1

migration from the seaboard slave states to the Southwest
during the first half of the nineteenth century was clearly revealed in the data concerning birthplaces of cotton belt overseers. Only 34 percent of those listed were natives of the
state in which they were residing in 1860. Only 12 percent of

the overseers in Lowndes County were born in Mississippi, but an additional 30 percent were from neighboring Alabama. The majority of overseers in the cotton belt had migrated to that region from the older plantation states—Virginia, the Carolinas, Tennessee, Georgia, and Alabama.

Table 8 discloses a striking disparity between the age, marital status, and property of overseers in Hinds and Yazoo counties, on the one hand, and those in Lowndes County and Natchitoches Parish, on the other. Adjacent Hinds and Yazoo were typical of many localities in the booming domain of "King Cotton." They were swamped with young men from the eastern slave states who had journeyed westward to make their fortunes in any occupation which seemed likely to prove lucrative. Many of these persons tried their hand at overseeing with results which frequently proved disappointing to their employers. It was this class—young, unmarried, inexperienced, and possessing little or no property—which largely pursued the overseer calling in Hinds and Yazoo counties. On the other hand, managers in Lowndes County and, to a lesser extent, in Natchitoches Parish were more nearly like their counterparts in the older slave states. The explanation lies in their date of settlement and in their geographic location, Lowndes being situated on the Alabama line and Natchitoches in northwestern Louisiana. Thus, 60 percent of the overseers in Lowndes listed some personal property, and at least 22 percent owned slaves. In Natchitoches Parish, almost three-fourths of the overseers possessed personal property and 18 percent had real estate.

Top overseers in the cotton states could not match the property accumulations of outstanding managers in the rice and sugar districts. Only a few had property valued in excess of $10,000, and most of those listed as slaveowners had only one or two Negroes. The richest property-holder encountered in the survey of cotton belt overseers was Richard D. Powell of Lowndes County. Powell, who exercised stewardship over the Cocke family interests in Alabama and Mississippi, owned twenty-one slaves and listed real property estimated at $12,000 and personal holdings of $30,000.

A composite statistical view of southern overseers, computed by averaging the results previously obtained in each of the four staple regions, is presented in Table 9. It must be stressed that this method of computation emphasizes the differentiation

Table 9

COMPOSITE STATISTICAL ANALYSIS OF
SOUTHERN OVERSEERS, 1860

	Upper South 166 Over- seers	Rice Coast 342 Over- seers	Sugar Parishes 228 Over- seers	Cotton Belt 808 Over- seers	Composite South- ern Aver- age
Average Age	34.0	33.8	33.8	30.6	33.0
Per Cent over Age 40	24	20	19	14	19
Per Cent Married	67	66	57	46	59
Per Cent Illiterate	10	4	3	–	6
Per Cent Owning Personal Prop.	56	66	40	44	52
Per Cent Owning Substantial Personal Prop.	4	13	12	8	9
Average Age, Owners of Substantial Personal Prop.	41.0	39.6	39.6	35.3	38.9
Per Cent Owning Real Property	10	24	15	10	15
Per Cent Owning Substantial Real Property	5	16	7	8	9
Average Age, Owners of Substantial Real Property	38.1	40.2	40.0	34.2	38.1
Per Cent Owning Slaves	7	19	16	14	14
Avg. No. Owned	3.9	7.2	5.3	3.6	5.0
Average Age, Overseer Slaveholders	40.0	38.9	39.5	35.1	38.4

of characteristics produced by regional variations instead of yielding averages based solely on sheer numbers. Thus, if the final averages were computed on a numerical basis alone, the results would most nearly resemble those obtained for the cotton belt, where the majority of overseers included in this survey were employed. But that method would obscure the important regional differences in overseer characteristics revealed by the census returns.

A number of general conclusions may be formulated on the basis of the data presented above. In the first place, the relatively low average age of the overseers surveyed adds additional credence to the contention that many overseers abandoned their profession after acquiring sufficient capital to enter more desirable occupations. The figures in Table 9 indicate that the average age of southern overseers was about thirty-three years, while only one-fifth of those engaged in overseeing were above the age of forty. The higher average age of those with substantial property holdings is evidence that it was possible to accumulate sufficient property while overseeing to escape the occupation after some years of service. Thus, in Georgetown District, South Carolina, the average age of fifteen managers possessing a personal estate of at least $5,000 was forty-one, while the average age of forty overseers listing no personal property was only about twenty-six years.

The statistics on the marital status of overseers show that in the older planting states about two-thirds of those listed were married. The percentage was somewhat lower in the Southwest, especially in the cotton belt where more than half of those surveyed remained bachelors. The low proportion of married overseers and the low average age of overseers in the latter region provide additional evidence of the existence in that area of a large floating population of nominal overseers, whose lack of competence provoked a deluge of abuse from the planter class. Some proprietors in the Lower South adopted the policy of hiring only married overseers, believing that marriage exerted a stabilizing influence upon the conduct of most young men. As one planter explained it: "Being married is a decided incentive to do good, since there is no *man*, with proper feelings and a due sense of honor, who will risk having his wife and children turned out of doors by any untoward act or imprudent conduct on his part." ' Be that as it may, about 40 percent of the overseers throughout the South remained single and still found employment.

Another fact disclosed by an examination of the census returns is that the number of illiterate overseers was relatively insignificant. This confirms the findings of Frank L. Owsley as to lower-class southern whites generally. Owsley, who also relied heavily on census data, concluded that "in comparison with the situation in most countries of the world at that time [1850] the Southern folk were one of the most literate major groups of the entire world." [8] This is not to imply that they excelled in their comprehension and use of the English language, but most were sufficiently literate to understand what they read and to impart information through the medium of letters. Like John Mitchell, who admitted that he was "know Scollar," [9] most overseers recognized their educational deficiencies and got along as best they could with the little knowledge they had acquired.

Finally, it is apparent that a considerable number of overseers, particularly on the rice coast, were men of substantial property. Although some might question whether one-tenth constitutes a significant proportion, the fact remains that such a percentage of southern overseers had substantial property holdings, and an even greater proportion were slaveowners. Moreover, about 15 percent possessed some landed property. As might be expected, there is strong evidence to support the assumption that the best class of overseers were in the employment of the largest and wealthiest planters. This confirms a view previously expressed by Lewis Gray, [10] and it accounts for the large amounts of property held by some overseers in the rice and sugar regions.

Such is the view of the southern plantation overseer as derived from the manuscript census returns of 1860. With this image in mind, it is now possible to proceed to a general discussion of the duties and responsibilities of this vital figure in the plantation establishments of the Old South.

4

Managerial Duties
and Responsibilities

MULTITUDINOUS duties and exacting responsibilities were associated with the management of southern plantations. Among the major responsibilities of the overseer were the welfare and discipline of the slaves, the care of livestock and agricultural implements, and the production of staple and subsistence crops. He assigned gangs to work, apportioned tasks, and supervised the labor of slaves in the field. He was expected to be sufficiently acquainted with contemporary medical practices to determine whether ailing Negroes needed professional attention and to treat minor complaints without outside help. To the overseer was given the responsibility for insuring that the slaves were properly fed and reasonably clean.

He was obliged to make periodic inspections of slave cabins and was responsible for the distribution of Negro clothing. Finally, upon the overseer depended, "to a large extent, the security of the whites against uprisings of slaves."[1] It is apparent that the life of a conscientious and energetic overseer was an arduous one.

Upon the assumption of his post, the overseer was usually given a set of written instructions which outlined his duties and detailed the wishes of his employer regarding the care and punishment of Negroes, apportionment of work, methods of cultivation, and other points respecting the management of the estate. The plantation rules for Andrew Flynn's "Green Valley" plantation, located in the Yazoo-Mississippi Delta just south of Memphis, illustrate the nature of these instructions. "Green Valley" was a relatively small cotton plantation with a slave force of just under forty. The following is a detailed exposition of rules for the government of the plantation as set forth in 1840:

1st   A good crop means one that is good taking into consideration every thing hands, breeding women, children, mules, Stocks, provisions, farming utensils of all Sorts & keeping up land, ditches, fences & C & C. The object therefore must be not to make a given number of bags of cotton but as many as can be made without losing as much or nearly as much in these particulars as is gained in cotton.

2nd   The overseer will never be expected to work in the field. but he must always be with the hands when not otherwise engaged in the Employer's business & must do every thing that is required of him, provided it is directly or indirectly connected with the planting or other pecuniary interest of the Employer at Green Valley Plantation.

3rd   He must never, on any account be absent a single night or an entire day, from the plantation without permission previously obtained. Whenever he goes to Church or elsewhere he must return without fail, before Sundown.

4th   He must keep all the keys carefully & where no one can have access to them but himself   He must never allow any one to unlock the Smoke House or corn crib except himself under any circumstances. He must lock the Stables every night. open them every morning & see personally that the mules are cleaned & fed twice a day at least & watered as often as necessary.

5th   He must visit the negro houses every morning by daylight. Once a week at least he must visit every negro house after horn blow at night.

6th   He must attend particularly to all experiments instituted by the Employer, conduct them faithfully, & report regularly & correctly. Some overseers defeat important experiments by carelessness or Wilfulness.

7th   He will be expected to give his opinions on all matters connected with planting & plantation affairs   the reasons for them, but if they are not adopted by the Employer, he must obey the instructions given, implicitly, thoroughly, & with a sincere desire to produce the best result.

8th   He will be expected to give minute information of every thing going on at the plantation or elsewhere that may be Known to him which may affect in any way the Employer's views or interests without being asked & of course, on all occassions [sic] to be very accurate in his Statements & sincere in his conjectures

9th   He is particularly charged to take care of the Stock, to obey all instructions whatever to them, to count them all at least once a month & to have them fed, salted & C. Every care must be taken of the mules

10th   The horn will be blowed by the Driver in the morning just before daylight & again just after daylight. At the latter the negroes will go to work   If it is very cold or rainy or if the Season is sickly the hands should not go out before Sunrise & not then if the rain continues. At night the horn will blow, in Summer at 9 & in winter at 8 o'clock after which no negro must be allowed to be out of his house on any pretence.

11th   The negroes must be Kept as much as possible out of the rain   It is much better to lose some time than to run the risk of Sickness & death. The Overseer must see that they have good fires after rains & of winter nights—

12th   They must be flogged as seldom as possible yet always when necessary. A good manager who is with the hands as much as he Should be can encourage them on with very little punishment. Violent threats must never be used & the Overseer is strictly enjoined never to kick a negro or strike one with his hand or a stick or the butt end of his whip. These things will not be tolerated. No unusual punishments must be resorted to without the Employers approbation

13th   The sick must be visited at least three times a day & at night when necessary & treated with every possible attention. Unless it is a clear case of imposition a negro had better be allowed a day's rest when he lays up. A little rest often saves much by preventing serious illness. Medicine must be given carefully & sparingly & when there is doubt what to give, let nothing be given. Never administer Calomal or Castor oil unless they are prescribed & insisted on by a Physician.

14th   The children must be very particularly attended to, for rearing them is not only a Duty, but also the most profitable part of plantation business. They must be kept clean, dry & warm, & wellfed & seldom [illeg.]. Plain food is necessary for them: bread, hominy or mush,

Soupes, Sugar & a little meat: molasses for those two or three years old, but not for those younger. Vegetables in general not proper for them.

15th   Pregnant women & sucklers must be treated with great tenderness, worked near home & lightly. Pregnant women should not plow or lift; but must be kept at moderate work until the last hour if possible. Sucklers must be allowed time to suckle their children from twice to three times a day according to their ages. At twelve months old children must be weaned.

16th   When any kind of business is done with, all the utensils Employed must be collected at once & put away carefully in their proper places. Waggons & carts must always be repaired & put under the shelter ready for use. So also with [illeg.] ploughs, spades   & C & C.

17th   The following is the order in which offenses must be estimated & punished. 1st   Running Away   2nd   Getting Drunk or having spirits   3rd   Stealing Hogs. 4th   Stealing. 5th   Leaving Plantation without permission   6th   Absence after Horn blows. 7th   Unclean house or Person. 8th   Neglect of work   The highest punishment must not exceed Fifty lashes in one Day.[2]

The above rules are typical of those drawn up for the government of plantation establishments throughout the South.[3]

Theoretically, most planters were in general agreement regarding the relative order of importance of the various functions performed by the overseer. This order was delineated in the introductory pages of Thomas Affleck's widely used *Cotton Plantation Record and Account Book*. The following paragraph from that source indicates the ideal criteria by which the planter judged the performance of his overseer:

In conclusion,—Bear in mind that *a fine crop* consists, first, in an increase in the number, and a marked improvement in the condition and value of the negroes; second, an abundance of provision of all sorts for man and beast, carefully saved and properly housed; third, both summer and winter clothing made at home; also, leather tanned, and shoes and harness made when practicable; fourth, an improvement in the productive qualities of the land, and in the general condition of the plantation; fifth, the team and stock generally, with the farming implements and the buildings, in fine order at the close of the year; and young hogs more than enough for next year's killing; *then*—as heavy a crop of cotton, sugar or rice, as could possibly be made under the circumstances, sent to market in good season and of prime quality. The time has passed when the Overseer was valued solely for the number of bales of cotton, hogsheads of sugar, or tierces of rice he had made, without reference to his other qualifications.[4]

In actual practice, however, many proprietors ascribed a great deal more importance to the production of staples than Affleck indicated. This emphasis upon crop results at the expense of long-range improvements remained dominant among most planters in the cotton belt until the end of the antebellum period.[5]

Despite differing views regarding the importance of staple production, there was universal agreement among planters that the welfare of their slaves was the paramount managerial consideration. This responsibility received the greatest emphasis in instructions to overseers throughout the South. It may be noted that six of the seventeen rules relating to the administration of "Green Valley" plantation were concerned exclusively with this subject. It is hardly surprising that the planter, who had a substantial investment in every slave on his plantation, should be interested in keeping them healthy and contented. The principal task of the overseer was to insure that these conditions were maintained among the Negroes under his supervision. Thus, P. C. Weston, a South Carolina rice planter, directed his overseer "most distinctly to understand that his first object is to be, under all circumstances, the care and well being of the negroes." [6] Similarly, Louisiana planter Maunsel White, distressed to learn of an outbreak of measles on one of his absentee cotton plantations, declared in a letter to his overseer: "I regret exceedingly to hear that my people are troubled with the measles—I feel confident you will take good care of them *let what may happen to the crop*." [7]

A duty of many overseers, especially on larger plantations, was the maintenance of various record and account books. The fact that countless overseers were able to discharge such a function adequately reinforces the contention, expressed earlier, that the vast majority of plantation superintendents were at least literate. The type of information which the overseer was required to enter in the plantation book is illustrated by the following rule of a Mississippi cotton planter:

The overseer shall keep a plantation book, in which he shall register the birth and name of each negro that is born; the name of each negro that died, and specify the disease that killed him. He shall also keep in it the weights of the daily picking of each hand; the mark, number and weight of each bale of cotton, and the time of sending the same to market; and all other such occurrences, relating to the crop, the weather, and all other matters pertaining to the plantation, that he may deem advisable.[8]

In addition to a plantation book, William J. Minor required his overseers to keep a separate record of slave births and deaths, a wood book, and "a receipt & forwarding book in which all articles received at the place or sent or shipped from the place are to be entered with the date of each transaction, prices & name of vessel or boat when known." [9]

The maintenance of plantation record books was especially important to an absentee owner as a supplement to the reports received from his overseer. Thomas Affleck contended that the use of his plantation book had promoted improvement in managerial practices. For example, recording the daily amounts of cotton picked by each hand compelled the overseer to institute an invariable and uniform system in the harvesting of that crop. In addition, said Affleck, the maintenance of a plantation book aided the overseer by providing evidence that the orders of his employer were being executed. [10]

There was considerable difference between the status of an overseer on an absentee estate and that of one on a resident plantation. The latter was often subjected to rigorous supervision by the master, and his duties might be confined to the daily execution of orders relating to supervision of the slaves in the fields and in their quarters. On the other hand, absentee owners frequently operated with comparative freedom of action. One authority expressed the view that under absentee ownership "the opportunities for abuses and misunderstandings increased." [11] Although there can be no quarrel with the argument that opportunities for abuses were greater on absentee units, it is certainly debatable whether misunderstandings between proprietor and overseer were more frequent on such plantations. Indeed, it seems more probable that friction between the two was reduced by their physical separation.

Most planters were painfully aware of the degree of power exercised by managers of absentee properties. James H. Ruffin, North Carolina lawyer and planter, displayed his knowledge of the powerful position occupied by his absentee overseer when he lamented: ". . . this man Dobbs will *ruin* and *beggar* me if he is not more closely watched than he has heretofore been. He is a man in my opinion totally devoid of principle and without the smallest regard to my interest when his own is not also consulted. He has under his management and control every thing I am worth to use or to abuse it according to his own will and pleasure." [12] The apprehension with which many planters regarded the installation of a new overseer upon their absentee property, and the most common abuses which occurred under absentee overseerships are clearly revealed in the following oft-quoted instructions from George Washington to one of his absentee managers:

I do in explicit terms, enjoin it upon you to remain constantly at home, unless called off by unavoidable business, or to attend divine worship, and to be constantly with your people when there. There is no other sure way of getting work well done, and quietly, by negroes; for when an overlooker's back is turned, the most of them will slight their work, or be idle altogether; in which case correction cannot retrieve either, but often produces evils which are worse than the disease. Nor is there any other mode than this to prevent thieving and other disorders, the consequence of opportunities. You will recollect that your time is paid for by me, and if I am deprived of it, it is worse even than robbing my purse, because it is also a breach of trust, which every honest man ought to hold most sacred. You have found me, faithful to my part of the agreement which was made with you, while you are attentive to your part; but it is to be remembered that a breach on one side relieves the obligation on the other. If therefore it shall be found by me, that you are absenting yourself from either the farm or the people without just cause, I shall hold myself no more bound to pay the wages, than you do to attend strictly to the charge which is entrusted to you.

There is another thing I must caution you against, not knowing whether there be cause to charge you with it or not, and that is, not to retain any of my negroes, who are able and fit to work in the crop or elsewhere, in or about your own house for your own purposes. This I do not allow any overseer to do. A small boy or girl for the purpose of fetching wood or water, tending a child, or such like things, I do not object to; but so soon as they are able to work out, I expect to reap the benefit of their labor myself.[13]

The overseer of an absentee estate was usually obliged to discharge additional responsibilities not required of resident managers. In addition to the normal obligations associated with crop production and slave management, he was frequently burdened with financial and logistical responsibilities inherent in the operation of a commercial agricultural enterprise. He might be called upon to institute law suits against debtors of the estate, order supplies from the commission merchant, negotiate loans, collect delinquent accounts, and, in general, to act for his employer in any matter involving the plantation under his cognizance. Moreover, the absentee manager was obliged to transmit, at frequent intervals, detailed reports covering every aspect of plantation operations. Alexander Telfair directed the overseer of his "Thorn Island," Georgia, plantation to "write me the last day of every month to Savannah, unless otherwise directed. When writing have the Journal before you, and set down in the Letter every thing that has been done, or occurred on the Plantation during the month." [14] Clearly, the post of overseer on an absentee plantation called for a man of uncommon ability.

The planter community was not reticent about offering advice to the overseer concerning the managerial practices he should pursue in the execution of his manifold duties. Most of this advice was focused upon the vital problem of Negro management. Those points most frequently stressed by proprietors in relation to this subject are illustrated by the following directions, drawn up by John Hartwell Cocke for the guidance of inexperienced overseers on his Virginia estate:

. . . never permit any order you give to be disobeyed, or disregarded, without a strict inquiry into it, & punish the offender if necessary.

Set the first example of strict attention to your duties & you may with the more justice, & propriety, inflict punishment upon others for the neglect of theirs.

Therefore never make an order without Punctually attending to it for if you make a rule & forget it yourself with what face could you punish others for neglecting it also?

If you punish only according to justice & reason, with uniformity, you can never be too severe, & will be the more respected for it, even by those who suffer.

Arrangement & regularity form the great secret of doing things well, you must therefore as far as possible have every thing done according to a fixed rule[15]

The two principles of slave management universally emphasized by southern planters in their directions to overseers were a firm discipline, tempered with kindness, and a uniform, impartially-administered system of justice. "No person," declared P. C. Weston, "should ever be allowed to break a law without being punished, or any person punished who has not broken a well known law. Every person should be made perfectly to understand what they are punished for, and should be made to per-

ceive that they are not punished in anger or through caprice."
Moreover, the South Carolina planter warned against the use
of abusive language or violence of demeanor as "they reduce
the man who uses them to a level with the negro, and are hardly
ever forgotten by those to whom they are addressed." [16]

Overseers were also cautioned against indulging in too much
familiarity with Negroes under their control. Joseph Johnson
advised the new overseer of his Warren County, Mississippi,
plantation: "Your experience & good sense has taught you, that,
familiarity with slaves will not do, an Overseer ought to have
but little Conversation with negroes under his care & that only
to tell them what to do & then to see that he is obeyed." [17]

There were differing views within the planter class concerning the degree of severity necessary to establish and maintain the overseer in an unassailable position of authority over the
slaves. Thomas Ruffin of North Carolina thought it desirable for
a new overseer to instill within the Negroes a fear of himself
at the outset of his administration. Slaves, contended Ruffin,
developed no respect for their overseer "unless he makes them
fear him at the beginning." [18] Another observer, however,
stressed the importance of a display of kindness toward the
Negroes by their overseer. "Kindness, and even gentleness," he
declared, "is not inconsistent with firmness and inexorable discipline." [19] This view was echoed by Virginia planter Hill Carter,
who advised his "friends, the Virginia overseers, to use a little
flattery sometimes instead of stripes." [20]

Although overseers were repeatedly cautioned against undue
familiarity with the Negroes, some slave managers apparently
failed to interpret this injunction as a prohibition against co-
habitation with sirens of the slave quarter. There has been
much speculation, but little concrete evidence, concerning the
degree of miscegenation which occurred in the Old South. With
regard to relations between white overseers and female slaves,
the preponderance of evidence indicates that such unions were
formed but that they were almost universally discouraged by
members of the planter community.

Illicit relations between overseers and slaves were most
common on absentee estates, where both temptation and opportunity tended to be greater than on resident plantations.
The gullible Fanny Kemble, during a brief stay on her husband's Georgia rice estate, found evidence that former overseer

Roswell King, Jr., had fathered several illegitimate slave children during his long term as absentee manager. One slave woman horrified the actress with the following account of her experiences under King:

> She told me a miserable story of her former experience on the plantation under Mr. K_____'s overseership. It seems that Jem Valiant . . . was her first born, the son of Mr. K_____, who forced her, flogged her severely for having resisted him, and then sent her off, as a further punishment, to Five Pound—a horrible swamp in a remote corner of the estate, to which the slaves are sometimes banished for such offences as are not sufficiently atoned for by the lash.[21]

Although Miss Kemble's intense antislavery bias seriously distorted her general account of affairs at Butler's Island, there seems little reason to doubt the veracity of her statements regarding King's conduct with the female slaves on that plantation. King and his father had operated the estate without any direction or interference from the owners for more than thirty years.

On his visit to John Burnside's Louisiana sugar holdings in 1861, William Howard Russell reported seeing a number of fair-complexioned slave children whose presence was attributed to the activities of previous overseers. It did not seem to the present manager, observed Russell, "that there was any particular turpitude in the white man who had left his offspring as slaves on the plantation." [22]

Extant plantation manuscripts contain few references to the problem of overseer-slave sex relations. A notable exception is afforded by the correspondence of Rachel O'Connor, who, perhaps because she was a woman and therefore sensitive to such relationships, had a great deal to say upon the subject. Mrs. O'Connor, who operated a plantation near St. Francisville, Louisiana, was driven nearly to distraction in the early 1830's by the disposition of her overseers to fraternize with the female slaves. In a series of letters to her brother and sister-in-law, David and Mary Weeks, she recounted the amorous exploits of overseers Patrick and Mulkey. Of the former, whom she regarded as "one of the best of farmers," Mrs. O'Connor remarked in one such missive: "Patrick behaves too mean to be a white man. his tracts are often found where he has been sneaking about after those negro girls." [23]

Accordingly, in the summer of 1832, Patrick was replaced by Mulkey, a married man with three grown sons, who made a good beginning, and for a time enjoyed the confidence of his employer. Shortly after engaging Mulkey for a second year, Mrs. O'Connor confided to her brother that "he dont appear to wish to abuse the negroes nor to have Wives amongst them, so far." [24] By the following fall, however, it became apparent that Mulkey too had developed a more-than-passing interest in the dark-skinned ladies on the place. In an irate letter to her brother, the proprietress charged that he was "a shameless being, nearly as bad as Patrick in the same way. if it was not for that he could oversee very well. but as it is, he has too many ladies to please." [25] As Mulkey's indiscretions became more flagrant, relations between employer and overseer deteriorated rapidly, culminating in the latter's enforced departure at the end of November. "Bad as Patrick acted," concluded the plantation mistress, "he was not one half as bad as this vilian, and his sons are as mean as himself." [26] Happily, the distraught proprietress had better luck with her next overseer, named Germany, who managed the plantation in splendid fashion for at least four years. After observing her new manager for more than two years, Mrs. O'Connor declared herself "perfectly satisfied with his management." He had refrained from "puting himself on a footing with those under his charge," and he had "no favorite misses to fight and abuse the boys about." But Germany, she concluded, was the only overseer she had ever employed who was entirely "clear of that meanness." [27]

Although such instances of overseer liaisons with female slaves were not isolated, they were certainly not typical. On many plantations such conduct resulted in the immediate discharge of the overseer. Alabama planter James Tait, plagued by difficulties resulting from interference with the slave women by his overseer, jotted down the following maxim: "A legacy to my children.—Never employ an overseer who will equalize himself with the negro women. Besides the morality of it, there are evils too numerous to be now mentioned." [28] Joseph A. S. Acklen, proprietor of one of the largest estates in Louisiana, imposed the following prohibition upon his overseers: "Having connection with any of my female servants will most certainly be visited with a dismissal from my employment, and no excuse can or will be taken." [29] Such restrictions undoubtedly had an effect in limiting nocturnal encounters between white overseers and slave women.

The lack of community of interest between overseer and slave was emphasized in a report prepared in 1846 by a committee of three, headed by John A. Calhoun, and presented to the Barbour County, Alabama, Agricultural Society. After alluding to the community of interest which governed the relationship between planter and slave, Calhoun observed: "There is one class of our community to whom all the motives referred to, to induce us to kindness to our slaves, do not apply. Your committee refer to our overseers. As they have no property in our slaves, of course they lack the check of self-interest. As their only aim in general is the mere crop results of the year, we can readily conceive the strong inducement they have to overwork our slaves."[30]

It is doubtful whether many overseers had any humanitarian feeling for the slaves under their supervision. One writer complained that the overseer had a low idea of slavery and did not see any reason to improve the conditions of the slave.[31] Upon cold reflection, however, it is difficult to discern why any overseer would have entertained thoughts of improving slave conditions, for to elevate the slave was to make him dissatisfied with his status, thereby increasing the already-formidable problems of Negro management. Kenneth Stampp has charged, with some justification, that overseers had a decided preference for physical force in dealing with slaves. "Overseers," declared Stampp, "seldom felt any personal affection for the bondsmen they governed. Their inclination in most cases was to punish severely; if their employers prohibited severity, they ignored such instructions as often as not."[32]

The observations of Frederick Law Olmsted during his stay on a large absentee cotton estate in Mississippi substantiate the view that overseers were inclined toward severe physical punishments. One overseer, asked by Olmsted whether the punishment of Negroes was not a disagreeable task, responded: "Yes, it would be to those who are not used to it—but it's my business, and I think nothing of it. Why, sir, I wouldn't mind killing a nigger more than I would a dog."[33] While visiting another unit of the same estate, Olmsted observed what he termed "the severest corporeal punishment of a negro that I witnessed at the South." The flogging had been administered to a young girl whom the overseer had discovered shirking her work. The overseer justified the severity of punishment in the following fashion: "If I hadn't punished her so hard she would have done the same thing again to-morrow, and half the people on the plantation would have followed her example. Oh, you've no idea how lazy these niggers are; you northern people don't know any thing about it. They'd never do any work at all if they were not afraid of being whipped." [34]

The typical overseer attitude toward slavery and the Negro was reflected by H. M. Seale, for at least fifteen years manager of the Houmas sugar estate in Ascension Parish, Louisiana. Resting after the labors of an August day in 1853, the veteran overseer contemplated events of the past year and evaluated slave morale on his plantation in these terms: "I am Getting on very well with my bisness this year   very little trouble with the Negroes. . . . My Negros Seem to be perfectly content." [35] Eight years later, William H. Russell visited Houmas and recorded his impression of Seale in these words:

The overseer, it is certain, had no fastidious notions about slavery; it was to him the right thing in the right place, and his *summum bonum* was a high price for sugar, a good crop, and a healthy plantation. Nay, I am sure I would not wrong him if I said he could see no impropriety in running a good cargo of regular black slaves, who might clear the great backwood and swampy undergrowth, which was now exhausting the energies of his field-hands, in the absence of Irish navvies.[36]

For his part, the slave did not ordinarily view his overseer with unconcealed admiration. Indeed, he looked upon the overseer as a symbol of all the odious features of the institution of slavery. As one writer has observed: "If a single individual of the slave regime may be singled out for the chief object of the slaves' hatred, it would be the overseer." [37] The slave recognized that his superintendent did not have the prestige of a property holder, and, as a result, the authority of the overseer "had to be maintained by fear of the lash rather than by respect." [38] The difficult position occupied by the plantation manager was rendered more precarious by the obvious conflict of interest between master and slave. An inefficient and incompetent overseer, who did not maintain strict discipline among the slaves, was often viewed with favor by the latter. On the other hand, "overseers who were vigorous in the prosecution of their duties and exacting in their demands on the slaves were the overseers who experienced the greatest difficulty in managing slaves." [39] Thus, a Tennessee proprietor who had engaged one of the latter sort was compelled to shift him to another plantation, after a term of only six months, because the "negroes . . . had such an unconquerable hatrid for the man, that I believe they would have done better without any." [40]

Slaves often went to great lengths to discredit an unpopular overseer in the eyes of his employer. One of the most common means of effecting this purpose was to go directly to the owner with tales alleging mistreatment and mismanagement by the overseer. Unfortunately, many planters declined to discourage this practice of tale-bearing and consequently undermined the authority of their managers. A more sophisticated stratagem was employed by the Negroes on John H. Cocke's "Hopewell" plantation in order to discredit their overseer, J. Walter Carter. Only the alert action of steward Richard D. Powell prevented the loss of the cotton crop at "Hopewell," an absentee plantation in Greene County, Alabama. Powell recounted the incident to his employer in the following manner:

The negroes attempted in a very friendly way in May to make Carter loose the crop. After finding himself in the grass he took the place of his head man, or Driver, & put him to work the first row & all the other hands to follow him, & all hands slighted their work by covering up the grass lightly, & not Cutting it up when small, & he became so restless that he did not take time to see how the work was done, & had his plows runing about, & plowing a spot here, & a spot there, & where they did plow, they would let the plows run over the grass, & not plow it up. All hands found I understood all about it, & from the first of June Overseer & negroes have done well—Carter never did have such a plain talking from any man before, I reckon as I gave him & it has made [him] see plainly all his foolish ways & C—The negroes understood me fully too, & all was done in friendship, & love, with a promise of punishment when the Crop was Laid by, or a good barbacue, & one or two days rest. They had the barbacue last Saturday. [41]

Notwithstanding the quaint phraseology of the steward, one may readily doubt whether the Negroes were motivated by sentiments of friendship and love in their efforts to oust Carter from his post.

Two basic types of labor organization—the gang, or time-work, system and the task, or piece-work, system—were employed on southern plantations. Operations on virtually all agricultural units in the tobacco, cotton, and sugar regions were conducted under the gang system, in which field slaves worked in gangs supervised by Negro drivers for a specified time period each day. Occasionally, however, the task system was utilized in those areas to perform certain types of labor for which it was better suited than was the gang method. Thus, on F. D. Richardson's "Bayside" plantation in St. Mary Parish, Louisiana, task work was sometimes used in ditching and scraping stubble.[42]

The task system of labor, in which individual workers were assigned specific daily tasks, was employed almost universally on the rice coast. The drainage ditches, which divided rice fields into half or quarter-acre plots, offered convenient units of performance in the successive planting, cultivating, and harvesting processes. Some planters found it expedient to deviate from the task method during actual planting operations. William Butler declared that in planting, the slaves "should be always Kept in gangs or parcels & not scattered over a field in Tasks as is too generally done, for while in gangs they are more immediately under the Superintendents Eyes."[43] Rice planters also might abandon task work in an emergency, "as in the mending of breaks in the dikes, or when joint exertion was required, as in log rolling, or when threshing and pounding with machinery to set the pace."[44]

The chief advantage of the task system was the ease with which it permitted a planter or overseer to delegate many of his routine duties to a Negro driver. It also gave some stimulus to rapidity of work by its promise of leisure time to those who finished their tasks early. However, for this incentive to be effective the tasks had to be so limited that the slowest field hand could finish in time to enjoy a few hours of free time. The performance of every hand therefore tended to be standardized at the usual accomplishment of the slowest and weakest members of the group.[45]

Olmsted had praise for the task system as he found it employed on the South Carolina rice coast. He noted that the tasks assigned would not have been considered excessively difficult by a northern laborer and mentioned several instances in which energetic and industrious slaves had finished their tasks by two o'clock. Commenting upon the advantages of the system, Olmsted declared: "The slave works more rapidly, energetically, and, within narrow limits, with much greater use of discretion, or skill, than he is often found to do elsewhere." [46]

The calculation of proper tasks for his Negroes called for a considerable amount of judgment on the part of the master or overseer. It was not desirable for any hand to be put in a task which he could not reasonably be expected to finish, for it was manifestly subversive of discipline to leave tasks unfinished and grossly unfair to punish for what could not be done. In general, the ordinary winter task in the rice belt was eight to nine hours, and the usual summer task required about ten hours to complete.[47] One proprietor, in an instruction to his overseer, defined a task as "as much work as the meanest full hand can do in nine hours, working industriously." [48] Alexander Telfair was more general in his definition, requiring simply "a reasonable days work, well done—the task to be regulated by the state of the ground and the strength of the negro." [49] It was not uncommon for the more active and industrious Negroes to assist the slower ones in the completion of their daily tasks.[50]

The determination of a proper work load for each slave was a vitally important function of the overseer on all plantations, regardless of whether the task or gang system was utilized. Although the proprietor might issue general instructions, a final judgment concerning what could reasonably be required of individual slaves could be made only by their immediate supervisor —the overseer. John H. Cocke issued the following directive to his overseers: "You are expected to have learned by your own experience what is a days work for a hand in every variety of Plantation Business, & daily compair [sic] what your people do with what they ought to do & thus perfect your judgment in such matters, enabling you to calculate beforehand what can be performed." [51]

Negro drivers were utilized on most southern plantations to assist the overseer in the execution of routine duties. Where drivers were not appointed, as on Telfair's "Thorn Island" plantation, the problems of Negro management were increased immeasurably. Telfair's policy was enunciated in the following instruction to his overseers: "I have no Driver. You are to task the negroes yourself, and each negro is responsible to you for his own work, and nobodys else." [52]

The maintenance of good relations between driver and overseer was essential to the proper functioning of plantation management. If proper slave discipline were to be maintained, it was imperative that the overseer support the authority of his driver. A Santee River, South Carolina, manager always required his Negro driver to dress better than the other slaves. The sagacious superintendent explained: "This caused him to maintain a pride of character before them, which was highly beneficial. Indeed, I constantly endeavored to do nothing which would cause them to lose their respect for him." [53] The driver was always reprimanded privately. He was required to report to his overseer every night in order to report the work of the day just ended and to learn what undertakings were scheduled for the following day. This practice "gave the driver a habit of regularity, and prepared him for a proper discharge of his duties should I be sick," declared the Santee overseer.[54]

The esteem in which an outstanding driver might be held by his overseer is reflected by the following notation of overseer Robert P. Ford in the plantation journal of Louisiana sugar magnate R. R. Barrow:

Andrew The Driver Died

The Residence has met with a great loss in the death of this valuable man, in the loss of Andrew I suppose the Plantation will materially suffer as his servises as a driver cannot be replaced   he was about 60 years old   he was well liked by all who knew him   he was a negro of uncommon good mind and I have regarded him one who possess good Judgement about Plantation work   he was Buried this evening and all the negroes on the Residence & Mertle Grove attended his funeral   he was aware of his approaching death and expressed an entire willingness to die   he conversed freely an hour before his death with many of his fellow servants and expressed a hope that he would meet them all in heaven—he was certain that he would go to heaven— before his death he bid all an affectionate farewell and died about 7 oclock in the morning triumphantly and thanked his god that he should soon be in heaven   his loss was generally and universally regretted and deep sorrow was depicted on the countenance of evry one who knew him   both white & Black   he was buried tonight[55]

The punishment of a driver by his overseer was obviously a matter which called for the exercise of considerable judgment and discretion. One planter issued the following directive to his managers: "The overseer must not punish the driver except on some extraordinary emergency that will not allow of delay, until the employer is consulted. Of this rule, the driver is, however, to be kept in entire ignorance." [56] If a driver's offense was sufficiently serious to warrant punishment, he was usually demoted and a more trustworthy slave elevated to take his place.

The hazards of arousing the hostility of Negro drivers are seen in the outstanding example of general demoralization which resulted from conflict between an overseer and his drivers on Ebenezer Pettigrew's North Carolina plantation. In the absence of his employer, then in Washington serving a term in Congress, Pettigrew's aggressive overseer Doctrine W. Davenport attempted to strip certain faithful and trusted slaves of special privileges previously accorded them by their master. The result was a swelling tide of discontent among the Negroes, beginning shortly after Christmas, 1835. While Davenport was absent on business, two old and trusted drivers led the Negroes in a great frolic. The Pettigrew Negroes gave a splendid feast for slaves from neighboring plantations, rode their master's horse about the countryside, and generally misbehaved. Upon his return, Davenport administered one hundred lashes to one slave for his part in the affair and placed three others in irons. The weary overseer continued to experience difficulty with the rebellious slaves throughout 1836, and his troubles did not finally subside until Pettigrew's return to North Carolina in February of the following year.[57]

As has previously been noted, slave medical care was a primary responsibility of the plantation overseer. Despite the fact that the best available medical care was provided for ailing Negroes on most plantations, the health problem was a serious one throughout the South. Many proprietors had their slave forces decimated by epidemics of cholera, yellow fever, malaria, measles, and other diseases which swept relentlessly from one plantation to another.

The problem of slave health was particularly acute on the rice coast. One visitor to that area noted that "the negroes do not enjoy as good health on rice plantations as elsewhere; and the greater difficulty with which their lives are preserved, through infancy especially, shows that the subtle poison of the miasma is not innocuous to them." [58] Nevertheless, one rice planter visited by this observer boasted a steady annual increase in his Negro force of 5 per cent—better than was averaged on many interior plantations.[59]

On many plantations in the rice belt the death rate exceeded the birth rate, and it was necessary to purchase additional slaves periodically in order to maintain a full complement of Negroes. The mortality rate of infants under two years of age on the "Comingtee" and "Stoke" plantations of John Ball, Jr., during the period 1803–34, was an alarming 33 percent for the former and 36.5 percent for the latter.[60] Slave lists for James B. Heyward's "Rotterdam," "Copenhagen," and "Hamburg" plantations during the period 1850–61 reveal a steady decrease in the total number of slaves on the three units from 394 to 332.[61] An identical trend was noted in the slave lists for Charles Manigault's "Gowrie" plantation during the years 1833–61. Particularly devastating were cholera epidemics in 1834 and 1854, which together wiped out thirty Negroes owned by Manigault. The latter was obliged to purchase additional slaves frequently in order to keep pace with the death rate on his plantations.[62]

The slave mortality rate in Louisiana was so striking that antislavery zealots accused sugar planters of deliberately working their Negroes to death. On the plantations of R. R. Barrow the natural increase of slave population lagged far behind the death rate, obliging Barrow to procure new slaves frequently. During the period from July, 1857, to March, 1858, he purchased no fewer than sixty-eight Negroes in three separate lots.[63] Louisiana planters lived in constant fear of cholera epidemics. That dreaded disease took the lives of twenty-eight slaves and the overseer on Lavinia Erwin's Iberville Parish plantation in the summer of 1835.[64] In May, 1854, twenty-six fatal cases were recorded on the Lapice plantation in St. James Parish.[65] Although he had no scarcity of cases, Effingham Lawrence was more fortunate than the proprietors cited above. After weathering successive epidemics of measles, whooping cough, and diphtheria with little loss of life on his "Magnolia" plantation, Lawrence entered the following comment in his journal: "We have had during the Past 18 months over 150 cases of measles and numerous cases of Whooping Cough and then the Diptheria all of which we have gone through with So far with But little Loss Save in the Whooping Cough when we lost Some 12 Children   We have otherwise enjoyed most excellent Health."[66]

To combat such outbreaks and to prescribe for minor ailments were important duties of the overseer. George Washington averred that "it should be made one of the *primary* duties of every Overseer to attend closely, and particularly to those under his care who really are, or pretend to be, sick." [67] Similarly, James R. Sparkman, a South Carolina physician and planter, declared that "on every well regulated rice plantation, the *sick* receive the *first* and if necessary the undivided attention of the overseer." [68] To enable the overseer to meet his medical responsibilities, the editor of a plantation and account book in the Upper South advised proprietors to supply their overseers with several medical books and the following medicines: "Calomel, Castor Oil, Epsom Salts, Spirits Camphor, Spirits Nitre, Spirits Hartshorn, Rhubarb, Ipecac, Jalap, Hive Syrup, Dover's Powder, Magnesia, Paregoric, Laudanum, Opium, Blister Plaster, Scales and Weights, Spatula and Mortar, 1 Thumb Lancet, 1 Gum Lancet, 1 pint Injection Syringe." [69] With such an assortment of supplies, it is a wonder that the overseer did not set up his own practice.

Moore Rawls, the outstanding overseer of Lewis Thompson's absentee sugar plantation, took his medical obligations seriously. In the following letter to his employer, Rawls outlines the precautions he has taken to prevent his Negroes from contracting the fever: "I have done every thing I possible could to prevent fever. The negros had around everry house, old troughs & Bbls to catch & keep water in I at last Dug a weel in the quater and even then they did not want to clean up around their houses. I think there must have been 200 vessels of one kind or other with water in them." [70] On another occasion Rawls gave Thompson the following account of an unorthodox, but apparently effective, treatment he had administered to an injured slave: "I have got Phill out wagoning   I commence on his foot in July. never let it be wet at all, applyed nothing but an ointment made of bacon rine & fat   light wood burnt together, mixt with burnt Leather. hope it may remain well." [71] Another Louisiana manager, plagued by numerous cases of the "Bowel complaint," reported to his employer: "I have given camphor and Laudnum and followed with calomel and rhuburb   I find it the best medcine I can give for that complaint." [72]

Such quaint remedies did not always benefit those to whom they were administered. Summoned to combat a cholera epidemic on a Concordia Parish plantation, a Louisiana physician discovered that two Negroes treated by the overseer had already succumbed. [73] Some professional practitioners sharply criticized what a New Orleans physician, Dr. D. Warren Brickell, termed "the almost universal practice on the part of owners and over-seers, of tampering with their sick negroes for one, two or more days before applying for medical aid. This practice may be in some measure excusable in the more common acute diseases of negroes, but during the existence of a malignant epidemic it is wholly unpardonable. . . ." [74] Although not entirely without merit, such a protest ignores the paucity of trained physicians —especially in the rural South—and the primitive nature of medicine in the early nineteenth century. Notwithstanding the infelicitous treatments prescribed by overseers and masters, the available evidence indicates that the health status of plantation slaves in the Old South was comparable to that enjoyed by the populace as a whole during that period. [75]

It was clearly in the interest of the overseer to keep his hands in the best possible physical condition. A general outbreak of sickness could have a profound effect upon the crop results if it occurred at a critical time. The harried overseer of Colonel J. B. Lamar's Georgia plantation penned the following account of his vicissitudes during a siege of illness, which reached its peak just as the cotton attained full maturity:

I hav bin Sick Since you left hear myself twice about too weeks but was only confined on the bed for 4 days   I am up at presant but not much acount   The Negrowes on this place Is verry Sickly & hav bin all the while since you Left us & the d[is]eases Is growin wors all the while as well as the attacks more numorous   18 on the Sick list today   16 of that nombr Field hands   too out of the croud Billous fever & very Bad caises   the Ballance chils & Fevers. Those that are out some of them unwell & unable to doo much   all of them has Bin Sick & some of them has Bin sick twice & Several of them down the third time   I hav so much Rain that It Is a hard mater to get one of them well   As Soon as one Gets out It Rains on him or he Is In a large due or in a mud hole & Back he comes again   this Is the way I'm getting on & I call this Rather Bad luck   At least Getting on Slowley   I hav used 2½ Gallons caster oile & ½ Gallon Sprts turpentine & 4 ounces quinine up to the presant   I am doin the best I can with them   Barron [a doctor?] has Bin hear 15 times . . . yours Truly,   Jonas Smith.

P.S.   Since I commenced Riting 4 hands hav come to the house with fever   makes 20 field hands down. I nearly hav a chill my Self. [76]

The experience apparently proved too much for the overseer, Jonas Smith, for, in October of the same year, he requested his employer to inform him of any proprietor in the vicinity of Macon "that wold hire to Go on ther plantation & Gave a Good price & a heathy place." [77]

Overseers often experienced great difficulty in determining whether a slave was really sick, or whether he was merely feigning illness in an effort to avoid work. The practice of "laying up" in order to enjoy the benefits of a unscheduled vacation was apparently common among southern Negroes. George Washington, who kept a close watch on affairs at his Mount Vernon estate even during his presidential terms, frequently questioned whether Negroes reported out for extended periods of time were actually sick. His thoughts on the subject are summarized in the following letter of March, 1795, addressed to Mount Vernon steward William Pearce:

> I observe what you say of Betty Davis & c^t—but I never found so much difficulty as you seem to apprehend, in distinguishing between *real* and *feigned* sickness;—or when a person is *much* afflicted with pain.— Nobody can be very sick without having a fever, nor will a fever or any other disorder continue long upon any one without reducing them: —Pain also, if it be such as to yield entirely to its force, week after week, will appear by its effects; but my people (many of them) will lay up a month, at the end of which no visible change in their countenance, nor the loss of an oz of flesh, is discoverable; and their allowance of provision is going on as if nothing ailed them.—There cannot, surely, be any *real* sickness under such circumstances as I have described; nor ought such people to be improperly endulged. [78]

Those suspected of "laying up" without cause were usually "cured" by a few judicious applications of the lash. The steward of a Mississippi estate, explaining why he had ordered to the field a Negro girl believed to be feigning illness, told Olmsted: *"We have to be sharp with them; if we were not, every negro on the estate would be abed."* [79] Moore Rawls gave one Negro, who had "been pretending to be Sick several weeks," what Rawls described as "a genteel whiping." The overseer expressed the view to his employer, Lewis Thompson, that the punishment had "done him more good than all medicne could have been given to him." [80] In like manner, Doctrine W. Davenport reported to Ebenezer Pettigrew that four of the latter's Negroes had attempted to feign illness. "I courd the hole four in fiftene minits," asserted Davenport, "and they have not been sicke since." [81] On Maunsel White's "Deer Range" plantation, a Negro was placed "in the stocks for feigning illness when not so." [82] Such punishments undoubtedly discouraged many slaves from taking advantage of their owners and overseers by pretending to be sick.

Running away was the most serious common offense charged to slaves on southern plantations. Although runaways occurred with monotonous regularity, they never ceased to evoke expressions of amazement from planters and overseers, to whom the reason for running away was usually a complete mystery. For example, a puzzled Mississippi overseer complained: "Lundy left no knowing Where nor what for." [83] Typical also was this terse entry in the diary of a Louisiana manager: "Calvin Ran off this morning for nothing." [84] In point of fact, however, the flight of plantation slaves was attributable to a variety of reasons—dislike of the overseer, fear of punishment, the desire to escape difficult or unpleasant work, reunion with another member of one's family.

Perhaps the most common cause was that revealed in a letter from Stephen Brown, overseer of George Austin's Peedee, South Carolina, estate, to Josiah Smith, Jr., Austin's Charleston agent. Brown reported that three Negroes had absconded early in December, 1773, "for being a little chastis'd on Account of not finishing their Task of Thrashing in due time." [85] Brown did not disclose the nature of the chastisement. Two Louisiana Negroes, Edmund and Peter, were apparently motivated by their desire to escape a similar correction when they decamped "without a word or a blow" in the summer of 1845. The only cause which the proprietor's son could "assign for their going off" was that "Peter was two days chopping behind: and Edm. 1½ days behind." He concluded, however, that both were "natural runaways and are just playing one of their favorite games." [86]

Occasionally, a particularly incompetent or severe overseer provoked the Negroes under his charge to depart en masse. Such a situation developed in the summer of 1844 on Levin Covington's Mississippi plantation, where the harassed overseer reported the departure of no fewer than eleven slaves within a period of less than two months. [87] The mass exodus of slaves from a small Jefferson County, Georgia, plantation is recounted in the following letter from overseer I. E. H. Harvey to his employer, H. C. Flournoy of Athens, Georgia:

Sir: I write you a few lines in order to let you know that six of your hands has left the plantation—every man but Jack. They displeased me with their worke and I give some of them a few lashes, Tom with the rest. On Wednesday morning they were missing. I think they are lying out until they can see you or your uncle Jack, as he is expected daily. They may be gone off, or they may be lying round in this neighbourhood, but I don't know. I blame Tom for the whole. I don't think the rest would of left the plantation if Tom had not of persuaded them of for some design. I give Tom but a few licks, but if I ever get him in my power I will have satisfaction. There was a part of them had no cause for leaving, only they thought if they would all go it would injure me moore. They are as independent a set for running of as I have ever seen, and I think the cause is they have been treated too well. They want more whipping and no protecter; but if our country is so that negroes can quit their homes and run of when they please without being taken they will have the advantage of us. If they should come in I will write to you immediately and let you know.[88]

It is clear from the above that a difference of opinion existed between Harvey and his employer regarding slave discipline, and it is equally certain that the overseer was disinclined to be lenient in the treatment of his charges.

Runaway slaves frequently camped in the vicinity of their home plantation, subsisting on supplies surreptitiously channeled to them by other members of the slave force. They usually returned voluntarily or were apprehended within a few weeks after their departure. Several methods were devised by southern planters and overseers to effect the return of runaways. Understandably, the overseer was inclined to rely upon rather severe measures' to combat this offense, which was so subversive of plantation discipline. For example, Archibald Hyman, the overseer of a small absentee plantation in Northampton County, North Carolina, sought permission from the proprietor to employ whatever means might be necessary in order to effect the capture of a recalcitrant runaway. Hyman's position is outlined in the following letter to his employer:

The boy washington who was in the woods came up this morning, I undertook to whip him for his Conduct. he raised his Hoe at Me and Swore that I Should Not whip him, I then ordered the Negros to take him, he then Swore that if one of them laid hands on him he would give them the Hoe. he then left for the woods again, if you dont want him hurt I will endeavour to take him without injury, but Should I Not Succeed in doing So I think he ought to be taken any how. You will please come up tomorrow or Monday and let Me Know what Course You wish Me to persue.[89]

J. E. Gill, manager of Andrew McCollam's "Ellendale" plantation in Terrebonne Parish, Louisiana, used a shotgun to bring about the capture of a Negro who had assaulted him in making his escape. Gill, whose overseership was a troubled one due to his incapacity to manage the McCollam slaves, recorded the following entry in his journal on the day of the unfortunate Negro's capture: ". . . spent the day in the woods after Isum shot him 2 in hips and Twice in legs." [90] Another Louisiana manager was actually commended by his employer for shooting a fleeing Negro, who, upon being warned to stop or risk being shot, "only ran the faster." The shotgun blast wounded the fugitive in the side but "did not stop him and it was only 2 Nights after that he was Caught. . . . The overseer was right. I sincerely hope it will stop this man from running away again." [91] It should be remarked that not all planters viewed the wounding of one of their slaves with such complacency.

Another method of inducing runaway Negroes to return to their plantation was noted by Louis Manigault in one of his plantation record books. Manigault had been plagued by runaways during the fall of 1860, but early in the following year he reported that "on 25*th* January 1861 all our Runaways (5 in number) were brought in through fear of the dogs." [92] This practice of tracking runaways with specially-trained dogs was common in many parts of the South. These dogs were hired out by professional slave hunters at the rate of $5 per day for tracking and $10–$25 for apprehending a fugitive Negro. [93] Unless he absconded in exceptionally dry weather when his scent did not stick to the ground, the runaway could usually evade detection by the dogs only by taking to a creek or river.

The utilization of professional slave catchers was more prevalent in the Lower South than in the other slave states. The overseer of a cotton plantation located about fifty miles north of Natchez, Mississippi, gave a visiting journalist the following account of methods utilized on his plantation to bring in runaways:

As soon as he saw that one was gone he put the dogs on, and if rain had not just fallen, they would soon find him. Sometimes, though, they would outwit the dogs, but if they did they almost always kept in the neighborhood, because they did not like to go where they could not sometimes get back and see their families, and he would soon get wind of where they had been; they would come round their quarters to see

their families and to get food, and as soon as he knew it, he would find
their tracks and put the dogs on again. . . . They had dogs trained on
purpose to run after niggers, and never let out for any thing else."⁹⁴

Trained dogs were also employed to track down runaway slaves
in West Feliciana Parish, Louisiana. Bennet H. Barrow reported
the capture of one of his fugitives in these words: "The negro
hunters came this morning, Were not out Long before we struck
the trail of Ginny Jerry, ran and trailed about a mile   *treed*
him, made the dogs pull him out of the tree, Bit him very badly,
think he will stay home a while." ⁹⁵ The use of dogs was obviously a highly effective method of discouraging runaways.

Another method which proved very persuasive in inducing the
return of absconded slaves was the policy of restricting the
privileges of the rest of the force until the absentees returned.
Since most fugitives depended for their supplies upon friends
and relatives at home, the latter could exert great pressure upon
the runaways to surrender.⁹⁶ Such a policy was pursued on
Maunsell White, Jr.'s "Velasco" plantation in Plaquemines
Parish, Louisiana, as the following notation by the proprietor
reveals: "Lit returned on Sunday thru the influence of the others
as I was working Seven negroes on Sunday to pay up for his
lost weeks work—they stood it the first Sunday but it seems
the 2nd they prevailed upon him to give up." ⁹⁷

Runaway slaves, upon being returned to their plantation,
were usually whipped and sometimes chained or placed in the
stocks for several days. Strong measures were frequently taken
to impress upon them the folly of repeating their offense at a
later date. In a letter to his employer dated November 14, 1861,
William Capers, manager of Charles Manigault's "East Hermitage" rice plantation, gave the following account of a severe
whipping which he had administered to a runaway slave:
"George (big) attempted to run off in presents of the entire
force and in my presents. He was caught by Driver John between Conveyor House and No. 1 door. I gave him 60 straps
in presents of those he ran off in presents of." Capers advised
Manigault to sell Big George or "you will loose him" and added
that "he should not be among a gang of Negroes." ⁹⁸ Returning
runaways on the Iberville Parish sugar plantation of Franklin
A. Hudson were confined in irons for several weeks and then
required to work on Sundays for an additional period of time.⁹⁹

A more sophisticated punishment was devised by another Louisiana planter, Bennet H. Barrow, who made one habitual troublemaker "ware womens cloths for running away & without the least cause." [100]
Slave discipline was clearly the decisive factor in the success or failure of an overseer. Although the chastisement of Negroes was a function of the latter, most planters placed limits upon the type and severity of punishment which their subordinates might administer. Typical of general regulations on the subject are the following rules, prescribed for the managers of William J. Minor's sugar plantations:

. . . he must not strike the Negroes with anything but his whip, except in self defense—He must not cut the skin when punishing, nor punish in a passion—He must not use abusive language to nor threaten the Negroes, as it makes them unhappy and sometimes induces them to run away—

When necessary to punish, he will inflict it, in a serious, firm & gentlemanly manner & endeavor to impress the culprit that he is punished for his bad conduct only and not for revenge or passion—[101]

Similarly, Mississippi proprietor Charles Clark specifically enjoined his overseers from using "the but [sic] of the whip or any instrument that will bruise the flesh   this will not be allowed," warned Clark, "except in case of absolute necessity arising from resistance." He further advised his managers to use "a whip with a suitable lash," rather than a cowhide, in punishing violators of plantation discipline.[102]
In order to diminish the likelihood of whippings being administered in a sudden passion, some planters required a specified time period to elapse between the commission of an offense and the chastisement of the offender. For example, P. C. Weston advised his overseers that it was "desirable to allow 24 hours to elapse between the discovery of the offense, and the punishment." Weston, a particularly benevolent master, forbade punishments in excess of fifteen lashes and, in all cases, preferred confinement to the plantation to whipping as a means of punishment. Indeed, added Weston, "the stoppage of Saturday's allowance, and doing whole task on Saturday, will suffice to prevent ordinary offenses." [103] On another South Carolina plantation, where all corporal punishment was administered by drivers, the

latter were required to leave their whips behind when they went into the field. Consequently, if the overseer wished to punish a hand while in the field, the driver was obliged to trudge a mile or two back to his cabin to secure a whip before the punishment could be applied.[104]

Limitations upon the number of lashes which could be applied at any one time were prescribed by most planters. On the Louisiana sugar estate of Governor Alfred Roman, the maximum number that could be inflicted without securing permission from the proprietor was ten.[105] Similarly, George Jones Kollock instructed the overseers of his Georgia plantations to give no "more than ten lashes unless I am present." [106] Kollock later raised the maximum figure to twenty, but such a punishment was still mild compared to those meted out on many plantations. A more common maximum was fifty—the number prescribed by Alexander Telfair for the overseers of his "Thorn Island" unit.[107]

Plantation slaves were subject to punishment for a variety of transgressions. When their master left on a visit to Kentucky at the height of the cotton harvest, the Negroes on a plantation in the Mississippi Delta subjected their manager to a particularly difficult time. The following entries by overseer T. L. Vandivier, recorded in the plantation book during the course of a single week, indicate a few of the minor offenses which slaves were prone to commit:

[November 12, 1855.] Whipt Betsey and black to day for changeing their places at the waggons
[November 13, 1855.] Whipt new Dave and matilda for fighting
[November 14, 1855.] all hands working Fine as I wish them to do
[November 16, 1855.] Whipt morgan For Telling Lies
[November 17, 1855.] Whipt Lancaster To day for picking Trashey Cotton[108]

Doubtless shaken by this series of events, Vandivier sought a salary increase of $200 for the following year.[109]

Accusations of mistreatment and, indeed, of brutality toward the slaves under their supervision have been leveled against members of the overseer class by numerous secondary writers and, during the antebellum period, by some plantation owners. George Washington, to cite one example, charged that most overseers seemed "to consider a Negro much in the same light as they do the brute beasts, on the farms; and oftentimes treat them as inhumanly."[110] More than a half-century later, a Mississippi planter, seeking the extradition of a man who had fled to Alabama after murdering one of his Negroes, complained to Governor John J. Pettus that "the shooting of negroes by overseers, and other irresponsible men of the country, is becoming too common a thing among us."[111]

Extant plantation records indicate that instances of brutality did occur, especially on absentee plantations where the overseer was not under the immediate eye of his employer. Thus, Benjamin L. C. Wailes, noted Mississippi planter and naturalist, was incensed to find, on a visit to one of his absentee units in 1858, that overseer Alexander Stanford had "neglected my sick negroes very much" and had maltreated others, "one of whom he has cut barbarously with his knife & afterwards whipped severely."[112] Stanford's successor proved no better and was peremptorily dismissed after five months. Although recommended to Wailes "as a religious man," he was in fact "passionate & profane & in short brutish in his disposition towards the negroes," asserted the angry proprietor.[113]

One of the most flagrant examples of overseer brutality occurred in 1859 on one of the units comprising the great Somerset estate, owned by John Perkins, Jr., and located in northeast Louisiana. A charge of cruelty was leveled against one King, the overseer of Perkins' "Backland" plantation, by Lewis Carter, overseer of neighboring "Viamede" plantation, which was also owned by Perkins. Carter's colorful account of the incident was contained in a letter to his employer, which read, in part, as follows:

Judg   them 2 litel garls that you Sent from your house to Backland is treated Badly   Mr Kings Wife was Sick last Monday an he sent for My Grany woman Mariah an She told me that Mr King nocked Selyan down and Stomped hir an your carpner Jim told me that Both of them was cut all to peces   Judg he dont half tend to his Busness in the feld he is at the house all the time an the house Servents Sees no pece atole   Judg I dont like to Say enything agenc a overseer But I think it is my Duty to Say this to you   I have talked to Mr Rhods [steward of Somerset estate] abut it untell I am out of heart for Mr King dos not Study your intrust   he don't Cear eny thing about nothing But your Mony and Judg when I see eny thing going rong on either of your places I must speak abut it and if the[y] will not hear me I must writ to you[114]

Carter continued to complain about King in subsequent letters to his employer, and, possibly as a result, King was not rehired the following year.

Despite occasional examples such as those cited above, it is likely that the majority of southern overseers treated the Negroes in their charge fairly well. Constant admonitions from the proprietary class, which obviously had a vital interest in the welfare of its slaves, deterred most overseers from abusing their wards. When an Alabama Negro came to his master "badly bruised up" following a severe beating by the overseer, proprietor James M. Torbert sharply rebuked his manager and wrote the following comment in his plantation journal: "this will not do   he can whip him if he wishes when he does wrong but to beat them up with Sticks and his fist Must not be." [115] In this instance, the overseer mended his ways and became the best manager ever employed by Torbert.

Where cases of severe treatment and unmitigated cruelty became known to the owner, the overseer usually received an immediate discharge. Virginia planter William Massie declined to reengage an otherwise excellent overseer, whom Massie described as "too savage and cruel in his infliction of stripes, and too brutal in taking every rag off the women, young and old when he chastises them." Massie responded to an inquiry from a distant planter with this evaluation of his former overseer: "He don't work himself, but has more work done than any man I ever had. . . . But, my Dear Sir, to use the vulgar phrase of a vulgar crew, 'he is hell upon a negro!' " [116]

On Effingham Lawrence's "Magnolia" plantation, assistant overseer J. Kellett was dismissed after shooting a Negro boy, who had apparently gone berserk with a cane knife. Joseph A. Randall, chief overseer of "Magnolia," entered the following version of the incident in his plantation journal: "The Boy Franke was Shot in a Runing position By J Kellett   The Ball Entering the Left arm near the Sholder Blade Goin through the Left Lung   Kellett seys he was Justifiable in shooting The Boy" [117] It is likely that the fact that Frank was "in a Runing position" when shot was the decisive factor in Kellett's discharge on the day following the incident. Another Louisiana overseer, William G. Etheredge, was charged $3 per day by his employer, R. R. Barrow, for every day lost by a Negro whom Etheredge had struck on the head with a hoe. [118]

An absentee planter often experienced considerable difficulty in determining exactly what kind of treatment his slaves were being accorded. Thus, in 1855 Georgia planter John B. Lamar informed his overseer, Stancil Barwick, that he had heard reports condemning the latter's treatment of slaves under his management. The reports were vigorously denied by Barwick, who dispatched the following missive to his employer:

Dear Sir: I received your letter on yesterday ev'ng   was vary sorry to hear that you had heard that I was treating your Negroes so cruely. Now sir I do say to you in truth that the report is false   thear is no truth in it. No man nor set of men has ever seen me mistreat one of the Negroes on the Place. Now as regards the wimin loosing children, treaty lost one it is true. I never heard of her being in that way until she lost it. She was at the house all the time, I never made her do any work at all. She said to me in the last month that she did not know she was in that way her self untill she lost the child. As regards Louisine she was in the field it is true but she was workt as she please. I never said a word to her in any way at all untill she com to me in the field and said she was sick. I told her to go home. She started an on the way she miscarried. She was about five months gone. This is the true statement of case. Now sir a pon my word an honner I have tride to carry out your wishes as near as I possibly could doo. Ever since I have been on the place I have not been to three neighbours houses since I have been hear   I com hear to attend to my Businiss   I have done it faithfully   the reports that have been sent must have been carried from this Place by Negroes   the fact is I have made the Negro men work an made them go strait   that is what is the matter an is the reason why that my Place is talk of the settlement. I have found among the Negro men two or three hard cases as I have had to deal rite Ruff but not cruly at all. Among them Abram has been as triflin as any man on the place. Now sir what I have wrote you is truth an it cant be disputed by no man on earth.[119]

Barwick, apparently in his initial year as overseer of Lamar's plantation, was confronted with a problem faced by all overseers in such a situation—that of asserting his authority over the slave force. In cases where the preceding overseer had been a lax disciplinarian, the new manager frequently incurred the enmity of the slaves when he attempted to enforce plantation rules and regulations. In the absence of additional data, it is impossible to determine whether Barwick was excessively harsh in his treatment of Lamar's Negroes.

Overseers occasionally encountered resistance when they endeavored to enforce unpopular edicts or to chastise refractory slaves. Although examples of slave attacks upon overseers are not difficult to find in southern plantation records, the available evidence indicates that such assaults were the exception rather than the rule. Ulrich B. Phillips estimated that only eleven Virginia overseers were murdered by slaves in that state during the period 1780–1864. By way of contrast, fifty-six slaveowners suffered fatal injuries at the hands of Virginia slaves during the same period.[120] Although one might anticipate a higher incidence of slave crime in the Lower South, the first recorded murder of an overseer by a slave in Oktibbeha County, Mississippi, did not occur until 1856.[121] Of course, the above figures are somewhat misleading since many overseers survived beatings administered to them by irate Negroes. Nevertheless, considering the total number of slaves who worked under the direction of white overseers during the antebellum period, instances of slave resistance to overseer authority were comparatively infrequent.

When such resistance occurred, it usually resulted from an attempt by the overseer to inflict punishment upon one of the slaves. A Mississippi overseer, who had twice been assaulted while in the act of administering a punishment, told Olmsted that "he always carried a bowie-knife, but not a pistol, unless he anticipated some unusual act of insubordination. He always kept a pair of pistols ready loaded over the mantel-piece however in case they should be needed."[122] Numerous examples could be cited to demonstrate that such precautions were not unwise. In May, 1823, Daniel P. Avant, manager of Robert Allston's "Matanza" plantation in Georgetown District, South Carolina, came to blows with a slave known as Jerry. The latter had annoyed Avant by blowing a horn for his own amusement —a diversion forbidden to slaves on most southern plantations. Avant attempted to whip Jerry for the offense, but the latter fought back. The overseer finally subdued the recalcitrant Negro, tied him up, and gave him twenty to thirty lashes.[123]

Less fortunate than Jerry was a Louisiana slave who defied both his driver and his overseer at the cost of his life. Details of the incident are contained in the following testimony of overseer Albert Foster, delivered at a coroner's inquest in Concordia Parish on July 5, 1857:

on Tuesday morning, the driver Bill came to me and stated that

Samuel had become unmanageable was destroying cotton, that he had ordered Samuel down to be whipped, that Samuel then swore he would not be whipped. Bill then told him that he would get the Overseer. Samuel swore, he might get who he choose, and followed the driver threatening to cut him to pieces with his hoe.

I went to the field along with the Driver, and found Samuel working, probably one hundred yards from the rest of the hands, he came to the end of the row as soon as I rode up. I asked him what was the matter, he said there was nothing, only the Driver had an ill will at him. I told him to wait till the driver got up as I always wished to hear both parties, as soon as Bill got up, I asked him what was the matter, he Bill immediately told me the same as he had done at the house. I then asked Samuel if he had refused to get down for punishment when the driver ordered him, he answered at once, yes, by God, I did and I am not going to be whipped by anybody, either black or white. I told him to stop, as I allowed no negro to talk in that way, and that he knew that. I then ordered him to throw down his hoe, and to get down, he swore God damn him if he would   I repeated the order, and he again swore he would not. I moved my horse nearer to him when he turned and ran off. I kept my horse standing and called to the rest of the hands to catch that boy, not one of them paid the least attention to me but kept on at their work. I then started after Samuel, myself, and overtook him and turned him. I ordered him to throw down the hoe and stand   he swore, God damn him if he would, and again ran off. I ran at him again and again turned him and repeated my order and got the same answer   he started again and I after him got again within 4 or 5 yards when he wheeled round, with his hoe raised in both hands and struck at me with his full force   my horse swerved aside and passed him his hoe descending I think within one or two feet of my head, pulled my horse up, and drew my pistol. Samuel was then standing with his hoe raised. I fired across my Bridle arm when he fell.[124]

Samuel died four days after the shooting. The overseer went free, although the postmortem examination revealed that Samuel had been shot in the back, the bullet lodging near his spine.

The punishment of a female slave aroused the ire of the woman's husband on another Louisiana plantation in 1837. Overseer William Jacobs recounted the episode in a letter to his employer's wife, Mrs. Mary C. Weeks:

as to the difficulty with Summer, it arose from my having hit his wife a few light liks when backward to procede to work, after which I proceeded to the field where Summer left his work to the distance of 20 or 30 yards with his Cane Knife in his hand & very much inraged, and Said that I had abused his wife & that he was not a going to put up with it & that I was an unjust man, and that I might go get my gun kill him & bury him but that he was not a going to put up with any other punishment of himself or family, and that he was instructed by his master Alfred & yourself that if his family was punished unjustly that he must report it to one of you.[125]

Several hours after this confrontation Summer ran away, presumably to join another slave whom Jacobs had struck with a riding cane after the Negro had given him "some impudance." Apprehensive lest Mrs. Weeks be disturbed by "these trifleing misfortunes," the self-possessed overseer assured her that "the buisness progresses as it has heretofore done and that my exertions according to the best of my judgement shall be used to promote your interest in the saving of the Crop." [126]

The severity of punishment accorded to any slave who defied or assaulted his overseer was an important factor in discouraging such misconduct. Swift punishment was meted out to Negroes guilty of any form of insubordinate behavior toward their overseer. Wealthy Louisiana sugar planter Alexander Pugh made a special trip to one of his plantations to chastise a slave for insolence to the overseer. "I do not think he will behave so again soon," he declared upon his return home.[127] Similarly, a Mississippi proprietor placed one of his Negroes "in the stock & gave him 39 lashes with the strap for being saucy & clinching his hands against the overseer." [128]

Most southern states had statutory provisions designed to deter slaves from physically assaulting their owners or overseers. For example, a Louisiana law of 1814 made it a capital offense for any Negro to strike his overseer "so as to cause contusion or effusion of blood." [129] In the same state, a slave who threatened his overseer or rebelled against him while being disciplined was punished at the discretion of the court.[130] Of course, legal formalities were often forgotten in cases of a particularly heinous nature. An Arkansas Negro, who committed a murderous assault upon his overseer by crushing the latter's skull with an axe, was captured, hanged without trial, and his body left hanging for a day to impress other slaves in the community with the gravity of the offense.[131]

So hostile was public opinion toward attacks by Negroes upon whites that even if an accused slave lived to stand trial, the latter was usually little more than a formality. A Columbus, Mississippi, lawyer, commenting upon the case of a slave charged with the murder of his overseer, noted that the defense was attempting to delay the case for, "as the case now stands, the negro stands a good chance to stand upon nothing with a cord of rope about his neck, one end attached to a beam above his head." [132] In the same state, the Kosciusko *Chronicle* of December 15, 1852, reported the murder of an overseer's wife and urged the community not to "spare its exertions to bring to condign retribution the foul and blood-stained villain." Five years later the *Federal Union* of Milledgeville, Georgia, reported the slaying of a Bibb County overseer by three Negroes following an attempt by the overseer to chastise one of the trio for alleged misconduct. The proprietor was said to be on his way to the plantation "and will," presumed the paper, "use his best efforts to bring the perpetrators of the diabolical deed to that punishment which their crime deserves." [133] Clearly, slave attacks upon overseers were not tolerated, nor could they be, if effective slave discipline were to be maintained.

5

Discord Between
Overseer and Planter

ESPITE the obvious need for harmony between proprietor and overseer, relations between the two were all too often characterized by dissension and misunderstanding. As a result of this friction, the problems of slave management were multiplied and agricultural production was hampered. Observing that "Negroes soon discover any little jarring between the master and overseer," Virginia planter Hill Carter declared that the two "should always pull at the same end of the rope." [1] So anxious was a Louisiana proprietor to establish harmonious relations with a new manager that he inserted this statement in their contract: "It is intended that a good understanding and Civillity will be pursued by both parties to each other &

thier families." ² Notwithstanding such efforts, the association between employer and overseer was clouded by a veritable war of opinions—a conflict which was aired freely in the agricultural periodicals of the antebellum period.

The divergent attitudes of planter and overseer were clearly reflected in their differing viewpoints concerning the relative difficulty of the managerial functions exercised by the overseer. Many planters failed utterly to appreciate the vicissitudes faced by their overseers as they sought to satisfy the rigorous demands imposed upon them by the former. A Burke County, Georgia, planter depicted the life of an overseer in the following terms:

Thus, master of his own actions, and responsible really to no one, he rides over the fields, and inspects the work and the stock, at his option; experiments with implements and with soils at pleasure, and always fruitlessly, since he is unaided by the knowledge of any scientific principle; and, knowing that neither his situation nor his reputation will be compromised while his crop can compare with those of his neighbors, the better paid of them, sometimes indolently visits his charge in a carriage, and often keeps his dogs and his boat, and indulges in the agreeable pastimes of the chase and the rod. Happy lot is that of overseer —for a man without education generally, and born to labor. He is well paid for playing the luxurious part of gentleman, and possesses, for the time, the plantation in his care, with all its means of contributing to his comfort and pleasure.³

To say the least, the life of the average overseer bore little resemblance to the idyllic existence portrayed above. Overseer Garland D. Harmon, the most vocal spokesman for his class in the Lower South, complained of being continually plagued by requests from his Negroes at night. "I can't even read at night, after the toils of the day is past," declared Harmon, "without being bedeviled with 40 niggers—here after everything you can mention." ⁴ Moore Rawls was another manager who had no illusions regarding the onerous nature of the duties borne by members of his class. Writing to his absentee employer during rolling season, Rawls gave this account of a day's service as overseer on a Louisiana sugar estate: "I left my house at 7 o'Clock last night   had to Stay at the Sugar house until 5 this morning   then in the field until 9 which was 14 hours and I know that there was not one minute in the whole without rain & hard too." The weary manager added that no Negro on the place would "make the hands work in Such times, any longer than I Stand by them." [5]

It remained for a Georgia overseer to furnish one of the most forceful expressions of disillusionment with one's occupation ever recorded. "If there ever was or ever will be a calling in life as mean and contemptible as that of an overseer," he declared, "I would be right down glad to know what it is, and where to be found. I am just tired of it, and will quit it, as soon as I can find a better business." [6] The overseer explained his disenchantment with the overseeing profession in this manner:

If there be good seasons, a favorable crop year, *the master makes* a splendid crop; if any circumstances be unpropitious and an inferior crop be made, it is the overseer. If the hands are runabouts, it is the overseer's fault; and if he flogs them to keep them at home, or locks up, or puts them in stocks, he is a brute and a tyrant. If no meat is made the overseer *would* plant too much cotton, and of course 'tis his fault. If hogs are taken good care of, the overseer is wasting corn, and 'the most careless and thriftless creature alive.' If he does not 'turn out' hands in time, he is lazy; if he 'rousts' them out as your dad and mine had to do, and to make us do, why he is a brute. [7]

The disgusted Georgian also charged that masters were too prone to accept the credibility of "negro news." Asserting that "every one conversant with negro character, knows well their proclivity for lying and stealing," he observed that any owner who formed the habit of interrogating his slaves about the management of his plantation could "soon get a budget of news, sufficient to hang any overseer." [8]

When the average planter undertook to employ an overseer he sought a man of good moral character, who was honest, sober, industrious, intelligent, faithful, and humane. Unfortunately, many who followed the calling of overseer were conspicuously deficient in one or more of these qualities. The overseers of Louisiana proprietor Joseph A. S. Acklen were enjoined to observe the strictest code of morality. "No man," warned Acklen, "will be retained on any of my places—who is not *strictly sober, moral* and *humane,* in his habits." [9] Francis Terry Leak announced that he would gladly pay a high salary "for the right kind of a man, in all respects; one who would be devoted to my interests; who would be just & kind to the negroes, at the same time that he maintained full authority among them; and who possessed a judgment equal to his duties." [10] Aside from

such fundamental qualities as honesty, sobriety, and faithfulness, the faculty most highly valued in an overseer was his
ability to make the slaves work. As one writer remarked, "any
fool could see that they were properly supplied with food, clothing, rest, and religious instruction." [11]

A veteran Alabama overseer, Daniel Coleman, writing in the
Southern Cultivator, presented an excellent summary of those
qualifications considered essential to achieve success in plantation management. The following characteristics, he said, distinguished a worthy overseer:

1. An overseer should be a moral and sober man, because he should
enforce the observance of morality on the farm. 2. He should be a fair
English scholar. This is indispensable, that he may keep plantation
accounts, cotton book, &c. 3d. He must be a man of sense and firmness,
and when entrusted with the entire control of a large number of hands,
he should be a man of experience; because a man of good mind may
acquire a moral influence over his hands, which is far better in its
results than the fear and eye-service produced by flogging. Many of the
hands are shrewd and cunning, and, under an incompetent overseer, they
soon learn to disregard all reasonable restraints. 4th. He should, in the
just acceptation of the term, be a gentleman, and have an ever abiding
regard for his own reputation; because the value and faithfulness of
servants depend much upon their moral training—and one who is a
dirty dog himself is an unfit preceptor. 5th. He should not be too wise
in his own conceit, to learn and profit by all modern improvements. A
bigot will not do well for an overseer.[12]

Perhaps because he expected too much, the typical planter
was rarely satisfied with his overseer. "To find an overseer
with the skill to operate a large estate, the self-discipline and
understanding of human psychology needed to control a body of
slaves, and the physical energy to perform the countless duties
assigned to him, was the dream of every planter but the realiza-
tion of few," observed Kenneth M. Stampp.[13] Whitemarsh B.
Seabrook, president of the United Agricultural Society of South
Carolina, probably expressed the sentiments of most planters
when he discussed the shortcomings of overseers in an address
delivered at the first anniversary meeting of the Society on
December 6, 1827. Terming the typical overseer a "needy wan-
derer . . . without education, without morals, or the incentive
to honourable emulation," he decried the necessity of placing in
the hands of such incompetents agricultural property consti-
tuting the entire wealth of certain districts in the state. "In

their hands," declared Seabrook, "is truly for a time, the whole fortune of their employers. Their ignorance cannot advance it: their indiscretion may forever blast it; and peradventure, shake the State to its centre." Happily, the South Carolina agriculturist added this qualifying footnote: "To the gloomy description here given of our Overseers, there are many and honourable exceptions; and I state with pride and pleasure, that as a class, they are gradually improving in morals, education and general worth." [14]

Southern overseers were berated by their superiors for a variety of deficiencies. Edmund Ruffin criticized them as a class for "being too wise to learn or to obey." [15] Dubbing professional overseers "the cowhide fraternity," Virginia planter William Massie termed that tribe of men "the most faithless and piratical of our population." [16] In Louisiana, Bennet H. Barrow expressed the hope that "the time will come When every Overseer in the country will be compelled to addopt some other mode of making a living—they are a perfect nuisance   cause dissatisfaction among the negros—being more possessed of more brutal feelings—I make better crops than those Who Employ them." [17]

A South Carolina proprietor, writing in the *Southern Cultivator* in 1846, complained of the scarcity of good overseers in South Carolina and eastern Georgia. Where, he queried, might competent overseers be found?

Can they be picked up at grog shops, muster fields, and political barbecues, where the young men destined to be the planters' agents are trained to a sufficient opinion of their abilities, and especially to their vast privileges as 'free, independent and equal citizens' of this republic, who are not to stoop to be any 'man's man,' or to do any man's business even when paid for it, unless allowed to do it after their own fashion? [18]

The disheartened planter lamented that local young men—those in need of capital but of industrious habits—were migrating to the Southwest, "where it is supposed there is a better field for enterprise. . . . The melancholy fact is that our region is nearly entirely destitute of even tolerably good overseers. And what is worse, they seem to be growing scarcer every year." [19] And so it went in the older planting communities throughout the South. Even in the Southwest, where the better overseers had supposedly taken employment, the cries of the proprietary group were no less shrill.

A complaint frequently voiced by plantation owners was that overseers lacked initiative and almost invariably took no permanent interest in the plantations under their supervision. A Georgia planter declared that overseers lacked the capacity to meet emergencies on the plantation and to adopt "new and improved methods of cultivation, erecting farm houses, &c. Having comparatively little interest in the result of his year's service, and none at all in the improvement and future value of the estate, it is not supposable that he will, of his own accord, direct his operations to any such object." [20] Another writer deplored the fact that an overseer who knew he was to leave at the end of the year ceased all exertions with regard to long-range considerations, such as agricultural implements, provision crops, livestock, and fences. "His intent is at an end as soon as he knows he is to leave, in every thing except to stretch the number of your cotton bags by packing light, that he may tell how many he made for you with such a start as he had." [21]

Since the overseer allegedly had only a temporary interest in the plantation under his charge, it is not surprising that he was frequently accused by members of the planter community of thwarting and sabotaging agricultural experiments. James H. Hammond of South Carolina attributed his lack of success in planting operations during the 1840's, in part, to the universal opposition of his overseers to agricultural experimentation. In 1845 he discharged J. J. Barnes, manager of "Silver Bluff" plantation, "because he would not weigh   measure & attend properly to the details of my affairs—experiments particularly." [22] Another South Carolina proprietor charged that overseers "uniformly set themselves against any improvement that is attempted, and in most cases will lose their places rather than permit any important experiment to succeed which they can thwart." [23] George Washington similarly criticized the overseer of his "Dogue Run" farm in 1794 for failing to measure his potatoes when they were taken from the fields. "It would seem," lamented Washington, "as if my blundering Overseers would forever put it out of my power to ascertain facts from the accuracy of experiments." [24]

In view of the sharply critical attitude assumed by many planters toward the overseer class, it is little wonder that many

proprietors experienced serious difficulties with their subordinates. Alabama planter Hugh Davis, who was not noted for his
sympathetic attitude toward overseers, returned home in the
summer of 1858 after a brief absence to find his fodder crop
almost ruined. "It is burnt badly—pulled badly—tied badly—
toted badly—Shocked Shockingly—& Stacked far worse than
any Similar work I ever Saw," exclaimed the angry proprietor.
It looked, added Davis, as if it had been "pulled before day, tied
up with the left hand—toted through the corn in a run & Stacked
in the darkness of midnight." [25] Several months later, the overseer responsible for this debacle tendered his resignation, assign-
ing as one cause "your great Tendency to become excited &
absence of mind while excited." To this communication Davis
responded with the following sarcastic observation in his farm
book:

The second reason he assigns, places me under very great obligations
for his candour & Sagacity—to wit that I am incompetent to attend to
my duties by reason of my absent mindedness—I have heard it stated
as the opinion of a great philosopher that all men are partially insane,
and went on blundering through the world, for want of a friendly moni-
tor to inform them of their lack of Sanity. I am more fortunate than
Common mortals to be thus posted up on my true Condition & feel as
grateful, as many others will feel astonished at the revelation—I really
breathe easier Since I have come to a knowledge of myself—& I shall
escape Some of my errors & their consequences by getting this note of
resignation—verily, verily—I believe So! [26]

Of course, in not a few instances the overseer was primarily
to blame for events which led to conflict with his employer.
James M. Torbert of Macon County, Alabama, became embroiled
with a particularly incompetent overseer, named Little Bustian,
in 1855–56. Characterizing Bustian as "a poor Chance," Torbert
hired him conditionally at a salary of $175 because "I am obliged
to have Some body." [27] The proprietor's apprehension proved
well founded, for within a month he complained: "I am affraid
Bustian will not do   he moves about too Slow." [28] On January
10, 1856, Torbert recorded a visit from a managerial aspirant
who had "Come to See if I would not turn of[f] Bustin and
employ him   I think I had better do it, I do not believe Bustin
has got good Since." The owner's patience was almost exhausted
by the end of January, when he wrote: "I do think they get
along Slower in the newground than I ever had hands in My

life   Bustin is not worth hell . . . I will let him Stay untill plough time and if he does, not improve I dismiss him." " Bustian apparently did improve after this but fell ill in midsummer and was obliged to vacate his post—a development which, doubtless, did not bring tears to the eyes of his employer, who soon engaged a more capable successor.

Even more exasperating were the experiences of Mississippi agriculturist Martin W. Philips, who was subjected to a succession of incompetent subordinates during the year 1856. Less than a month after engaging one Champion to overlook his "Log Hall" plantation, Philips had become disenchanted with his new overseer. The latter had been drunk continually, didn't "seem to desire to govern negroes," and refused to enforce plantation rules requiring Negroes to attend preaching. "He says it is a sin to *make negroes* attend, and against his conscience," recorded Philips.[30] The overseer was discharged, but, on the following day, Philips decided to allow him to remain after Champion pledged himself "to abstain from liquor while here; also to join a temperance society, if one be in Raymond." [31] The reformed overseer retained his post until July 6, when he departed vowing vengeance against Philips because of a misunderstanding which had developed between the two men over the ownership of a slave.[32] Philips employed two more overseers during the balance of the year without finding one who proved to be satisfactory.

Difficulties between planter and overseer were no less frequent on small plantations than on larger units, as the tribulations of David Gavin, a small South Carolina proprietor, illustrate. Gavin's problems with overseer H. J. F. Griffin, whom he had engaged to manage his place during the year 1859, centered around the conduct of Griffin's wife. Shortly after the arrival of the Griffins, Gavin entered the following notation in his diary: "I am afraid my overseer H. J. F. Griffin and wife will be a great pest to me, they have taken a ham of pork already out of my smoke house without my knowledge or permission and said not a word to me about it, his dogs are a pest and children not much better." Protesting that "Mrs. Griffin seems to want as much waiting on as the mistress of the plantation should expect," the irate planter further asserted that she "has even been hiring my negro women to sew and work for her." [33]

As the year progressed, the overseer's wife became even more

COTTON-GIN—GINNING COTTON

overbearing, and relations between employer and manager deteriorated accordingly. Early in May the proprietor confided these thoughts to his diary:

> Mrs. Griffin has been cutting high capers this evening, as soon as I left the house or yard she fell aboard of one of my little negroes, Rachael and beat her unmercifully, with her feet and hands, She has been makeing a fuss on the place ever since she has been here, she commenced first with the large negroes and now without any cause has beat this little negro, It has done my health more injury a great deal than my worrying with the hogs in the swamp field, I see plainly I cannot put up with her conduct without a great alteration for the better and that quick, I have for some time been afraid to go off the place for any length of time on account of her high capers, but if I cannot leave the yard, it is rather more than I am disposed to bear if it can be avoided, and there is at least one remedy, I think.[34]

So incensed was Gavin that he could not refrain from further comment on this incident three days later:

> Mrs. Griffin the she-D. . . . could not do without a negro, she had Wesley at her house to-day to wait on her, I expect she will be beating him before long, she did without two whole days, I do not wish the She-devil to strike one of my people again, large or small, She may devil Mr. Griffin as long as he is willing to allow it, but I am tired of it already and do not think I shall bear more than one other kick-up like that of tuesday last.[35]

Mrs. Griffin showed no disposition to improve her conduct, and a month later Gavin commented: "Mrs. Griffin is annoying me again, wants me to give her my riding mare or stop a plow for her to ride, this is Grand!" [36] Finally, on August 15, Gavin dismissed Griffin as overseer "on account of the conduct of his wife." One only wonders that he bore the "capers" of Mrs. Griffin for so long a time.

Gavin fared little better with his next overseer, Henry G. Syphret. After about three months of the latter's management, it became clear to Gavin that the new overseer did not possess the ability to extract the maximum amount of work from his slave force. The decisive factor in Syphret's dismissal in February, 1860, was a fight between the overseer and a slave girl named Betsey. Gavin's final evelution of the unfortunate Syphret was that he was "some better than none but not much." [37]

An overseer might be dismissed from his post for a variety

of reasons. Among the most frequent causes of the discharge
of a plantation manager, some of which have been discussed
above, were drunkenness, absence from the plantation without
permission, failure to get along harmoniously with the Negroes,
cruelty to the Negroes, chronic illness, incompetence in managing the plantation, and failure to attend to duties. Ordinarily,
a proprietor would not sever his relationship with his overseer
merely because the latter had made an honest mistake.

A few specific examples will serve to illustrate the circumstances under which an overseer might be expected to have his
period of service abruptly terminated. Isaac H. Dismukes, overseer of James K. Polk's absentee plantation in Yalobusha County,
Mississippi, was discharged because "he had too much company
and neglected his duties on account of it." [38] Overseer John Harman displayed such a fondness for alcohol that after one week
in the employment of South Carolina planter, John Ewing Colhoun, he received "notice to remove himself off, as a great
drunkard & a person unfit to be on any Plantation as an Overseer." [39] On the Iberville Parish sugar plantation of Franklin
A. Hudson, overseer F. Joly's predilection for hunting precipitated his dismissal before the end of his initial year of
service. Joly obtained permission from his employer to absent
himself from the plantation on Sundays until 6 P.M. in order
to enjoy this pastime. Unfortunately, Joly fell into the habit
of returning considerably later than the hour set by Hudson.
On August 17, 1856, the proprietor noted: "Overseer absent all
day   did not return until 1. a m Monday morning   was to
have been home by six, according to agreement." [40] As the year
progressed, Joly's absences became more frequent and Hudson's
patience began to wear thin, finally culminating in the overseer's discharge at the end of November. [41]

Ineptitude for slave management cost many an overseer his
position. Observing that "a very decided and commanding man
must be had to make anything on a plantation without the
presence of the owner," an Arkansas proprietor dismissed his
manager because the latter had not pushed the Negroes sufficiently hard. [42] On the other hand, Edmund Ruffin discharged
three successive overseers of his Virginia plantation during the
1820's for what he termed "cruel or other abusive treatment of
some of the slaves." [43] Another Virginia planter, William Massie,
declined to rehire the overseer of his "Pharsalia" plantation

after his initial term. Massie gave James Fulcher credit for being courteous and accommodating, "but in the general management of my stock, and in fact all other business, he is entirely incompetent. . . . He also causes my hands to leave their work and go into my pastures for horses for his children to ride. His children are very decent, but this thing won't do." "

An overseer usually accepted his dismissal with good grace, but such was not the case with James K. Metcalfe, manager of William J. Minor's "Waterloo" plantation. Metcalfe took charge in mid-December, 1852, but at the end of his first year, Minor "declined to reengage him for another year—at which he was much enraged & left vowing vengence." " Similarly, a Mississippi overseer, discharged in the spring of 1862 for stealing meat from the smokehouse and "for his utter incapacity to carry on the place," retaliated against his former employer by leading Confederate authorities to twenty-seven bales of cotton, which had been hidden by the proprietor with the intent of circumventing a government order to burn all cotton in the district."

Occasionally, the estrangement of proprietor and overseer led to more serious consequences. Thus, an altercation with a former overseer whom he had discharged for improper conduct resulted in the fatal shooting of Colonel Joseph Bond, probably the most affluent cotton planter in Georgia on the eve of the Civil War. Upon learning that one of his Negroes had been severely whipped by Lucius Brown for allegedly trespassing upon the plantation which Brown was managing, Bond accosted his former superintendent, knocked him off his horse with a stick, and was then shot to death by Brown. The latter was released from custody following a preliminary hearing before a magistrate's court."

Quite different was the outcome of a feud involving two Louisiana planters and their respective overseers. The dispute began in the summer of 1858 when proprietor Dick Christmas and his overseer assaulted the manager of neighboring "Burnlea" plantation, one Fly, whom they accused of punishing one of their Negroes. Several weeks later, Christmas was fired upon from the mill on "Burnlea" as he passed with a party of friends. The irate Christmas immediately swore out a warrant charging Fly with attempted murder, but the latter posted bond and was soon back at his job. The next incident occurred early in September when Fly's employer, while en route to New York on private business, was severely beaten in Memphis by persons whom his wife termed *"hired assassins*—relations, of Dick Christmas." Finally, "a few weeks after this *brutal,* cowardly attack," overseer Fly was assassinated—"shot dead in the middle of our *own field* attending to *his business,"* raged the proprietor's wife in a letter to Judge Alonzo Snyder. "About day-light," she recounted, "the assassin or assassins were concealed in the corn and had made an arbor of *pea-vines*—from whence they shot poor Fly *dead*—as he was passing. There is no doubt in the minds of the community who is the instigator of this foul deed." [48] Unfortunately, no data remains to indicate whether the guilty party was ever brought to justice.

It is not intended to imply, by the foregoing discussion, that plantation owners always viewed their overseers with hostility and never extended to them fair and compassionate treatment. Occasionally, proprietors tempered the blow of a dismissal with the payment of a larger sum than that to which the unfortunate overseer was entitled. Thus, South Carolina planter John Ball, Jr., discharged overseer John E. Moreton after only one month's service, "but in consideration of his extreme poverty and 4 small children dependent on him for sustenance—I allowed him ¼ yrs. wages which was more than he deserved." [49] Similarly, Maunsel White dismissed the manager of his "Deer Range" sugar plantation in March, 1861, and paid him for "3 months altho he Only Worked two." [50]

White also displayed compassion by reemploying an overseer who had proved unsatisfactory in an earlier term as the manager of "Deer Range." In the summer of 1855 White encountered his former overseer in New Orleans "full of regret & Sorrow that he Should have acted so foolishly" and begging to be given a second chance. The forgiving proprietor agreed to try him once more "on Condition that he would promise to learn & turn his whole Soul & attention to what he was about." Prior to the overseer's arrival at "Deer Range," White dispatched a letter to his son, then residing upon the plantation, in which he urged the latter to "speak mildly & encouragingly to him so as not to hurt his feelings Poor fellow. his not understanding the Language is his great misfortune. but he promises to apply himself faithfully." [51] Few planters were as sympathetic as White in the treatment of their subordinates.

Of course, there were many able overseers who, as a consequence of their industry and ability, enjoyed amicable relations with their superiors. After enduring managers Patrick and Mulkey whose principal interests were directed toward the female slaves on the plantation, Louisiana proprietress Rachel O'Connor finally procured the services of a superintendent who proved entirely satisfactory.[52] The new overseer, Germany, was industrious, stayed constantly in the field, never left the plantation, took particular care of the corn and horses, did not meddle with the Negro girls, and was attentive to the mistress of the plantation when she suffered a prolonged illness. In short, concluded Mrs. O'Connor, "I think him the best overseer I ever knew." [53] As Germany commenced his third year of service, the proprietress evaluated him in these terms: "If ever an overseer done his duty he has done his since he commenced on this plantation & continues to do so. . . . I never knew one to behave so well before and scarcely ever expect to experience it in another. and what is still better, he is an honest man in every respect." [54]

John Carmichael Jenkins of the Natchez region probably experienced as little trouble with overseers as any plantation owner in the Old South. His diary contains frequent expressions of pleasure at the progress of farming operations on his three Mississippi plantations. After receiving a report that the hands on one of his plantations had picked 36,000 pounds of cotton in a single week, the enthusiastic proprietor exclaimed: "Hourrah for River Place." [55] Following a visit to the same unit two years later, Dr. Jenkins noted: "The past week I spent at River Place & found the Plantation matters getting along admirably—a good deal in advance of last year—as they have scraped over a greater part of the Cotton ground—& the stand a very fine one—" [56] Apparently he was blessed with overseers of a better sort than most, probably because he displayed greater tolerance and understanding toward his subordinates than did most of his planter colleagues.

Appreciative employers sometimes gave special dispensations to particularly outstanding overseers to compensate them for long periods of distinguished service. Georgetown District rice planter Robert F. W. Allston left legacies in his will for two of his most esteemed overseers, Jesse Belflowers and Harman Pitman.[57] In Plaquemines Parish, Louisiana, the chief overseer of Effingham Lawrence's "Magnolia" plantation was rewarded for his many years of faithful service by the proffer of a permanent home on the plantation. Upon his retirement from the active management of "Magnolia" in September, 1862, for reasons of health, Lawrence offered Joseph Acquilla Randall "a Home here as long as He choose to accept it." [58] Had more planters displayed such a benevolent attitude toward faithful employees, it is likely that the overseeing profession would have held a greater attraction for competent young agriculturists.

The most fundamental cause of friction between planter and overseer concerned the division of managerial responsibility between the two and the consequent degree of supervision to which the overseer was subjected. Lack of independence in management was a chief complaint of the overseer, and one that few planters took measures to alleviate. Typical was the remark of an Alabama proprietor that his manager was "getting too big for his pants." [59] The overseers of "Brookdale" farm in Amite County, Mississippi, were subjected to particularly close oversight by the owner, as the following rules indicate:

He is to change no order or arrangement by me given or established unless with my consent. And in the cultivation of the crop to conform to my directions as far as possible.

He is to see me, if at all possible, every night and inform me of the business of the day and learn my wishes for the ensuing day and of mornings also to see me if convenient before going out. [60]

Another Mississippi planter allowed his overseer to "pitch the crops, and work them according to his own judgment, with the distinct understanding that a failure to make a bountiful supply of corn and meat for the use of the plantation, will be considered as notice that his services will not be required for the succeeding year." [61] Such an arrangement was probably preferred by most overseers, since a failure to harvest sizable subsistence and staple crops frequently led to dismissal, whether the manager exercised control over planting operations or not. One observer reported that the overseer was usually given a free hand on plantations where the cotton yield was of paramount importance. "If he makes cotton enough, they don't think they ought to interfere with him," commented the writer. [62]

The typical planter view respecting the division of managerial responsibility between owner and overseer was expressed by a correspondent in De Bow's Review, who contended that the first duty of an overseer was subordination to his employer. Arguing that subordination was not subjection, he asserted that the master must exact obedience from the manager "for the same reason that the husband is allowed to rule the wife. There cannot be two heads; and he who owns the property, bears all its burdens, and takes all its risks and responsibilities, must have the entire control, and a discretion of delegating it in such way and proportion as may suit himself." [63] This general viewpoint was echoed by members of the proprietary class throughout the South. A Darlington, South Carolina, planter declared: "The employer has a right to his own way—though it might be the wrong way—where no moral responsibility is involved, and the Overseer ought cheerfully and fully to carry out his instructions." [64] Virginia proprietor Hill Carter maintained that "no overseer, however high his standing, should hesitate to obey implicitly the orders of his employer; for how can he require those under him to obey him, unless he obeys those over him? The first duty of those who expect to command, is to learn to obey." [65]

In 1854 a vigorous debate was waged in the pages of the *American Cotton Planter* over the degree to which an overseer should be supervised by his employer. The principal protagonists in this literary controversy were Mississippi planter Martin W. Philips and Garland D. Harmon, a renowned Georgia overseer. Philips initiated the conflict with a scathing indictment of the overseer group, in which he ridiculed the idea of relinquishing control of his hands to a hired manager. [66] Shortly after the publication of this article, a Burnsville, Alabama, overseer leaped to the defense of his class. "I should like to know," he countered, "why any man would employ another to do what he intends doing himself. Does he employ a man that he may have one more to give orders to?" He argued that no man who had to be ordered what to do was qualified to be an overseer. [67] Harmon then entered the debate, contending that a failure to invest the overseer with proper authority relegated him to the position of a driver. He advised his fellow overseers "never to agree to oversee for a man who wants you to 'go by directions'; for I assure you, that man is mistaken; he only wants a 'driver,' and you will be more troubled by him than forty negroes." [68]

Philips returned to the attack in September, 1854, with the argument that subordination of the overseer to his employer carried with it no derogatory implications regarding the former's capacity or competence. "To me," he declared, "it is monstrous, to think that a master, when employing an agent, whether a doctor, a merchant, a mechanic, or what not, cannot, direct his own affairs. In planting, I would myself require absolute, unconditional obedience, and if any man be too proud for this, he will never suit me; and I cannot conceive of any thing derogatory to the gentleman." [69] So far as the degree of supervision was concerned, Philips asserted that planter directions were not intended "to cover every act, every thought," but only *general* details of plantation management. [70] Harmon responded that he had no objection to "general directions," but did "object to employers ('monstrous' as it may seem) giving directions to overseers as to planting, cultivating the crop, and the management of the negroes, requiring him to be guided by those directions, and if a poor crop is made, charging it upon the overseer, as I have known to be the case!" The Georgia overseer concluded his remarks with this trenchant point: "To make the overseer responsible for the management of the plantation, he must have control of it; otherwise he cannot be responsible, because no man is, nor should be, responsible for the acts of another! My motto is, that every man should stand or fall upon his own merits. This is all I ask, and I think it is fair." [71] It is interesting to note that Harmon later served a single term as the manager of Philips' "Log Hall" plantation.

Additional factors engendered friction between proprietor and overseer. Stringent regulations relating to the demeanor of the overseer in the presence of his employer irritated the former group. For example, a rule submitted by an anonymous planter and printed in the July, 1849, issue of the *Southern Cultivator* cautioned the overseer against the use of "disrespectful language in the employer's presence—such as vulgarity, swearing, &c.; nor is he expected to be guilty of any indecencies, such as spitting on the floor, wearing his hat in the house, sitting at the table with his coat off, or whistling or singing in the house." [72] The publication of such an insulting regulation prompted a South Carolina manager to defend his colleagues against "those contributors who seem to delight in rendering our business less desirable than it even is at present. Such ill-assorted rules . . . have a tendency to not only lower their business in their own estimation, but also humble their position in the eyes of others, and serves effectually to prevent men of education and of superior standing, from engaging in such a pursuit." [73]

Strife between planter and overseer also arose out of the practice, pursued by some absentee proprietors, of checking on the performance of their subordinates by making inquiries of planters residing in close proximity to their absentee property. In the fall of 1847 a dispute arose between Maunsel White and James N. Bracewell, overseer of the former's "Concord" plantation, located on Bayou Boeuf in Louisiana. Bracewell, apparently a sensitive and insecure personality, was angered to learn that his employer had been corresponding with neighboring planters regarding the progress of operations at "Concord." The dispute reached a climax in November when White dispatched to his overseer a sharply-worded letter, a portion of which reads as follows:

. . . I am not a little surprised at your remarks relative to my correspondence with Mr Elgee, Mr Compton, or Mr Any body else, & that had you rec^d my letter of the 14th, previous to the receipt of mine of the 25th you would have made other arrangements for business & that even now after your acknowledgement of my liberality, you insinuate that you only agree to stay with me, provided 'this' & provided 'that.' What you can possibly mean by such, I cannot conceive Unless you mean, that I am by no means to make any inquiry about your conduct, on the plantation. What you mean by insinuations, is too far beneath my notice, & now Sir if you are *a faithful overseer, an Honest man, & a good Christian*, you need not be afraid that your conduct will not bear the test of enquiry—you are perfectly right in endeavoring to introduce 'provisions' to the contrary in any new engagement But I now tell you distinctly & to use your own beautiful phrase 'flatfooted,' that while you stay with me, I shall *examine, Scrutinise,* & enquire about your conduct & proceedings, & if I find them unworthy of my confidance; you shall quit, were it to cost me the crop. You have mistaken your man, I can never be driven into any measure, you must therefore on receipt of this letter, state decidedly & explicitly & without provisos, or conditions, whether or not you are willing to remain on Concord plantation on the terms proposed in my letter of 25th October.[74]

Faced by this ultimatum, the sensitive Bracewell reluctantly acceded to the conditions imposed by his employer. White remarked that it was "not done without 'Snarling' but it matters not. It is in your nature & cannot be eradicated; I shall be satisfied if you do your duty as a faithful Overseer, & that is all I want." [75]

Even more exasperating to the overseer than the practice
of checking on his activities through neighboring planters, was
that of making such inquiries among the slaves under his
control.[76] Such reports were manifestly unreliable and, moreover, were unwise since they tended to undermine the authority
of the overseer. Nevertheless, the practice was widespread
throughout the South and tended to inflame relations between
owner and manager wherever it existed. A regulation promul-
gated for the guidance of overseers on one plantation stipulated
that the owner would "not encourage tale bearing," but, continued the directive, he "will question every negro indiscrimi-
nately whenever he thinks proper about all matters connected
with the plantation, and require him to tell the truth." Should
such interrogation reveal "any thing derogatory to the overseer,"
he promised to communicate it to the latter immediately.[77]

The policy of allowing slaves to carry complaints over the
head of the overseer directly to the master was vigorously
opposed by plantation managers. An Alabama overseer complained that proprietors seeking information about plantation
business "seldom, if ever, inquire of the white man, but call up
some negro, and ask him questions that ought to make any
gentleman blush to think of asking a negro about a white man.
With so little confidence manifested for a man, is it any wonder
that he feels no interest in raising children, enriching lands,
and improving livestock?"[78] At least one planter recognized the
danger of relying upon slave news and made it his policy to
whip any slave who complained of the overseer. "The impropriety and absurdity of listening to what negroes have to say
about their overseer," he reasoned, "is perfectly evident to any
who will reflect a minute on the subject."[79]

Some planters weakened the authority of their subordinates
by allowing special privileges for favorite Negroes or by interfering with the punishment of slave offenders. The effective
discipline of a slave force was clearly impossible under such circumstances. The following letter from Samuel L. Straughan to
his employer, Robert Carter of "Nomini Hall," illustrates the
consequences which could result from the granting of special
privileges:

Sir: I understand by Suckey that she has leave of you to stay at
home and wash her Clothes at any time when she pleases & to goo to

Eviry place to meeting in the week She pleases Let the worke bee in
what condition it will: for Last Saturday I hadn't bout 40 Thousand hills
of Tops & Blads of foder out & was very likely for Rain & Did Rain &
I sent for hir to Come in the morning to help Secoure the foder but
She Sent word that She would not come to worke that Day, & that you
had ordered to wash hir Cloaiths & goo to Any meeting She pleased any
time in the weke without my leafe, & on monday when I come to Recken
with hir about it She Said it was your orders & She would do it in
Defiance of me, I Never Refuse to Let wone of the people goo to meeting
If they ast my leafe, but without that If they that is under me Doo
Contrary to my Direction they will Sufer for it As one of the people is
as much to me as a other & I shall treat them as Such & I hope if Suckey
is aloud that privilige more than the Rest that she will bee moved to some
other place & one Come in her Room.[80]

Complaints such as that contained in the following communication from Gabriel Ellis to Robert F. W. Allston were also
common: "Things goes on very badly here   Mrs Allston has
divested me of so much of my authority and the Negroes is
aware of it that I can not Manage them as they aught to be
if one Runs away and goes to her she will not sufer me to
punish it at tall." [81] A Georgia overseer, harassed by similar
interference, gave vent to his feelings in this manner:

flodg grace this day for covering corn bad, then flodg her again
for insolence, which Mr. Kollock did not seem to like, when the owner
takes the part of the negro against the Overseer who wishes to forward
the interest of the owner It never fails to bring Mr. dont care on the
place and ruin the Negroes and make the owner a bankrupt   the reason
that existed Mr. Kollocks dislike for Graces flodging was an accidental
cuff close her eye which he Mr. Kollock thought was done through temper
or intention.[82]

There appears to have been considerably more justification for
the owner's intervention in the latter case than in those previously cited.

Conflict between planter and overseer sometimes centered
around the emphasis upon staple production at the expense of
long-range agricultural improvements—a practice which was
particularly prevalent in the cotton states, where on many plantations the professional reputation of the overseer depended
altogether on the quantity of cotton he was able to produce and
prepare for market. Manifestly, such a policy encouraged the
manager to overwork his slaves, exhaust his land, neglect his
stock, and allow his equipment to deteriorate.

It was indeed audacious for the proprietary class to blame its overseers for the existence of such a pernicious practice; nevertheless, some planters did so. In an address delivered before the Beech Island Farmers' Club of South Carolina in June, 1856, William J. Eve of Augusta, Georgia, criticized overseers for their failure to take an interest in livestock. "To make a good crop is the object of their ambition; and the *height* of it, to pick out more clean cotton to the hand than any overseer in the State," declared Eve.[83] Alabama planter John H. Dent, writing in the *American Agriculturist,* complained that plantation owners could rarely "procure a man that will keep an eye to the whole interest of the plantation." Most overseers, said Dent, looked upon cotton as "the elevator of their reputations." [84] Such was undoubtedly the case in many areas, but he neglected to point out that the *planter class* established the standards by which the reputation of an overseer was judged.

Some overseers readily perceived the deleterious effects of an undue emphasis upon cotton production and sought to induce the proprietary class to alter its standards for reckoning the worth of plantation superintendents. A Georgia overseer utilized the device of a fictitious dialogue between "Colonel Cottonbags" and an overseer to ridicule the former in the pages of the *Southern Cultivator.* Remarking derisively that "our farmers pride themselves upon being Captains, Colonels, Majors, and Judges, far above the honor of being the President of an agricultural society," the Georgian declared that overseers were simply following the lead of their employers in valuing their services by the amount of cotton produced.[85] Mississippi overseer William H. Cook urged planters to consider "whether moderate crops of cotton, with good cultivation, and a proper and diligent attention in taking care of property on plantations, will not enhance the wealth of the planter in a greater degree, than the driving, exhausting mode of cultivation practised in some sections of our country." [86]

The more perspicacious planters discerned that the overseer was not primarily to blame for the ruinous policy of neglecting slaves, stock, and land in order to harvest bumper staple crops. John Taylor of Caroline observed that it was not the fault of overseers "if their employers have made their wealth and subsistence to depend on the impoverishment of half a continent. The most which the land can yield, and seldom or never, improvement with a view to future profit, is a point of common consent and mutual need between the agriculturist and his overseer; and they generally unite in emptying the cup of fertility to the dregs." [87] A South Carolinian informed his fellow planters that no reform of the overseer class or increase in the wealth of the country would be possible until proprietors "generally come to the opinion, that it is necessary to attend to other things besides making cotton, to get rich by agriculture." It was no wonder, he declared, that the overseer demanded complete control of the plantation, opposed all agricultural experiments, overworked the Negroes, and neglected the sick. "He has no other interest than to make a big cotton crop," asserted the South Carolinian, "and if this does not please you and induce you to increase his wages, he knows men it will please, and secure him a situation with." [88]

During the 1840's and 1850's, when farsighted southern agriculturists began arousing the people to the need for improved methods of farming, proprietors in the older staple regions gradually receded from their policy of directing their attention solely to staple production. Some progress was made even in the Lower South, where such men as Martin W. Philips, Noah B. Cloud, Daniel Lee, and Thomas Affleck led the fight for a more scientific approach to agriculture. Despite these efforts, however, many cotton-belt proprietors, especially those of absentee estates, continued to exert strong pressure upon their overseers to devote the bulk of their energy to the production of cotton.

The failure of many plantation owners to compensate their overseers with salaries commensurate with their responsibilities was a cause of much dissatisfaction within the overseer group. "For the responsibility they bore and the work expected of them," one authority has written, "they were probably the most underpaid workers in all our economic history." [89] Some contemporary observers professed to believe that members of the overseeing profession were rewarded handsomely for their services. For example, a Natchez physician, R. Butterfield, remarked in 1859 that "scarcely any business, requiring the investment of no capital, *pays better*." [90] Realistic planters, however, repeatedly urged the payment of higher wages in order to elevate the standards of the overseeing profession. One proprietor asserted that a good overseer could not be secured for an annual salary of less than $400 to $500. Cheap overseers, he averred, were, "like most cheap things, worthless." [91] In similar fashion, a Virginia planter declared that real economy demands that "we should look more to the overseer's ability to manage our matters profitably, than to the few extra dollars he may demand for his services." [92]

Contemporary plantation records tend to support the conclusion that there was a distinct correlation between competence and pay in the procurement of plantation managers. Hugh Davis, who operated a medium-sized cotton plantation in central Alabama, found it impossible to secure a satisfactory overseer for less than $350 per year. Davis was slow to perceive this fact, however, and for years was disappointed by the performance of subordinates engaged at cheaper rates. [93] Another proprietor who consistently paid low wages to his overseers was Dr. Walter Wade, owner of "Ross Wood" plantation in Jefferson County, Mississippi. Like Davis, the Mississippian experienced a rapid turnover of plantation superintendents, most of whom distinguished themselves by their incapacity to manage his interests. Two of the most competent managers of "Ross Wood," Hiram Reeves and John W. Bennett, departed voluntarily to accept more lucrative positions with neighboring planters. [94] Wade was certainly aware of the problem, for, in his last contract with Reeves, he stipulated that the latter could "quit whenever he wants to or can *get better wages*." [95] But, like so many other proprietors in the Lower South, Wade stubbornly refused to raise his pay scale in order to attract more competent managers.

One planter who reversed his position with regard to the adequacy of overseer pay was Martin W. Philips. In 1854 he expressed the opinion that plantation managers in his state were paid "as much as planters can afford, up to a fair price, and the best evidence is, many of them become rich." [96] Two years later, however, Philips declared that the two most important positions in society—those of preacher and overseer—were the most ill-paid. "I would have an overseer paid more than a mere hireling," he asserted. "I would have him paid according to his talent, education, responsibility and fitness." Why, queried the Mississippi agriculturist, should "Robert Jones, behind a counter [i.e., clerk in a store] get $600 or $800 per year, when David, his brother, his class-mate and his equal at least, can only get $300 or $400 as an overseer?" [97] On the other hand, Edmund Ruffin contended that the payment of liberal wages did not necessarily guarantee the procurement of a competent overseer. "It is the only business known to me," complained the disillusioned Ruffin, "in which good abilities & services cannot be obtained by paying for them liberally." In fact, said he, "the increase of wages often operates to lessen the value of the services." [98]

The more articulate overseers joined progressive planters in demanding the payment of higher salaries to members of the overseeing profession. A veteran overseer, writing in the *Southern Cultivator* in 1861, deplored the tendency to hire as overseers those who would work for the lowest wages. "It would be much better to give double wages" and procure a capable man, he asserted, "than to take one at half pay and get a half overseer and have your business half managed." [99] Garland D. Harmon complained in 1850 that overseers were the only class not benefiting from the high price of cotton at that time. "Whilst they pay 20 cts. per lb. for Coffee and for other things in proportion, there has been no increase of their wages, which I think rather unjust to them, as every thing else has risen to correspond with the price of cotton." [100] Despite pleas from overseers and enlightened planters, few proprietors showed a disposition to increase the salaries of their subordinates during the waning years of the antebellum period.

An additional factor which irritated the overseer class was the propensity of plantation owners in some areas to change overseers frequently, even in cases where the manager was executing his duties in a satisfactory manner. As has been noted previously,[101] the terms of overseers in the older planting states tended to be less abbreviated than those of their counterparts in the Southwest. Louis Manigault noted that a well-known axiom in the rice districts was "Never Change an Overseer if you Can help it." [102] Virginia planter William Bolling, however, upon giving notice to an overseer who had lived with him eight years, remarked: "They all seem to wear out after a while and to require changing." [103] In like manner, a Tennessee proprietor who changed managers in 1839 reported no serious trouble with his departing overseer; he was just "wearing out." [104]

The position of those in the Lower South who adhered to the practice of changing overseers annually was presented by Milton Baggs, Jr., in the July, 1860, issue of the *Southern Cultivator*. Writing from Milliken's Bend, Louisiana, Baggs frankly opposed the view of many "that the longer a planter retains his Overseer, provided, of course, that he is a good one, the better." His argument ran as follows:

In the first place, I argue that an employee is never so energetic, industrious and careful as whilst he is new in a situation. In the second place, there is almost always a desire in a manager to remain two years in a place where no former one has remained more than one. Hence he will naturally do his best one year in hopes of being continued for a longer time, especially if the salary is fair and the place is not objectionable. In the next place, when a manager goes on a place where he expects all his energies will be taxed to the utmost in order to remain even one year, he immediately girds himself to be up and doing. Grass will not grow under his feet, I warrant you. If there is any good in the man you will get it out of him without a doubt. For, any man who is worth anything at all, will do his utmost rather than submit to the disgrace of a dismissal.

When, on the contrary, he undertakes with a planter who has the reputation of being easily pleased, with whom, to use his own expression, he can remain as long as he wants, he immediately sets himself up to live upon a sinecure. To be a gentleman, and not an overseer.[105]

The Louisiana proprietor noted the belief of some that an overseer became more valuable the longer he remained on one place, because an extended term enabled him to become better acquainted with the cultivation of the soil, the drainage of the land, and, above all, with the character of individual Negroes on the plantation. Taking issue with the last point, Baggs argued that it was not necessary to learn the character of each slave since all should be treated alike. Indeed, he "would rather an Overseer knew as little about my negroes as possible." [106] Finally, the Louisianian reasoned that an overseer might successfully suppress his faults and undesirable qualities for a single year, but if allowed to remain longer he would inevitably drop his guard, and his failings would begin to appear.

The fundamental flaw in the above argument is that no competent and conscientious overseer would be likely to seek employment with a planter who had the reputation of discharging his manager at the end of his initial year, no matter how satisfactorily the latter had performed his duties. A Tennessee planter, A. T. Goodloe, wasted little time in challenging the validity of Baggs's remarks. Goodloe expressed the opinion "that when a planter is fortunate enough to engage the services" of a good overseer, "he should give him employment as long as he will remain, overlooking a great many secondary faults for the reason that we are all liable to a commission of error." [107] In addition, Goodloe disputed the Louisiana planter's contention that all Negroes should be treated alike. "When a negro is generally disposed to act well," observed Goodloe, "it is right and proper that we should overlook his errors to a greater extent than we would do if he was habitually disposed to meanness and rascality; and that we should reward him more liberally when we have presents to give." [108] Negroes should be treated alike only insofar as all should be subjected to rigid discipline, concluded the Tennessee proprietor.

An Alabama manager, writing in the *American Cotton Planter* in 1854, observed that brevity of tenure had a detrimental effect upon the performances of members of his profession. "No man," he wrote, "can prove his talents as a good manager the first year, because everything is new; he has just learned the disposition of his employer and negroes, the qualities of the lands, &c." Frequent overseer turnover, in his opinion, was a major cause of the widely-lamented failure of the overseer to take an interest in long-range agricultural improvements. [109] These sentiments were echoed by a writer in the *Southern Agriculturist*, who declared that no agricultural improvements could be effected "if overseers are invested with the chief authority, and changed every two years. Each one has his peculiarities in managing affairs; plants differently, works differently, establishes different rules for the government of negroes, wants other implements, and has different views about feeding working-animals and rearing stock." [110] By a process of reasoning, the logic of which is not readily discernible, this observer placed the responsibility for frequent managerial changes on the shoulders of the *overseer*. Describing the latter group as "fond of change," he intimated that many of the best overseers demanded wage increases which they knew their employers could not grant and then removed to other plantations at a lesser salary than that which they had received from their previous employers. Notwithstanding this incredible argument, it is clear that the *planter*, rather than his subordinate, was chiefly to blame for the rapid turnover of overseers on southern plantations.

Despite the severe criticism heaped upon overseers by the planter community, the latter group recognized the importance and even the indispensability of the managerial class in the plantation regime of the Old South. One proprietor declared: "These men stand at the helm of the productive interest of this country, and it is in this light that we are enabled to appreciate the worth, the great value of overseers as a community of men." [111] Another asserted that "every thing in the slave-holding states depends on their conduct." [112] Remarking that it was impossible for a man to spend all his time with his slaves, a Virginia proprietor termed the overseer "an indispensable agent" on farms larger in size than eight hundred acres. [113] Similarly, a writer in the Columbia *South Carolinian*, after severely condemning the overseer class for its deficiencies, concluded with the observation that "no planter, who attends to his own business, can dispense with agents and sub-agents. It is impossible, on a plantation of any size, for the proprietor to attend to all the details, many of which are irksome and laborious, and he requires more intelligence to assist him than slaves usually possess." [114]

In like manner, some proprietors recognized the formidable responsibilities associated with the oversight of a large agricultural unit. "No class of our community have any more responsibility resting upon them than does an overseer," asserted Martin W. Philips in 1854. [115] Similarly, Natchez physician Butterfield, charging that the importance and welfare of overseers was too often neglected by their employers, declared: "No business requires its superintendents to be men of good habits, industry, intelligence, sound judgement and a constant exercise of the same, than the management of a plantation." [116] "Justus," writing in the *American Cotton Planter*, acknowledged that "few positions in life are more responsible than that of an overseer on a Southern plantation." The overseer, he continued, occupied a post as responsible as that of "the head clerk to whom the merchant would entrust the management of his mercantile affairs; or the superintendent to whom the capitalist would confide a manufacturing establishment; or the teacher to whom a parent would commit the education of his children." He urged overseers to impress upon their minds a sense of this vast responsibility and to refrain from carelessly undertaking duties which controlled the annual income and indeed "the peace of mind and consequent happiness of those who employ you." [117]

A few planters undertook to defend their less articulate subordinates in the pages of contemporary agricultural periodicals and in speeches before local agricultural societies. One of the most vigorous defenses of the overseer class was delivered by James Barbour, president of the Agricultural Society of Albemarle County, Virginia, at a meeting of the Society on November 8, 1825. Barbour's remarks are so significant that they merit extensive quotation. After remarking that obviously there was something radically wrong with the treatment accorded overseers in the administration of southern plantations, he made the following observations:

Undue prejudices are indulged against this class of people. That such a class is necessary to the state of society, their existence and employment unquestionably prove. A prejudice against that which is indispensable, cannot be defended on rational grounds. That there are vicious men in this class is unquestionable. But are there not vicious employers too? And it is very well worth the inquiry, whether this very prejudice, and its consequent ill treatment, is not calculated to produce the causes of complaint on whose existence this prejudice seeks to justify itself. Penurious salaries—suspicion—harsh treatment, tend to degredation, and debasement. Add to this, a continual restlessness, and a disposition to an annual change—and you have summed up the general treatment to which they are exposed. Thus you move on in one continued circle, and not infrequently from bad to worse. We are all aware of the dilapidation of a tenement which changes hands every year. It cannot be expected, either from an overseer, or a tenant, that he will take much heed to the future, in which he does not feel himself at all interested. Indeed, it is impossible that he can succeed so well the first year. He has to learn the wishes of his employer, and the disposition of the hands under him; the capacity of the latter for labor; the different kinds of soil he has to cultivate, and a long list of details which cannot be acquired in a year. Why not try a different course? In my own case, and I draw frequently on my own experience, for one fact is worth a hundred theories—I give liberal wages, abundant finding, and many indulgences. I treat them kindly and make them feel a respect for themselves. I avoid frequent change. In return I have received honesty and zeal. My principal manager has lived with me between twenty and thirty years. I cannot ascribe my success altogether to accident; fortune may, for a short time, exercise an influence; but uninterrupted success, for a long series of years, must be rooted in a deeper and more permanent cause—and instead of grudging their wages, I rejoice to see that while they are securing my independence, they are acquiring one for themselves, due to their honesty, industry and zeal.[118]

These comments by Barbour, a leading Virginia agriculturist and secretary of war in the Cabinet of John Quincy Adams, indicate an amazing comprehension of the difficulties which plagued the overseer class, and they specify remedies which, had they been followed by other planters, would have resulted in a general elevation of the condition and standards of southern overseers.

Another proprietor who came to the defense of the overseer group was A. T. Goodloe of Green Hill, Tennessee. Writing in the *Southern Cultivator* in 1860, Goodloe disclaimed setting himself up "as the peculiar advocate of this class of men" but offered his remarks from a sense of duty, "as one who feels an interest in the advancement of Southern Agriculture." He found it strange that so many of his fellow planters encouraged the view that overseeing was "a calling unfit to be followed by a man who possesses any gentlemanly principles, or has respectable parentage." Such an attitude discouraged numerous honest and capable young men from entering the overseeing profession, "thereby leaving openings, and consequently offering inducements for men possessed of more 'brass than brains' to apply for and receive employment as overseers, who disgrace, with their inefficiency, an honorable profession." [119]

The Tennessee proprietor advised planters to encourage capable managers "by treating them with the respect they are entitled to, giving them liberal wages, and retaining them in service as long as possible." Incompetent overseers should be dismissed in a "friendly" fashion and encouraged to undertake some other vocation, counseled Goodloe. Asserting that a good overseer was "in every quality that constitutes the gentleman, the equal of his employer," he denounced the tendency to equate respectability with the possession of wealth or admission into affluent society. Goodloe concluded with a plea for "young men of limited circumstances" to attend agricultural schools and prepare themselves for the overseeing profession

instead of adopting, with false notions of gentility and professional dignity, those *so called* more elegant and honorable employments; of being, perhaps, what the country is already too much flooded with, the *important* and pedantic pedagogue in some country log-cabin, or that lazier and more inefficient dignitary, the *pettifogger*, in his lonesome and neglected law office, or the *quack*, with his patent pills, which he cannot dispose of 'for the general health and prosperity of the land,' for love nor money. The young man competent to be an overseer can obtain a ready and lucrative salary; he will be an ornament to the profession he has had the independence to embrace, and he will have the gratification of knowing that he has elevated it to some extent in the estimation of mankind.[120]

Overseers themselves were not slow to answer attacks directed against them by their superiors. Alluding to a particularly vehement diatribe against his colleagues by a correspondent in the *Southern Cultivator*, a Georgia overseer remarked sardonically that "the *wise* and *good* should show some *charity*, and *instruct* and *pull* us up out of the *mire* and *dirt*, rather than getting on our *shoulders*, and bidding us GOD *speed*." [121] In like manner, a charge that overseers were primarily responsible for the deterioration of southern soil provoked a cynical response from Garland D. Harmon. "What a pity," remarked Harmon, "that the fertile farms of the South should be literally wasted by the ignorance and negligence of 'overseers'." Why, he asked, did not planters dispense with overseers and "attend to the business themselves?" Harmon acknowledged the desirability of overseers "becoming 'better read' " but added that many of their employers might also profit from such a suggestion. "We are all too ignorant," observed the Georgia overseer, "and until we become more enlightened, Southern Agriculture must forever remain in the background." [122]

A Burnsville, Alabama, overseer complained that the members of his class received the blame for everything. Replying to a scathing indictment of the overseeing profession by Martin Philips, he declared that the overseer, "after having been confined from the beginning to the end of the year, Sundays not excepted, has barely sufficient to pay for what he was compelled to have, to say nothing of the little comforts he ought to have, and is oftener blamed for not doing more than praised for what he has done. . . . There are some persons in the world that never suffer one chance to escape to say something derogatory to the reputation of poor overseers." [123] Reflecting a conviction held by many of his colleagues, he concluded with the observation that "most of the rich, that hire men to attend to their business, inherited their property, and have poor judgment about farming." [124]

The case for the overseer was never more forcefully stated than by a Columbia, South Carolina, overseer writing in the September, 1849, issue of the *Southern Cultivator*. Said he:

For wages scarcely if at all in advance of that given to the Irish ditcher, an Overseer is obliged to manage the interests of a planter whose estate yields him from five to twenty thousand dollars a year. He has to expose himself to the noxious vapors on plantations bordering and some situated in swamps. He has to punish and keep in order the negroes, at the risk of his life, and besides all this, he is virtually excluded from his kindred, and fellow creatures, and compelled to lead a life as secluded, in fact more so than the inmates of Sing-Sing prison, and all this is expected from him without any profit to himself whatever.[125]

This writer joined progressive planters in urging proprietors to adopt some means of elevating the character and respectability of the managerial class. A step in this direction, he observed, could be achieved by giving the overseer a fair percentage of the returns from the plantation, and by allowing him to cultivate for his own use a few acres of land. By such means he could establish for himself a respectable footing in society.

The South Carolina correspondent pointed to England where stewards and overseers were men of talent and enjoyed considerable respectability. According to the Carolinian, agricultural managers in that country received, in addition to their regular salaries, a farm rent free, thus enabling them not only to live comfortably but also to "save an independence in a few years. To such men the loss of their situation is a matter of serious consequence, and they therefore exercise all their powers and energy for the benefit of their employer, and strive, in every way, to please him." [126] This incentive to please one's employer was conspicuously absent in the temperament of many southern overseers. The South Carolinian concluded his remarks with the following illuminating comment: "I feel a pride in my profession, and hope yet to find overseers holding a respectable footing in society." This was certainly a formidable answer to the deluge of planter criticism which rained upon the heads of plantation overseers.

There is little doubt that the general reputation of members of the managerial profession was materially injured by the incapacity of the large transient group in the Lower South, who offered their services to those planters ready to sacrifice experience and ability for the sake of reduced expenditures. John H. Hairston, explaining his decision to retain a veteran North Carolina overseer as the manager of his uncle's plantation in Lowndes County, Mississippi, complained bitterly of the quality of overseers in that state. "I was determined," said Hairston, "not to employ a half way overseer without I should have been takin in as there is plenty of that kind in this Country, and others very scarce." [127] Unfortunately, not all proprietors were as exacting as Hairston in their choice of a manager. The conclusion seems inescapable that this inept group would have disappeared had not plantation owners continued to employ such persons merely because they would work for lower wages than more competent overseers.

The better class of overseers recognized that the character of all members of their profession was affected detrimentally by the actions of the drifters, and they repeatedly warned planters to exercise more discrimination when choosing a manager. Alabama overseer Daniel Coleman, charging that the reputation of his profession had been seriously damaged by the activities of "charlatans and pretenders," urged proprietors "to give good wages to a man fully qualified, rather than to pick up at a low rate a mere pretender." [128] Another veteran overseer complained that there were "too many farmers who do not give the subject of getting good overseers the right bearing, and for the sake of getting a man for a few dollars less, will take a man into their employment, to manage their domestic affairs, who is wholly unfit for the place, or occupation for which they are employed." If proprietors would strive to procure experienced managers by offering them adequate compensation, he continued, "our country would soon get rid of a floating population, as overseers, and our farmers would have honorable men following, what every man should look upon as an honorable occupation, which would do honor to themselves and to that class of men who are willing and expect to do their employer's justice." [129] Despite such pleas, the "charlatans and pretenders" continued to find employment, and the reputations of their more competent colleagues suffered accordingly.

A few planters charitably admitted that the proprietary class was largely to blame for many of the deficiencies in the overseer system. Martin W. Philips tempered his criticism of the overseer group with a plea for planters to treat their subordinates more as equals. If such a policy were inaugurated, observed Philips, "we would then see the business more respected, and men would have a better opinion of their calling." [130] The Mississippi agriculturist also admitted that it was the fault of the planting community—not the managerial class—that a large crop of cotton was considered the touchstone of success in the overseeing profession.[181] Similarly, John A. Calhoun, in a report to the Barbour County, Alabama, Agricultural Society, declared that "if masters would lay less stress on the mere crop results of the plantation, and place more stress on the proper treatment of their slaves, and the systematic management of their plantations," many of the evils attributed to the overseer system would be materially alleviated.[182]

Numerous suggestions were offered by both planters and overseers to elevate the standards of the managerial profession. Agricultural education was the method most frequently advocated to achieve this end. Whitemarsh B. Seabrook, president of the United Agricultural Society of South Carolina, urged the South Carolina legislature to provide funds for the establishment of agricultural schools in which prospective overseers might receive training.[183] As the initial step in such a program, Seabrook recommended that "a Professorship of Agriculture" be established "in our College at Columbia." [184] Jefferson Davis was another who advocated the foundation of agricultural schools for the purpose of training more competent managers.[185] Citing the crucial importance of the overseer class, a Louisiana planter proposed to establish a model farm near New Orleans, where youths desiring to embark upon an overseeing career could acquire "the instruction indispensable to the accomplishment of its various duties." [186]

Other concerned planters were more general in their recommendations. A South Carolina proprietor, asserting that the overseeing profession could be made respectable only if the quality of the persons engaged in it were raised, urged his fellow planters to encourage their young sons to enter the occupation. This would aid in converting the overseer class "from being ignorant and undeserving of confidence, into intelligent, valuable and industrious citizens, not only respectable, but adding respectability to their country," he declared.[187] It was the duty of the plantation owner, asserted the South Carolinian, to do his part to make the profession a respectable one. "Patronize and encourage young men of industry, give a tone to the pursuit, and you will rapidly command those of talent, industry and merit, as superintendants [sic] of your property," he counseled.[188]

John H. Dent of Cowikee Creek, Alabama, sought to encourage the formation of a body of career overseers—"a class who would enter into it as a business for life, or a profession; not as places for temporal employment or a home, but as an honorable profession, with a desire to learn both the theoretical and practical part of the duties. Such a class of men would add more to the agricultural interest of the South than all the new modes and theory now in operation." [139] On the other hand, Natchez physician Butterfield sought to encourage young men to enter the overseeing profession by citing the opportunity for advancement from that occupation to an independent planting status. The Mississippian, observing that "very many of our best planters were formerly overseers," declared that the ambitious plantation manager had "a great advantage over those who have followed other avocations, inasmuch as he can bring to bear the results of past experience" in initiating his own agricultural undertaking. [140]

In addition, Butterfield advised overseers to strive to improve themselves by devoting their entire industry and energy to the interests of their employers, and by adding to their knowledge of agricultural affairs through the reading of farm magazines and by contributing the results of their experience to such journals. [141] This plea for overseers to take the initiative in raising the standards of their own profession was echoed by Garland D. Harmon, who advised his fellow overseers: "If we would raise the standard of our profession, let us act uprightly, and attend to our business closely, and be paid for our trouble." [142]

A broader distribution of contemporary agricultural periodicals was another reform which planters and overseers alike believed would contribute to the general improvement of those who followed the overseer calling. A Mississippi manager, William H. Cook, recommended that all proprietors furnish their overseers with one or two papers of that kind. "Although books alone," conceded Cook, "cannot teach a man the business of planting and farming, yet a good agricultural paper will give every overseer many useful hints in plantation business during the year, if he will read it with attention." [143] An identical recommendation was advanced by a Georgia seaboard planter, who remarked that, in addition to increasing their agricultural knowledge, "it would . . . cultivate a greater desire to stay at home and read this [the *Southern Cultivator*] and similar papers, after the fatigues of the day, instead, perhaps, of participating in other matters of questionable benefit either to them or their employers." [144] Editors of agricultural journals even appealed for contributions from their overseer readers. Expressing a desire to receive more communications from intelligent overseers, John M. Daniel, editor of the *Southern Planter*, declared in 1848: "They have better opportunities for observation than any other class; and when they are intelligent men, as a large number of them are, they can furnish just the sort of information needed by the farming community." [145]

It is impossible to determine the extent to which farm journals were disseminated among southern overseers. That many managers read them and a lesser number penned contributions to them is clear from a perusal of the journals themselves. It is known that Colonel Joseph Bond, who operated a number of cotton plantations in southwest Georgia, supplied each of his six overseers with copies of the *Soil of the South* during the 1850's. One of Bond's overseers was an occasional contributor to that periodical and in one such article attributed much of his success in producing a high ratio of cotton, corn, and pork to his employer's generosity in providing him with a subscription to the *Soil of the South*. The editor, of course, welcomed such an observation and urged other planters to emulate Bond in providing their superintendents with his publication. [146] It is not clear how many heeded his plea.

Essays, prizes, and contests were other devices utilized by progressive agriculturists to arouse an interest in improving the standards of the overseeing profession. Thus, a writer in the *American Farmer* inquired "whether it would not be beneficial to the Agriculturists of the South, if a prize should be proposed for the best essay on the duties of overseers or managers, in the form of an address, to persons engaged in that employment." [147] In 1855 an Edgefield District, South Carolina, planter offered a fine watch to "the Overseer (working not less than ten hands) who will report the best managed farm, largest crop per hand of Cotton, Corn, Wheat and Pork, for the present year." [148] Such contests undoubtedly served to stimulate interest among some overseers, but the maladies which plagued the managerial profession could not be cured by such a superficial remedy.

Had all the suggestions advanced by the proprietary class for the improvement of the overseer system been adopted in the years immediately preceding the Civil War, it is still doubtful whether the result would have been a measurable elevation of the overseer in the eyes of his employer. The differences between the two were quite fundamental and, to a large degree, inherent in the nature of the system itself. No matter how able and humane an overseer might be, his self-interest simply did not inspire concern for the conservation and welfare of plantation implements, soil, and slave force—matters in which the proprietor had a decided interest.[149] Such contradictory self-interests between owner and overseer made conflict between the two almost inevitable. Certainly the planter class could have done much in the areas of wages, tenure, crop emphasis, and overseer respectability to improve the standards of the managerial profession and reduce friction in the plantation establishment. But, in the final analysis, it is difficult to see how the conflicting views of proprietor and overseer could have been resolved with mutual satisfaction to both parties.

6

The Overseer
During the Civil War

$\mathbf{W}$HEN the long-smoldering sectional conflict erupted into open warfare in the spring of 1861, most southern proprietors adhered to the normal planting routine as long as local conditions permitted them to do so. In one of the great ironies of all history, the slaves for whose benefit the war was allegedly being waged, remained docilely at their posts and continued to produce the crops which enabled their masters to delay the advent of their freedom. Not until Federal troops penetrated into their immediate neighborhood did the Negroes in large numbers flee their homes, thereby throwing agricultural operations in the locality into complete chaos. Nevertheless, the war's progress had a profound impact upon the plantation system, not

138

only in those areas directly affected by military operations, but throughout the South. An alarming shortage of experienced overseers, government requisition of slaves and livestock, the burning of cotton by order of Confederate authorities, and the insatiable demand for food supplies to provision the army—all contributed to the ultimate demoralization of the southern agricultural system.

The role of the overseer assumed even greater importance with the departure of hundreds of thousands of able-bodied southern whites for the fighting front. In many localities the security of the remaining whites against possible slave insurrections was entirely dependent upon the authority wielded by overseers. It is not surprising, therefore, that the drafting of plantation managers into Confederate military service provoked a storm of protest from the planter class. The general temper of southern planters is reflected in the following letter from South Carolina proprietor James B. Heyward to the Confederate military authorities in his area:

> This will be handed to you by Overseer Mr. C. R. Hains. He informs me that he is compelled by his engagement with you & the order of his captain to return to camp. I beg that you will excuse the liberty I take of protesting against the withdrawal of the Overseers from this neighborhood. They all have large numbers of negroes under their charge who though an orderly set are very dependent upon their Overseer for direction & care. In his absence the timid become panic struck & the bold mischievous. I think in a short time not only individual interests but the whole community will suffer evil consequences. It is necessary that these people should be looked after either in a civil or military way. I recommend the former as the best for both parties, & the Overseer system as the best civil police system that can be invented. Overseers who have lived long on plantations know the individual character of the negroes & by means of a system of espionage know every thing that is going on. Let us not interfere with this if it can be [illeg.]. By all means spare men who are unsuited by years & bodily infirmity for active military duty. I will also mention that the plantations will be able to render more effect[ive] aid in the way of supplies for the army if the direction is [illeg.].[1]

No greater testimony to the utility of the overseer system could be offered.

In response to pressure from the proprietary group, the Confederate Congress provided for the exemption of overseers from military service under certain conditions. The Confederate Conscription Act of April, 1862, which inducted into military service all white men between the ages of eighteen and thirty-five, exempted one owner or overseer for each plantation having a slave population of twenty or more.² This provision, however, applied only in those states which did not have laws requiring the residence of an adult white male on each plantation. Exigencies produced by the war led to revisions of this statute in May, 1863, and again in February, 1864, which considerably reduced the number of exemptions granted under it.³ Thus, an act of May, 1863, provided for exemption from military service only upon the payment of $500 to the government.⁴ At the end of 1863 the number of plantation overseers exempted by authority of the Confederate Congress was only 200 in Virginia, 120 in North Carolina, 301 in South Carolina, and 201 in Georgia.⁵

Regulations governing the exemption of overseers varied considerably from state to state and, as military pressure upon the South increased, were altered to suit the needs of individual army commanders. In the spring of 1864 Henry Parnell, steward of the planting interests of John Perkins, Jr., in Ellis County, Texas, complained to his employer that the military authorities in that state, "in trying to carry out what *I* consider an excellent law use no discretion in trying to supply the wants of some communities & the absolute necessities of others. I refer to the order to put into the army all details for agricultural purposes who raise any thing but provisions." ⁶

As the plight of the South became more desperate, other suggestions were offered to limit the number of overseers excused from military obligations. The assistant surgeon of the 3rd Georgia Regiment proposed that superficially-wounded soldiers be detailed to oversee plantations, thereby releasing exempted, able-bodied, professional managers for military duty. "I believe there are enough Georgians now detailed in hospitals and other useless situations," said he, "to supply the places of nearly all the able-bodied men now exempted in that State to oversee plantations." ⁷ This suggestion, however, was apparently never adopted.

In order to obtain the release of an overseer from wartime service it was the normal practice for the planter to secure an affidavit from a civil magistrate stating that the overseer's services were indispensable. Two other persons familiar with the facts were required to verify the statement under oath. The following affidavit, filed in August, 1863, by Robert F. W. Allston illustrates one procedure by which southern planters procured exemptions for their managers:

> Nightingale Hall 26ᵗʰ Aug 1863
> This is to certify that Joseph M. Thompson my overseer at this place is also overseer at *Guendalos*, where there are about one hundred negroes the property of Col Ben Allston of the Confederate Army, now serving with Genl. E. Kirby Smith, beyond the Mississippi River. That after reasonable delay, and diligent enquiry, having failed to procure a satisfactory person, I employ'd my own overseer J. M. Thompson to look after the police of my son's plantation above named. He has been with my people since January, 1861, and I trust will ensure the police and government of guendalos as well. If J. M. Thompson can be spared from the conscription, it would be a satisfaction to retain him in his present employment. It would contribute materially to the Police of the locality in which he resides.
> witness—
> F. W. HERIOT
> JA R. SPARKMAN[6]

Allston was only partially successful in his endeavor to retain the services of Thompson, for in 1864 the latter left for military service.[9]

In the waning months of the war some proprietors found it necessary to petition the Confederate Secretary of War for the release of their overseers. Others simply appealed to the military commander in their area in an effort to secure exemptions for key managerial personnel. Such was the course pursued in the summer of 1864 by Dudley Avery in an attempt to forestall the induction of Joseph P. Kearney, overseer of his father's sugar plantation in St. Mary Parish, Louisiana. Avery, then serving as an officer in the Confederate Army, dispatched the following letter to Major General Richard Taylor:

> Genl.
> I received a letter a few days since, from my uncle, Mr Henshaw, informing me that my Father's Over-seer Mr Kearney, had been ordered to report at Camp Hunter for enrollment. We have thirty working hands, still remaining on the Plantation and three hundred acres of Corn under Cultivation. Our place is in fact, one of the few in the Parish of St Marys where any crop will be raised. My Father is in Texas and my Brother and myself are in the Army; Mr Kearney is the only white person remaining on the plantation and has been supplying the people in the adjoining Parishes with Salt. I would therefore, General, most respectfully request that Mr Kearney, be allowed to remain upon the Plantation, at least until my Father can come from Texas and make some other arrange-

ments. I would not, Sir, have taken the liberty to write to you, had my
Father been present to attend to his interests. With high esteem and
respect, General I have the honor to remain your obedient Servt
                    Dudley Avery Lieut Co "E" 18th La Regiment[10]

Avery's request was granted and Kearney remained on the
plantation until long after the war had ended.

Another method by which proprietors secured the release of
overseers threatened with induction into military service was by
the procurement of substitutes. North Carolina planter Peter
Wilson Hairston paid $200 for a substitute in July, 1862, in
order to retain in his employment John S. Giles, who had held
the overseership of Hairston's "South Yadkin" farm since
1852. [11] In Clarendon District, South Carolina, the salary of
overseer G. V. McMillan was to be governed in 1864 by whether
a charge was made for the latter's exemption from conscription.
It was agreed between McMillan and his employer, James R.
Sparkman, that if the overseer were exempted "without cost or
charge by the Government for said Exemption," he was to
receive a salary of $300. But if a charge were exacted, to be
paid by the owner, then McMillan was to receive only $200. [12]

Despite the release of some overseers from compulsory military duty, an acute shortage of slave managers developed during
the war. Many overseers patriotically volunteered for military
service, while others were forcibly inducted into the army. Moreover, the enlistment of many marginal planters, the size of
whose holdings had not previously justified the employment of
a superintendent, left many slaves unattended and increased the
demand for overseers. Various expedients were devised to combat this shortage of managers. Perhaps the most obvious was
that of simply getting along without an overseer. Thus, in
August, 1861, F. A. Metcalfe, proprietor of "Newstead" plantation in Washington County, Mississippi, entered this notation
in his diary: "Clary left this morning to go to the wars. I'm
without an overseer." [13] Metcalfe was unable to secure a replacement for his departed overseer and, as a consequence, assumed
full managerial responsibility himself. Women and children were
called upon to assume the managerial function on many plantation units. The mistress of a large cotton plantation in the
Yazoo-Mississippi Delta, jolted by the sudden departure of her
overseer, remarked apprehensively: "I hope the Negroes will not

give me any unnesary truble." [14] Happily, she was able to locate a new manager within a short time, but others were not so fortunate. Planters doubled up in some localities, and a single overseer was entrusted with the general oversight of a number of plantations. In Terrebonne Parish, Louisiana, Charles Minty, a carpenter by trade, was pressed into service as the overseer of William J. Minor's "Southdown" plantation during the period 1863–66. [15]

Notwithstanding numerous instances of effective management by the substitutes referred to above, there can be no doubt that the southern agricultural system suffered appreciably from the shortage of overseers during the war. Not only was it difficult to procure *any* overseer in some localities, but the likelihood of obtaining a *good* slave manager was extremely remote. Seeking a replacement for an overseer whom he had just discharged, steward Henry Parnell observed to his employer, John Perkins, Jr., that "temptations are now so strong for roguery that I am affraid to trust any one." Parnell remarked that both of the men he was considering for the position were "too severe for the times," but, said he, "I hope to Controll their management." [16] After enduring the bungling efforts of several wartime over-lookers, a disgusted Mississippian exclaimed: "God help those who are at the mercy of these times of Overseers & negroes." [17]

So severe was the shortage of competent managerial personnel during the war that many proprietors were obliged to retain in their employment men who would have been summarily dismissed in normal times. Remarking that "overseers are scarce," Mississippi planter James Allen elected reluctantly to keep an overseer, who, according to Allen, knew "nothing about making corn." Since "I will remain at home," concluded the harried owner, "I may get along with him." [18] Similarly, Louisiana proprietor William J. Minor, plagued by difficulties with the manager of his "Hollywood" sugar plantation, was obliged to retain his unsatisfactory subordinate during the year 1863 because he could not locate a replacement. In a letter to Andrew McCollam, Minor characterized overseer Ewing Chapman as "a great rascal & not to be depended on in any way," and added that if there were any chance of getting off his crop he would move his family to neighboring "Southdown" plantation, where "with the aid of my sons I may be able to do without an overSeer." [19]

It is difficult to measure the degree of patriotism which

characterized the managerial class. Some overseers enthusiastically volunteered their services to the Confederacy. To cite one example, Seneca Pace, veteran manager of Phanor Prudhomme's "Bermuda" plantation in Natchitoches Parish, Louisiana, joined a volunteer unit known as the Prudhomme Guard and, in March, 1862, departed for active military service with his company.[20] In Colleton District, South Carolina, overseer Stephen Lofton joined a volunteer company as early as January, 1861. His employer, David Gavin, after criticizing an Orangeburg planter for discharging his overseer when the latter volunteered for a similar unit, stated his position in these terms: "Mr Stephen Lofton my overseer has volunteered, and if he has to go and fight will put me to inconvenience, and perhaps loss. But I expect to feed his family just the same as if he was here attending to my business." [21] Lofton departed for army duty in the summer of 1861, and Gavin, true to his word, continued to provide for Lofton's family although he had engaged a new overseer. Another plantation superintendent who offered his services to the Confederacy at an early date was Smith Powell, overseer of John Hartwell Cocke's "Hopewell" plantation in Greene County, Alabama. Powell joined a military company shortly after the outbreak of hostilities and was called into active service during the latter part of 1861. He emerged safely from the war and returned to "Hopewell" about the middle of 1865. Powell reported to his employer that he had been "wounded twice but not to injure me in any way." [22] A somewhat less patriotic reaction was displayed by the overseer of Cocke's "Lower Bremo" plantation in Fluvanna County, Virginia, when he was declared fit for military duty in February, 1864. Albert Wood's lack of enthusiasm for army service is reflected in the following comment, contained in a letter to his employer: "Well Gen. I suppose you have heard that there is some body medling about me liveing here and doing business for you so that they are trying to put me in the army but I trust to the Almighty that they may not succeed in sending me there as they say that if you sent a requisition that it would get me of[f] S[o] that I must trust to you and the almighty to clear me." [23] Cocke did his part by requesting an exemption for Wood, but it is not clear whether "the Almighty" was able to persuade Confederate military authorities to honor the petition. Another Virginia overseer who showed little disposition to cross swords with the Yankees

was L. P. Wallace, who remarked to proprietor Samuel Mc-
Dowell Reid in February, 1862, that he would "hold to the
militia, for if they run it will be no more than will be expected
of us." ²⁴ Shortly thereafter, Wallace was called to active duty
as a militiaman.

It is impossible to state with certainty the attitude of overseers toward political affairs generally and toward the North
in particular, as the divided nation approached the tragic crisis
of April, 1861. Few members of the managerial class expressed
their views on these subjects in the correspondence which has
survived to the present time. However, judging by the position
which they occupied in the plantation system of the Old South,
it seems unlikely that many overseers viewed the North with a
sympathetic eye. William W. Smart of Rapides Parish, Louisiana, was apparently the only overseer to serve as a delegate to
a secession convention in the South. Smart, who owned property
valued at approximately $5,000, entered the Louisiana conven-
tion as a Unionist, but on the final ballot he supported seces-
sion.²⁵

One plantation superintendent who did not hesitate to record
his estimate of the northern invaders was Joseph Acquilla Randall, for many years the chief overseer of Effingham Lawrence's
"Magnolia" sugar estate in Plaquemines Parish, Louisiana. In
June, 1861, Randall offered the following prayer, which has
been described by Ulrich B. Phillips as "the most rampant fire-
eating expression" he ever encountered:

This Day is set a part By presedent Jefferson Davis for fasting &
praying owing to the Deplorable condishion ower Southern cuntray is
In   My Prayer Sincerely to God is that Every Blacke Republican in
the Hole combined whorl Either man women & chile that is opposed to
negro slavery as it exsisted in the Souther[n] confederacy Shal be trubeled
with pestilents & calamitys of all Kinds & Dragout the Balance of there
exsistance in misray & Degradation with scarsely food & rayment enughf
to keep sole & Body togeather and o God I pray the to Direct a bullet or
a bayonet to pirce The Hart of every northern Soldier that invades
southern Soile & after the Body has Renderd up its Traterish Sole gave
it a trators reword   a Birth In the Lake of fires & Brimstone   my
honest convictsion is that Every man wome[n] & chile that has gave
aide to the abolishionist are fit Subjects for Hell   I all so ask the to
aide the Sothern Confedercy in mentaining Ower rites & esstablishing the
confederate Government Beleiving in this case the prares from the wicked
will prevailith much—Amen—²⁶

The colorful Randall also had some caustic comments to make regarding the patriotism of his fellow Southerners and the conduct of military operations by Confederate leaders. The failure of the men in his parish to respond to a call for volunteers in the spring of 1862 produced the following comment from Randall: "The military of this parish Being called to Geather at point alahast under special orders of the Govner There was but a bout 200 men present when There Shold of bin 600   Col Wilkinson gave them an opertuinty to volinteer but There was but 2 come forth   Patriotism is very Low In this parish." [27] The dissemination of Randall's fiery prayer might have served to fan the flame of patriotism among his neighbors. The Louisiana manager also had harsh words for General Albert Sidney Johnston following the fall of Fort Donelson and the subsequent evacuation of Nashville by Confederate forces in February, 1862. Terming the "ware neuse . . . very unsatisfactory," the veteran overseer asserted that Johnston "ort to be Hung for not making a Stand at Nashville   he is an old ass to my opinion enney how," concluded the disgruntled Randall.[28] In like manner, Randall was sharply critical of the defense offered by the forts below New Orleans shortly before the fall of that city to Union troops. Both Randall and Lawrence were present as spectators on the night of April 23, 1862, when Admiral David G. Farragut successfully ran the forts and commenced his bombardment of the city.[29]

During the war southern authorities were obliged to requisition large numbers of Negroes from surrounding plantations to work on Confederate fortifications. These impressments frequently came at inopportune times and, as a consequence, retarded the progress of agricultural operations. Faced with a requisition for Negroes to work on the Vicksburg fortifications in the spring of 1862, Mississippi proprietor James Allen stated flatly: "declined sending any—cant walk negroes 25 miles to work 1 night & no overseer to work them when they get there." [30] The following week, a Mr. Tucker threatened to "send a posse after me & team" if Allen did not send his team and a negro to Vicksburg. "Who the devil *he* is dont know," declared the irate owner. "I have paid no attention to any of their requisitions, thinking more than half are by scoundrels to get planter's teams to haul private property." [31]

Stewards and overseers were no less vociferous than their

employers in denouncing such requisitions. Richard D. Powell, steward of John H. Cocke's Alabama holdings, complained bitterly of the action of the government in taking hands from the Cocke plantations to work on the fortifications at Mobile in December, 1863. "I wish our own Government may not ruin us, before the Yankees get a Chance at us up here," declared Powell in a letter to his employer.[32] During the winter three of the Cocke Negroes died in Mobile, and several others were sent home sick. Following the return of the remainder in April, 1864, Powell remarked: "I have got all the hands at home once more, & do hope the Gov. will do without them for the future & will give the idle soldiers employment." [33] In April, 1862, 105 hands, including 24 from "Magnolia" plantation, were requisitioned from Plaquemines Parish to bolster defenses at the forts below New Orleans.[34] Several weeks later, Joseph A. Randall noted the departure of 10 additional "Magnolia" Negroes to work on a Confederate ram, which was hurriedly being constructed in order to oppose the anticipated attack by Admiral Farragut. The latter impressment was recorded by overseer Randall in the following inimitable fashion: "The St Petony came Down colecting negros to work on The mississ[i]ppi Gun Boat or Ram   The Pople feels that the security of New Orleans res Solely a pon the completion of the Ram." [35]

In addition to military supervisors assigned by the Confederate government, slaves working on fortifications were often subjected to the supervision of overseers sent by their masters. "The laws of Alabama, Louisiana, Mississippi, and Virginia permitted any owner, or any group of owners, who sent 30 slaves to the works to send an overseer to look after them, his salary to be paid by the Confederate Government." [36] Although their own managerial responsibilities were increased during the absence of their overseers, many planters preferred to send civilian overseers with their slaves, believing that the presence of such operatives would insure better treatment for their Negroes while in government service. Frequently, the failure of Confederate military personnel to give proper attention to the welfare of laboring blacks engendered friction between these civilian overseers and the military supervisors.[37]

The advance of Union troops produced a variety of reactions among southern overseers. In October, 1862, F. D. Richardson, proprietor of "Bayside" plantation in St. Mary Parish, Louisiana, recorded the following note in his plantation journal: "Overseer left—cause fear of yankees." [38] The manager's flight was somewhat premature, since the plantation was not evacuated until the end of December. A few unscrupulous overseers took advantage of the chaotic conditions engendered by the proximity of Federal soldiers to forward their own interests at the expense of those of their employers. Louisiana planter William J. Minor wrathfully discharged overseer Ewing Chapman after a long series of transgressions capped by the latter's incessant tattling to both Federal and Confederate troops. When the Union army overran "Hollywood" plantation, the overseer pictured Minor as a strong Confederate sympathizer; but when the Confederate forces of General Richard Taylor surged into the lower Louisiana sugar parishes in the summer of 1863, Chapman characterized his employer as "a d - m yankee." After the Federals reentered Terrebonne Parish, Chapman again accused Minor of interfering with the management of the Negroes so as to discourage them from working. But, at the same time, "he told the negroes they were all free & there was no use trying to conceal it any longer." Storming that "the impudence of this man exceeds belief," the incensed proprietor finally discharged his insubordinate manager in the fall of 1863. [39] Almost a week after Chapman's dismissal, Minor reiterated his denunciation of the departed manager and his two sons in a lengthy entry in his plantation diary. Charging that "this man & his Son Charles . . . has demoralyzed my Negroes as much as that rank Abolitionist Wm. Fauss did while he was working the two places last year," the Louisianian characterized the Chapmans as "three of the most unprincipled men I ever met with." Had he not gotten rid of them, concluded Minor, "the Three would have ruined me." [40]

Similar instances of overseer misconduct occurred in the Upper South. On Charles Friend's "White Hill" plantation, located two miles east of Petersburg, Virginia, the overseer "joined in the general pillaging about him" when the approach of Federal troops forced the Friend family to flee the plantation in the summer of 1862. [41] Grief G. Mason, who for more than seventeen years had managed Peter Wilson Hairston's "Cooleemee Hill" plantation in Davie County, North Carolina, was discharged in 1861 for misbehavior which followed his employer's departure for the army. [42] Despite these unfortunate examples, most southern overseers remained faithfully at their posts and joined their employers in combating the hardships produced by the war.

As the war progressed, agricultural operations in the South were affected in a number of ways. One such effect was a greater emphasis upon the production of subsistence crops and a consequent reduction in the number of acres devoted to staple production. In January, 1864, steward Richard D. Powell advised his employer, John H. Cocke, that it would be prudent to concentrate on subsistence crops on the latter's Alabama plantations. "I intend planting more largely of the Sugar Cain," said Powell, "& think it wise, if this war continues, to make all corn we can this year, if we make no more money than to pay expenses." [43] Apparently disappointed with his corn yield during the initial year of the war, Louisiana proprietor Alexander F. Pugh declared that he would "make enough for all purposes" the following year, "if I have to plant the whole plantation in corn." [44]

Another consequence of the war was the embitterment of relations between overseers and slaves, particularly in those areas directly affected by military operations. Following a temporary reoccupation of the Lafourche district of Louisiana by Confederate forces, overseer James Walkinshaw reprimanded a Negro for permitting another slave to do twice as much plowing as he. When the Negro protested, Walkinshaw allegedly declared: "Don't contradict me. I don't allow anybody white or black to do that; if you contradict me again, I'll cut your heart out; the Yankees have spoiled you Niggers but I'll be even with you." During the course of the ensuing altercation the incensed overseer stabbed the Negro in the breast. When the Federals reestablished control over the district, Walkinshaw was arrested and sentenced to a term of six months in the parish prison. [45] Some overseers fled for fear of reprisals from the Negroes during Federal occupations. One Louisiana manager was murdered by freedmen in October, 1862, and another was attacked and severely beaten by ex-slaves the following year. [46]

In areas threatened by Union forces, plantation owners took elaborate precautions to safeguard their valuable slave property. Pierre Phanor Prudhomme, proprietor of "Bermuda" plantation in Natchitoches Parish, Louisiana, took the following action in May, 1862: "Had two Loads of planks put along Bayou Congo, to put up Shanties in Case the Yankees trouble our

Negroes—" [47] In May of the following year a double watch was instituted at night, as Federal forces approached the vicinity of "Bermuda." [48] Happily, the invading "Yankees" bypassed the plantation, and agricultural operations at "Bermuda" continued without serious interruption until the end of the war.

The disruption of farming activities by the advance of Federal forces in Virginia is clearly delineated in the plantation journal of Edmund Ruffin, Jr. Ruffin, the proprietor of "Beechwood" and "Evelynton" plantations in Prince George County, Virginia, apparently entered the Confederate Army in May, 1861. At the end of his initial year of service he declined reelection to his post as captain of cavalry and returned home to prepare for the evacuation of his farming units, then menaced by the advance of General George B. McClellan's army. [49] The first sign of restlessness among the "Beechwood" Negroes occurred on May 25, 1862, as Ruffin recounted in these words:

Strong proof of the effect of presence of the enemy this morning—Eight of my men left last night and went off to the enemy—generally young and likely—of them one was my carriage driver—one the House boy—& one a young carpenter whose apprenticeship ended last xmas & who had just returned home—With 8 others employed on the fortifications near Richmond, this leaves me a weak force to save a crop of corn already in the grass—to send off corn & c—and to save a crop of wheat—besides how few of the remainder may be left within a few days! [50]

Ruffin's fears were realized in what the master described as "another heavy stampede" on the night of June 8, bringing to twenty-five the total number of slaves who had absconded from "Beechwood" and "Evelynton" by that date. [51] As McClellan continued his advance toward Richmond, the number of defections increased rapidly until the proprietor reported on June 25:

All farming operations came to a halt on Saturday [June 21]—Wheat crop will be lost, unless my offer of one half for the other is taken by some one—Corn that has been worked looks well—but will now receive no more work—69 of the best negroes have escaped from this place and Evelynton & all from Marlbourne [Hanover County plantation of Edmund Ruffin, Sr.], of which last 2/5 were mine—

On June 23 Ruffin transported the remaining fifty-nine women and children to Petersburg, where he remained for a brief period before removing his family and slaves to "Marlbourne."

HARVESTING THE RICE

The approach of Meade in the fall of 1863 precipitated another flight, this time to "Redmoor," a poor tract of three hundred acres in Amelia County, Virginia, where Ruffin continued farming operations on a modest scale for the balance of the conflict. "Beechwood," "Evelynton," and "Marlbourne" were all virtually destroyed during the war.[52]

The Vicksburg campaign profoundly affected the agricultural routine in the river counties of Mississippi during the spring and early summer of 1863. As early as May 6, the manager of "Fonsylvania" plantation in Warren County reported apprehensively: "Exspecting the yankes enny hour." [53] The enemy, however, did not reach "Fonsylvania" for nearly three weeks. Overseer Alfred Quine, obviously a man of few words, recorded the effect of their arrival in the following entry, which must rank as something of a classic in succinctness: "All hands went to work and worked up to 12 Oclock and the yankees came and set the Negros all Free and the work all stoped." [54] Apparently, the work at "Fonsylvania" did not resume to any measurable degree after this date, for, almost two weeks later, the discouraged overseer commented: "holiday all the time now with the Negros." [55]

Conditions in the Bayou Lafourche region of neighboring Louisiana were equally distressing in the fall of 1862. Shortly after Federal troops landed at Donaldsonville, sugar planter Alexander Pugh reported "great excitement among the slaves." [56] Three days later, he recorded the following notation in his plantation diary: "Found our negroes completely demoralized, some gone and more preparing to go. I fear we shall lose them all They go off in carts—" [57] The proprietor's apprehension proved justified, for the Negroes continued to decamp on subsequent days, some leaving every night. "The Plantation will probably be completely cleaned out in a week," predicted the gloomy owner.[58] The situation became even more serious on November 5, when Pugh reported a rebellion among the Negroes on a nearby plantation. The rebellious slaves, according to Pugh, had overpowered both their overseer and master, tied them up, and carried them to the neighboring town of Thibodaux, where they were detained until Pugh secured their release. By the end of November, the Louisiana proprietor, who had been an ardent secessionist in 1861, could only observe philosophically: "Times are very gloomy, and the future promises to be worse." [59]

One of the most interesting accounts of the demoralization of agricultural operations engendered by the invasion of southern territory is contained in the plantation journals of Effingham Lawrence's "Magnolia" sugar estate. The war had little impact upon the planting routine there until the late spring of 1862, after the capture of New Orleans by Union troops. Less than a week after the fall of New Orleans, the "Magnolia" slaves began to desert in small groups. On May 14 overseer Joseph A. Randall, accompanied by two other whites, "went to Fort Jackson and Had a convesation with Col Jones In regard [to] the negros That Thay have in there possession   We learned From Him that the negros would not be Givin up Untill ordered to Do so By Washing City." [60] Defections from the "Magnolia" slave force continued to mount until the total number of absentees reached twenty-nine on May 26. However, at the end of May the Negroes began to return from the Federal camps. On May 30, 1862, Randall noted: "Ralph Moses Eldridg and Jacke Hubard Returned from the forts This morning   Say thay Have Seen the Eliphant and are Glad to get Home." By mid-June all the slaves had returned voluntarily or had been turned over to Randall by Federal authorities at Fort Jackson and Fort St. Philip.[61]

Ominous signs of insubordination began to appear among the Negroes on adjoining plantations during the late summer. On August 11 Randall recorded the following account of slave defiance on neighboring "Woodland" plantation:

The negros on woodland Plantation was rather In a state of munity [sic] this morning   Thay refused to go to work and Presented them selfs Befor the Overseer Mr T. J. Decker and sead Thay wold not worke eney moore unless they go[t] pay for there work   That there time had Expired some Time Since   after a longe Talke Mr Decker succeeded in geting them to a gree to work   there Language was we will Try it a nother week.

A similar incident occurred on another plantation in the vicinity during the same week, and Randall reported that neighboring overseers were growing apprehensive about the future conduct of the Negroes under their supervision.

White on Browns place and Mr Decker apprehend a grate deal of Trobel a mong the negros and say thay fier Inserrection Rebelion and midnight muder and say they will not Stay on there places unless there is some Decisive steps taking and Have Ritten to There agents to that Effect   I apperehend no Danger from magnolia of That Kind   we may Have a stampeed and all the negros ru[n] away But I Do not Belive that Horace Greely cold get up an Inserrection a mong the negros her   my views Differ very much from Deckers & Whits Both In the management of negros at the present time and the move the negros will make.[62]

Despite this manifestation of confidence in the peaceful intentions of the "Magnolia" labor force, signs of discontent began to appear during the latter part of August.[63] Randall retired from the active management of the plantation on September 3, 1862, and was apparently succeeded by W. C. White, who had been serving as assistant overseer since the beginning of July.

Confronted by a rising tide of insubordination among his slaves, Effingham Lawrence attempted to appease them by promising a handsome present if they would remain faithful and harvest the sugar crop. The following notation by overseer White indicates that the effect of this new pronouncement was not immediately apparent: "New arrangement with poeple on this place to day and has not had the effect to acellerate their movements but little—*very Leetle.*"[64] During September and October slave discipline on "Magnolia" deteriorated rapidly, with the Negroes working only when they chose to do so. Lawrence complained in mid-October that Federal officers were inciting Negroes in the parish to resist the authority of their overseers and masters. The demoralized state of affairs was portrayed by the proprietor in the following journal entry:

Great Demoralization and want of Discipline   impossible to do anything with slaves when every effort is made by the Federal officer Lieut Carson to Destroy the Plantation if Possible by urging the Slaves to drive their overseer and master from the Plantation for the Purpose of having General Dow or Government officers take Possession of it as is being done at McManus Dr Borlands Browns and Smiths.   everything now is as dark as Possible and we have a Terrible Prospect before us in attempting to manage the negroes.[65]

Overseer White expressed the hope that "every negro would leave the place as they will do only what pleases them. go out in morning when it suits them. come in when they please &cc."[66]

Slave insubordination in the neighborhood reached a climax on October 21, when Lawrence reported:

We have a Terrible state of affairs Here negroes Refusing to work and women all in thier [*sic*] Houses. The negroes have erected a gallows in the Quarters and give as an excuse for it that they are told by Lieut Carson they must drive their master mr Corneluis [sic] Lawrence & Mr Randall off the plantation—Hang thier master &c and that then they will be Free—no one now can tell what a Day may bring Forth—we are all in a State of Great uneasiness   McManus' negroes drove the overseer off and took Possession of the Plantation after Genl Dow made the Raid upon it and took off the Bal⁶ of the Sugar & Molasses leaving some arms in Possession of the negroes who Immediately Rose and destroyed everything they Could get Hold of   Pictures Portraits & Furniture were all Smashed up with crockery and everything in the House.

Alarmed by these ominous developments, Lawrence finally induced a Federal officer, Colonel Weed, to join him in urging the Negroes to settle down and take off the sugar crop. This appeal was miraculously successful in producing a change of heart among the Negroes, and early in December Lawrence declared that it was "most Gratifying to See the Good Conduct of the negroes—They have taken My advice, and I believe feel well Satisfied that they have done it." [67]

Except on Christmas Day, when they commenced work in the morning, "but came Home at Breakfast Saying that never having had a chance to Keep it before they would avail themselves of the privalege [sic] now they thought," [68] the "Magnolia" slaves conducted themselves in exemplary fashion for the balance of the year. Lawrence praised them for their faithful service and in January, 1863, distributed among his servants the sum of $2,500 as a reward for their good conduct. Although he still considered the Negroes his slaves and remained adamant in his refusal to pay them wages, the Louisiana proprietor recorded these lavish words of praise for his slave force:

. . . the negroes have Remained So far Faithful and obedient and are now going on with Planting a new Crop under the full Belief that Justice will be done them in Future let what will Happen as it has been done heretofore   There Conduct certainly has been [good?] when I think of the Terrible ordeal they have Passed thru and the attempts made to Demoralise and Disturb their former Relations most extraordinary—But they See now the great advantage to them of Remaining under my Protection   they are and almost I may say the only Plantation w[h]ere a vast number of the Slaves have not been Scattered and destroyed by means of Destitution and the Consequent Diseases attending the Federal Camps w[h]ere thousands were Huddled together like Hogs without the Least chance of any Protection. [69]

Unfortunately, the plantation journal ends with the above entry, and there is no clue as to whether planting operations continued on "Magnolia" throughout the remainder of the war. It is known that Lawrence leased his plantation to another planter at the end of 1862, but the effect of this transfer upon the conduct of the "Magnolia" labor force cannot be determined.[70]

Prevented by the war from marketing their cotton in Europe, many southern planters were faced with a shortage of liquid capital and, consequently, lacked the ready cash with which to pay their overseers. Thus, when settling with her manager for his services during the year 1861, a Mississippi proprietress was obliged to give him a note "payable when she *sells her cotton*." [71] This tenuous credit basis was soon obliterated when Confederate authorities ordered the burning of cotton to prevent it from falling into the hands of advancing Federals. In desperation some overseers began seizing the property of their employers as security to compel the eventual payment of their salaries. Profoundly disturbed by such activities, H. B. Shaw complained, during the winter of 1861, of the behavior of many overseers in Concordia Parish, Louisiana. "Some refuse to attend to their business, & by force hold possession of plantations, committing outrages on them," he asserted in a letter to Judge Alonzo Snyder. Observing that "unless some prompt remedy shall be provided, much evil will ensue, probably productive of violence," Shaw urged the judge to use his influence to secure the passage of a law which would protect plantation owners from such depredations. "Let the overseer have any proper process to enforce the payment of his salary," concluded Shaw, "but, at the same time, let there be some remedy for the planter to protect his property from neglect, mismanagement & abuse." [72]

Some proprietors solved the problem posed by the scarcity of ready capital by entering into profit-sharing agreements with their managerial subordinates. For example, in 1865 Alexander F. Pugh engaged an overseer to manage one of his Bayou Lafourche plantations in Louisiana for one-eighth of the profits.[73] A slightly different agreement was formulated in January, 1864, between Mrs. John Hampden Randolph and the overseers of her "Forest Home" and "Blythewood" plantations in Iberville Parish, Louisiana. Each overseer was to receive one-third of the net proceeds from the crop produced on his plantation, and each was "to furnish himself with everything the place does not afford free of charge." For their part, the overseers were "to pay one third of the expenses for the year, and one third of the taxes" on their respective crops.[74] This arrangement was almost identical to the old colonial practice of leasing developed plantations to overseers on a crop-share basis.[75]

The transition from slave to hired labor following the war produced a shift in emphasis in the employment of overseers. Tact and the threat of docking wages, in large measure, replaced the old reliance upon physical force as means of inducing Negroes to work. As a consequence, plantation owners began to seek employees who had had experience in dealing with wage laborers, or who thought they could adjust to the new system.[76]

Of course, there are numerous examples of antebellum overseers who retained their positions after the termination of hostilities. Reference already has been made to Joseph P. Kearney, who secured an exemption from military service and managed the "Petite Anse" sugar plantation of Daniel Dudley Avery throughout the period 1861–74, before retiring from the overseeing profession to undertake his own planting enterprise.[77] Another Louisiana overseer, Robert R. Peebles, managed Maunsel White's "Deer Range" plantation during the years 1858–59 and again from 1863–69. Peebles left "Deer Range" in April, 1869, after Maunsell White, Jr., refused to increase his salary from $1,650 to $2,000 per annum.[78] The most remarkable example of an overseer continuing in his occupation after the war is afforded by Johnson G. Giles, who served continuously in the employment of Peter Wilson Hairston from 1843 until 1876— an uninterrupted term of thirty-four years.

One authority has asserted that these holdovers from the antebellum plantation regime were reluctant to dispense with the lash and other instruments of physical punishment after emancipation of the Negroes.[79] Hence, he has reasoned that "the Negroes worked better under the newcomers from the North than under those who had directed them in slavery."[80] This appears to be a dubious conclusion, since the southern overseer was far better acquainted with the Negro character and knew those methods which would be most likely to spur him to a productive effort. Unfortunately, time limitations have precluded an investigation of the changes in managerial personnel and practices which accompanied the transition from slave labor to free labor in the South. It is a separate subject and merits the attention of some future scholar in the field of southern history.

7

The
Overseer Elite

THOUSANDS of overseers—good and bad, ambitious and indolent, transient and settled—were engaged in the management of southern plantations and slaves. Although the lives of many will remain forever hidden, sufficient contemporary material has survived to reveal some instances of singularly successful careers. The reader should keep in mind, however, that the men discussed in the following pages are not to be considered typical representatives of their class. But, on the other hand, their achievements are no more remarkable than those of many of their colleagues. Some of these men devoted their lives to the efficient and conscientious discharge of their responsibilities as plantation managers without acquiring the material possessions which so many persons regarded as the standard of success and respectability in their society. Others advanced to positions as stewards or independent agricultural proprietors, and a few became prosperous planters. All were worthy representatives of a group which played a vital role in the progressive development of southern agriculture during the antebellum period.

A few overseers made important contributions in the invention and development of agricultural implements during the nineteenth century. Professional overseer Joseph Delaplane invented in 1822 a "substratum" plow for use in deep plowing.[1] During the 1850's an overseer in Claiborne County, Mississippi, patented a combination turning plow and cotton scraper, which was enthusiastically acclaimed by one agriculturist as "the best cotton Plow ever invented."[2] Among those present when the inventor, George W. N. Yost, gave the first public demonstration of the implement was Colonel Thomas S. Dabney, who immediately ordered twenty-four of the plows. Lacking the capital and facilities to manufacture his device, Yost was obliged to sell his patent rights to two wealthy Mississippi planters, who contracted with a firm in Pittsburgh to manufacture the implement. Yost left Mississippi in 1856 and later entered the plow manufacturing business in the North.[3] Another plantation manager who displayed inventive genius was Georgia overseer J. Alston Reynolds. Announcing the invention of a rice planting machine in 1861, Reynolds declared in a letter to South Carolina proprietor Robert F. W. Allston that his device would "plant 14 to 16 acres per day with 5 hands attending to it."[4] Notwithstanding such examples, most members of the overseer elite achieved distinction as a result of their managerial—rather than their inventive—skill.

Reference has been made in the preceding chapter to the uncommonly long tenure enjoyed by overseer Johnson G. Giles while in the service of planter Peter Wilson Hairston.[5] Giles managed Hairston's "South Yadkin" plantation in Davidson County, North Carolina, from 1843 to 1851 at an annual salary of $200. In 1852 he was shifted to "Camp Branch" plantation in Henry County, Virginia, where he remained for fourteen years, again drawing a salary of $200 per year. Following the Civil War, Giles moved to "Leatherwood" plantation near Danville, Virginia, and apparently assumed a general stewardship over all absentee holdings of the Hairston family in Henry County. He retained this post until 1876, when he retired from the active management of the Hairston interests at the age of sixty-six. As agent for the Hairston family in Henry County, Giles received a salary of $250 until 1874 when his compensation was raised to $300 per annum.[6] The latter sum represented the highest amount ever paid to an overseer by Peter W. Hairston, a proprietor not noted for his generosity in the dispensation of wages. Giles apparently accumulated little property of his own during the thirty-four years he was associated with the Hairstons. In 1860 he owned no slaves nor real estate and listed personal assets of only $45.[7] Nevertheless, the remarkable length of his term bears eloquent testimony to the high regard in which he was held by one of the leading planting families in the Upper South.

One of the most successful farm managers in Virginia during the antebellum period was Andrew Nicol, a native of Scotland, who immigrated to America in the early 1830's. Nicol's first significant overseeing engagement in Virginia was with Edmund Ruffin, at a time when the latter was devoting the bulk of his attention to the editorship of the *Farmers' Register*. While serving as overseer of Ruffin's Coggin's Point farm (later named "Beechwood") during the period 1836–39, Nicol undoubtedly learned many beneficial farming techniques from the famous southern agricultural reformer. Characterizing his subordinate as "a man of some education, and much more subsequent reading," Ruffin praised Nicol for his "attentive intelligence, fidelity to & regard for my interests—& moreover gratitude to myself." Some years after the Scotsman had left his employment, Ruffin evaluated his former manager in these terms: "Mr. Nicol took good care of my affairs, & endeavored to carry into effect my plans as well as the means permitted. . . . But the most important value of my new overseer, & especially in my situation, was that he treated my slaves with kindness as well as justice, & they were well cared for in health & in sickness."[8]

Such inordinate praise from a man whose general dissatisfaction with the overseer class was so pronounced that he later dispensed entirely with their services was indeed remarkable. Ruffin was so delighted with Nicol that in 1851 he enclosed one of the latter's letters in his own missive to Governor James H.

Hammond of South Carolina in order to illustrate the education and intelligence of his former overseer. Hammond agreed that Nicol's letter was "certainly a very creditable one" and added that if "Mr. N. could stand the Rice Swamps he would answer admirably to manage for a nest of Rice Planters," as Jordan Myrick, a celebrated South Carolina overseer, had done.[9]

After serving four years with Ruffin, Nicol received, through his employer, a flattering proposal to undertake the stewardship of Robert B. Bolling's Sandy Point estate, described by Ruffin as "the most valuable & extensive farm in Virginia." The offer was so advantageous to his overseer that Ruffin agreed to sever their connection, and the two "parted with feelings of mutual respect & regard." [10] Sandy Point estate was located on the James River in the lower end of Charles City County, Virginia. It contained 7,000 acres, of which 2,700 were under cultivation in 1849. The total slave force on the estate numbered 180, of whom one-half were working field hands largely employed in the production of wheat and corn, the chief staples of the planting establishment.[11] The cultivated portion of the property was divided into four farming units, which, until 1840, were operated under the management of separate overseers. Because of "the expenses, inconvenience and frequent misunderstandings incident to such an arrangement," a change was instituted in 1840, whereby all units were placed directly under the management of Nicol, who was assisted by two suboverseers.[12]

In 1841 Nicol presented an account of agricultural operations on the Bolling estate in a series of four articles which appeared in the *Farmers' Register*. In the following extract from the first of these articles, Nicol indicates his awareness of the inferior status generally accorded to members of his class and proceeds to make some illuminating comments regarding his conception of the obligations of an overseer to his employer and to the agricultural community in general.

I am . . . aware that communications of this nature from a source so humble, will, with many, subject the writer to the charge of egotism. To such I have no other apology to offer than to state, that though I own neither a slave nor one foot of land, but fill the humble station of manager of a farm, I am willing to communicate my practical experience, not only with the view of benefiting others, but in the hope, that by eliciting remarks from others of more experience and sounder judgment, I may by that means be enabled to attain such additional knowledge as may not only benefit myself, but may also enable me thereby to render my services more efficient and profitable to my esteemed employer. I consider it my imperative duty that my employer shall not only reap the full benefit of whatever practical knowledge or experience I may now possess of agriculture, but that I should use every effort in my power to increase and improve such knowledge, not only for my own, but his benefit. . . . There are also some of your readers who I know not only consider the attempt of a farm manager to commit his views and practical experience to the pages of an agricultural journal as an unpardonable offence, but who also consider the reading of such periodicals as being entirely beyond his province; and who will also censure the proprietor who keeps an individual so presumptuous in his employment. To such there need no excuse or apology be offered. It cannot but be matter of regret to every liberal mind, that so many of those whose livelihood is obtained as overseers of farms, are not only incapable of committing their views to writing, but who from ignorance are incapable of reading or appreciating the important benefits which they, and, through them, their employers, might derive from the perusal of such periodicals; perhaps some will say, 'Where ignorance is bliss 'tis folly to be wise.' [13]

It must have been gratifying to Robert Bolling to be able to entrust his extensive planting interests to the management of such a capable man as Nicol. The latter retained his stewardship of the estate for more than ten years, still serving in that capacity as late as 1851. [14]

Even more spectacular than the career of Andrew Nicol was that of another Virginia overseer, Richard Sampson. The latter "began his farming at daily labor, between the plough handles, on his father's poor farm, in Goochland—and from that humble beginning," he rose to become one of the most progressive and farsighted planters in eastern Virginia "solely by his hands and head—his labors, his knowledge, and his attentive care, as a cultivator of the soil." [15] Sampson spent the first twenty years of his adult life as manager of the large James River estate of John Wickham, in which capacity he was earning an annual salary of some $1,500 by 1810. [16]

By 1816 the ambitious overseer had accumulated sufficient capital to purchase a tract of 670 acres, situated on the James River about eighteen miles above Richmond. Utilizing the knowledge gained from his many years of overseeing, he soon prospered, and by 1837 had increased the size of his farm to 1,050 acres. After experimenting for three years with tobacco, Sampson abandoned it as unprofitable and concentrated instead upon the production of wheat, corn, hay, cattle, and hogs. The regular laboring force of the farm numbered fifteen males and five females in 1837. [17] Following a visit to Sampson's Goochland County farm in that year, Edmund Ruffin reported that "the general appearance of every thing on Mr. Sampson's farm indicates a system of good order, and unremitting attention." The proprietor, added Ruffin, was "a frequent and bold experimenter" in his agricultural undertakings. [18] Sampson continued to acquire wealth and eminence with the passing years, and in 1856 the *Southern Planter* labeled him "the best farmer in Virginia." [19] Such was the stature attained by one former overseer in the Old Dominion.

The career of Thomas Ferguson affords striking evidence of the mobile character of American society in the eighteenth century. Born in 1726, the son of a Cooper River, South Carolina, ferryman, Ferguson worked initially as a sawyer with two slave helpers and then became successively a plantation overseer, steward, and rice planter. He later married the daughter of Christopher Gadsden and, by 1774, was the proprietor of nine plantations near the Ashley River. [20]

One of the most outstanding overseers in the South Carolina low country was Jesse Belflowers, who served for twenty-five years in the employment of Robert F. W. Allston, a leading Georgetown District rice planter. Belflowers managed Allston's "Chicora Wood" and adjoining plantations from 1842 until his death in 1866 at an annual salary which rose from $300 in 1842 to $1,000 after 1852. In addition, he purchased several Negroes, whose hire was bringing him an annual return of $800 by 1856. [21] In 1860 Belflowers owned property valued at $7,000, of which $1,200 was invested in real estate. [22]

In response to some critical remarks concerning Belflowers by Allston's son, Benjamin, in 1858, the elder Allston commented:

You must bear a great deal with Jesse Belflowers, he is a man of few words, of fix'd habits and those solitary. You will rarely meet with him on so large a place [as "Chicora Wood"], for he is always circulating and no one knows where to find him. The negroes dislike him mortally on this very account. . . . I have never required him to wait for me, but to attend to business as it came in his way. Having his report weekly I had no need to question him. . . . It will be an advantage for you to have the benefit of B's experience in going over the crop, but you must humor him, he is a crooked stick. [23]

Notwithstanding his eccentricities, Belflowers enjoyed the confidence and affection of the Allston family throughout his long period of service. His death in 1866 was a blow to the surviving members of the family. Commenting upon the faithful overseer's last illness, Robert Allston's widow wrote to Benjamin: "I am truly grieved at the report of Mr Belflower's illness. I scarcely hope for his recovery. He is old and his constitution much shattered and enfeebled. He is one of our *true* friends, and a link connecting us with the past. He is a great loss." [24]

William Capers was another overseer of high standing on the rice coast. Following many years of service in Georgetown District and two years as manager of Governor Aiken's estate on Jehossee Island, Capers was engaged in 1859 to undertake the management of Charles and Louis Manigault's "Gowrie-East Hermitage" unit on Argyle Island in the Savannah River. Capers, described by Louis Manigault as "a fine looking man 44 yrs. of age," was accompanied by a wife and six children when he assumed his new post on April 8, 1859. His employer noted that although Capers had "numerous enemies," he was recognized even by them "as a Competent Manager of a Rice Crop, & a Capable & intelligent man." The new overseer was engaged at the rate of $1,000 per year—"the highest Salary We have yet paid," observed Louis Manigault. [25]

As a result of inept performances by his two immediate predecessors, Capers found conditions on the plantation in a bad state when he took charge. The capable manager entered upon his duties with enthusiasm and initiative, however, and soon had affairs in good order. At the conclusion of his initial year as overseer, Louis Manigault recorded the following expression of confidence in his new superintendent:

Mr Capers has not made a large Crop but he says it was much on a/c. of the bad Condition in which he found the plantation, & I believe him, & am satisfied thus far with him, feeling that he has had no Chance. . . . During the past winter Mr Capers has done much work. He has Cut a new Canal through two Squares, on the upper portion of the plantation, which I think will be of Service. . . . I place Confidence in Mr Capers. He has had a good beginning this year, & all the Rice which is up thus far looks as well as I have ever seen Rice in this Stage looking.—[26]

Unfortunately, a tremendous storm on July 7, 1860, did great damage to the rice, and the crop of that year was again small.

Capers, nevertheless, continued to enjoy the confidence of his employers and remained as overseer of "Gowrie-East Hermitage" throughout the vicissitudes of the wartime period. Capers was especially noted for his skill in the management of slaves. Although a rigid disciplinarian, he was patient and understanding with the Negroes who adhered to plantation regulations and who performed their tasks in acceptable fashion. On the other hand, the veteran manager could be quite severe when circumstances warranted such action. Thus, stern measures were employed by Capers following a slave suicide in June, 1860. As he recounted the incident to Charles Manigault, Capers returned to his plantation after a brief absence and found all

going on quite well excepting the death of London who was drowned on Monday morning about 9 ocl. The cause of this sad calamity is this, viz., George brought London & Nat to Ralph, saying they deserved punishment, they were taken to the Barn, when Ralph went for the key to put them in George allowed London to leave him, an when spoken to by Ralph about not making an exertion to stop London his answer was he would not dust his feet to stop him. London went on to Racoon sqʳ then took the River at the mouth of the canal, in the presents of some of Mr. Barclay's negroes and Ralph who told him to return, George should not whip him until my return, his ans[wer] was he would drown himself before he would and he sank soon after, the remains of him is now quite near no 15 Trunk, Gowrie. My orders have been no one is to touch the corpse and will there remain if not taken off by the next tide, this I have done to let the negroes see when a negro takes his own life they will be treated in this manner. My advice to you about George is to ship him, he is of no use to you as a driver and is a bad negro, he would command a good price in Savannah where he can be sold in a quiet manner.[27]

George and Ralph were both broken as drivers shortly after the above incident, and in August, 1860, driver John was purchased from James R. Pringle of Charleston for the sum of $500. Capers, who had previously utilized John as a driver while overseeing for Pringle, had advised Manigault to "buy him by all means, there is but few negroes more competent than he is, and was not a drunkard when under my management, & was not ruptured." [28] The veteran overseer's confidence in John was well founded, for in October Capers reported to his employer: "I have found John as good a driver as when I left him on Santee, bad management was the cause of his being sold & am glad you have been the fortunate man to get him.[29] The rehabilitation of driver John is a conspicuous example of Capers' success in the realm of slave management. Capers died in October, 1864, much to the sorrow of Louis Manigault, who evaluated the character of his late overseer in these laudatory terms:

30th October 1864   We met with a very sad loss to the Plantation. Mr William Capers our experienced Overseer died on this day. He was a remarkable man in some respects, & Knew more of the Negro Character and how to manage a Plantation than any of our former Overseers. Mr Capers belonged to the best blood of Carolina. His G. Father and my G.G. Father (Peter Manigault) married Sisters Mary & Elizabeth Wragg, consequently he and I were 3d Cousins. He was a perfect Gentleman, and I made more of a Companion of him than merely regarding him as a Simple Overseer. He often remarked to me that His Uncle (Mr White) who first gave him instructions in managing Negroes, would frequently say that 'if a Man put his confidence in a Negro He was simply a Damned Fool,' and that he had proved that true all his life.—Mr Capers assisted me in numerous ways during our four years War, and in the midst of all our plantation troubles. He sent me regularly vegetables and other articles from the plantation to my half starved family in Augusta Ga., & he on several occasions advanced me money which I always returned. His Remains are deposited in the Church Yard, Cherokee Hill, not far (one mile) from the Camp, where he died.[30]

It is interesting to note that Capers was regarded as the best of the Manigault overseers, despite the fact that rice production on "Gowrie-East Hermitage" during his six-year term fell considerably below the crops produced on that plantation in the early 1850's.

A renowned overseer on the Georgia rice coast was Roswell King, Jr., for more than three decades the manager of the Butler estate near Darien, Georgia. The estate was founded in the 1790's by Major Pierce Butler, a native of Ireland, who came to the colonies prior to the Revolution as an officer in the British Army. Upon the death of Major Butler in 1822, his estate passed jointly to his grandsons, Pierce and John, the sons of a Philadelphia doctor. In 1834 the elder brother, Pierce Mease Butler, married the famous English actress Fanny Kemble.[31] During a brief sojourn on Butler's Island in the winter of 1838–39, the bitterly antislavery Englishwoman kept a journal of her observations of life on the estate.[32] Although this journal, as has already been pointed out, is unreliable, reflecting as it does the extreme bias of its author, it is one of the principal sources of information concerning the management of the Butler property.

King assumed the active management of the Butler holdings about 1819, succeeding his father, Roswell King, Sr., who had been in charge of the estate since 1802. For almost twenty years, the estate, which consisted of three separate plantation units and more than seven hundred slaves, was governed by the younger King with no direction or assistance from the absentee owners.[33] Although King enjoyed the complete confidence of the Butler family throughout this entire period, he was excoriated by Fanny Kemble for his alleged mistreatment of the slaves under his supervision. After conversations with Negroes on the Butler plantations and with neighboring proprietors, Miss Kemble, who arrived two months after King resigned his position as overseer, indicted the latter on the following counts: (1) a failure to correct the deplorable condition in which he found the slave hospital when he assumed his post; (2) an unrelenting opposition to religious instruction of the Negroes; (3) the fathering of a number of illegitimate slave children;[34] and (4) the abusive treatment of young slave mothers and older Negroes.[35]

With due respect for Miss Kemble, it seems probable that her evaluation of the younger King is seriously distorted. That the noted overseer was a rigid disciplinarian is not doubted, for this quality was a mark of all efficient slave managers. But other evidence indicates that King's administration was not nearly so harsh as the impressionable actress would have had her readers believe. Writing in the *Southern Agriculturist* in 1828, King proclaimed his distaste for the lash as an instrument of slave punishment. "When I pass sentence myself," said he, "various modes of punishment are adopted; the lash least of all.—Digging stumps, or clearing away trash about the settlements, in their own time; but the most severe is, confinement at home six months to twelve months, or longer." [36] King's method of discipline was apparently effective, for in ten years of management he had lost, by Negroes running away, only forty-seven man-days from a slave force which numbered nearly six hundred at that time.[37]

In a letter to his employer, written in 1827, King reported that he had "killed twenty-eight head of beef for the people's Christmas dinner" and remarked that he could "do more with

them this way than if all the hides of the cattle were made
into lashes." [38] The veteran overseer also believed in the efficacy of a system of rewards for the efficient performance of
assigned tasks. Negro drivers on the estate were accorded
special consideration. Affirming an observation by his employer, King declared in 1828: "If punishment is in one hand,
reward should be in the other. . . . We save many tons of rice
by giving one to each driver; it makes them active and watchful." [39] In the final analysis, the conclusion seems inescapable
that King was an exceptional overseer. As Fanny Kemble herself observed, before her opinion of King was altered by conversations with the Negroes: "The mere fact of his having
charge of for nineteen years, and personally governing, without any assistance whatever, seven hundred people scattered
over three large tracts of land, at a considerable distance from
each other, certainly bespeaks efficiency and energy of a very
uncommon order." [40]

Although the facts concerning King's disciplinary measures
are not clear, it is certain that his overseership was profitable
to himself as well as to his employers. He became so prosperous
that he frequently sent his wife and children, accompanied by
a Negro servant, to the North during the summer months. In
addition, he accumulated sufficient capital to acquire slaves and
to purchase two agricultural units to which he removed upon
his retirement from the active management of Butler's Island
in October, 1838. [41] On the two plantations, designated in his
journal as "South Hampton" and "Col^n Island," King experimented with an amazing variety of crops—rice, sugar, sea
island cotton, corn, and short staple cotton. Reserving "the
Island" primarily for use as a summer residence, the former
overseer established the center of his farming enterprise at
"South Hampton," located about twenty-five miles from Butler's
Island. [42]

Following the untimely death in January, 1841, of Thomas
Oden, King's successor at Butler's Island and formerly manager
of James Hamilton Couper's "Hopeton" plantation, King once
more became associated with the Butler estate. Serving in the
capacity of steward, he made periodic trips to the Butler holdings on Butler's Island and St. Simons Island, where he assumed
responsibility for the books and accounts, rode over the crop
with the two overseers, gave out Negro clothing, and reported

to Captain John Butler during the latter's infrequent visits from Charleston, South Carolina.⁴³ During one period of more than a week, King was engaged "at Butlers Island making & putting up new Brush Screen, & Middling Screw &c &c at the Steam Mill." ⁴⁴ King retained his position as general agent for the Butler interests in Georgia until at least the mid-1850's all the while operating his own planting establishments.⁴⁵ He was, without doubt, an extraordinary man.

The most celebrated overseer in the rice belt during the nineteenth century was, in all probability, Jordan Myrick. A native of Brunswick County, Virginia, Myrick moved to the South Carolina low country in 1803, at the age of seventeen, and sought employment as an overseer. His first position was as manager of the "Villa" plantation of David Deas on the eastern branch of Cooper River.

> His chief or distinguishing excellence as a planter was in the cultivation of rice—the accuracy with which he could discern, the true state of the fields, with the proper time for flowing, &c. &c.; next his judicious, kind, but firm and efficient management of the negroes under his care; and lastly his skill in constructing and repairing the banks of ricefields. His reputation for these qualifications, added to his high character for integrity and industry, soon brought his services into demand, and at one time, he had the superintendence of thirteen plantations, in the adjoining parishes of St. Thomas and St. John. These he managed successfully by having an intelligent young man, residing on each place, subject to his control.⁴⁶

By 1828 Myrick had acquired sufficient funds to launch an independent planting venture. He purchased 140 acres of rice land on the eastern branch of Cooper River and acquired a force of thirty-three Negroes to work his land. During the period from 1829 to 1833 he sent an average of 347 barrels of rice to market each year, yielding an average annual gross profit of $5,000. Myrick died in September, 1834, leaving property estimated to be worth $40,000.

The former overseer was twice awarded gold medals by the Agricultural Society of South Carolina for excellence in planting and in the management of Negroes. In response to a request from the Society, he published in 1824 a detailed account of his method of cultivating rice, and received wide acclaim from members of the planting community. James Hamilton Couper, a Georgia rice planter and scientific agriculturist of the first order, considered Myrick's report so significant that he entered it verbatim in the pages of his "Hopeton" plantation journal."' In assessing Myrick's influence upon managerial practices in the rice belt, one writer credited him with inspiring, "by his good example" and oftentimes by his instruction, "a great improvement in the morals, manners, and character of overseers in South-Carolina generally, but especially on the rice plantations. . . . Much emulation and rivalry was excited by his success . . . and the usual criterian [*sic*] of excellence in the character of an overseer was 'to raise as good crops as Myrick.' " [48]

Two of the most successful Louisiana overseers, Moore Rawls and Joseph Acquilla Randall, have been discussed so fully in preceding chapters that little remains to be added here. Rawls, a native North Carolinian, managed one of Lewis Thompson's Bertie County farms for ten years before being shifted to his employer's Rapides Parish sugar plantation in 1857. He was a man of little formal education, deeply religious, and imbued with a sincere desire to please his superior. His administration of Thompson's Louisiana estate was characterized by the exercise of common sense, initiative, and an unswerving fidelity to his employer's interests.

The letters from Rawls to Thompson throughout the former's period of service in the Lower South comprise one of the most illuminating commentaries upon the trials and tribulations of the plantation overseer which can be found anywhere. The following passage from one of these letters reveals the apprehension with which many slave managers viewed their isolated position in a sea of blacks:

Mr Thompson as I see in the yesterday parpers that the slave Isaac belonging to Mr Stafford and charge whith murder of Stephen Tier has had 2 mistrials. I can but call your attention to such *outrages* by *Slaves*

Why Sir I have said & I say now that there two grate causes of this eveil, which I think future history will develop and I hesatate not to say that Amalgamation, and forcing emigration will be the ruination of this Country.

Where is it to terminate   we hear of attempts to take the lives of white men every day. If allowd to go on further, what will be the consequnce.   who can say to the black and troubled waves, thus far shalt thou go, may it not prove a nucleus, from which will follow scens, Such as beathed in Gallic blood the Ill fated Island of St. Domingo (I hope not)

it is time that owners of slaves should open their Eyes to this matter, for their lives are no more secure than that [of] their overseer's

but there are some slave owners who think that a white man's life is worth nothing in comparison with that of a slave, because he can be easey transfered to his pocket.[49]

The fear of slave insurrection was apparently quite profound among at least some members of the overseer class.

Rawls returned to North Carolina in November, 1861, having accumulated savings of more than $4,000 during his five years of service in Louisiana.[50] Unfortunately, no information is available concerning the activities of the veteran overseer after his return to his native state.

Like Rawls, Joseph A. Randall was a simple man, deficient in formal schooling but abundantly endowed with those qualities essential to success in his occupation. Randall was accorded generous treatment by his employer, Effingham Lawrence, and following his retirement from the active management of "Magnolia" plantation in September, 1862, he gratefully accepted Lawrence's offer of a home on the estate for as long as he chose to remain.[51] Unlike many other outstanding southern overseers, Randall accumulated little property during his long managerial career and apparently had no ambition to secure an agricultural unit of his own—as late as 1860 he owned no real or personal property whatever.[52] Nevertheless, he achieved an enviable record as the overseer of one of the largest sugar plantations in the South.

An overseer who successfully made the transition from an overseeing to a planting career was Julius A. Johnson of St. Mary Parish, Louisiana. While managing the interests of sugar planter John Moore during the 1850's, Johnson was entrusted with far greater responsibilities than most members of his class were ever called upon to accept. Moore was so impressed with his overseer's managerial capabilities than in 1856 he made Johnson his partner.[53] By 1860 Johnson had amassed total property holdings in excess of $40,000, and had increased the size of his planting establishment to such an extent that he was himself obliged to employ an overseer.[54]

Another outstanding Louisiana overseer was W. W. Bateman, manager for at least a decade of Colonel J. L. Manning's extensive sugar holdings in Ascension Parish.[55] English war correspondent William H. Russell encountered Bateman during his travels through the sugar parishes in June, 1861, and described the veteran overseer as "a dour strong man, with spectacles on nose, and a quid in his cheek." Questioned by Russell about the large knife which he carried in a leather case attached to his belt, Bateman explained: "I keep this to cut my way through the cane-breaks about; they are so plaguey thick." [56] Bateman, a native of South Carolina, moved to Louisiana in the late 1840's and by 1860 had acquired twenty-five slaves and a total estate valued at more than $30,000. [57] The size of his estate provides ample evidence of his exceptional ability as a plantation overseer.

Few overseers in the cotton belt could match the record of Elisha Cain, for nearly a quarter-century the overseer of Alexander Telfair's "Retreat" plantation in Jefferson County, Georgia. Cain assumed the managerial post at "Retreat" about 1825 and retained the overseership of the plantation until 1848. His long term was by no means devoid of instances of misconduct by the slaves under his supervision. In the fall of 1829 Cain reported that a slave named John had run away "for no other cause than that he did not feel disposed to be governed by the same rules & regulations that the other negroes on the land are governed by." [58] John soon returned and displayed an apparent willingness to conform to the rules of the plantation.

In 1833 Cain encountered considerable difficulty from a female servant named Darkey. Following the application of what the overseer termed a "moderate correction," Darkey had retaliated by threatening to poison her housemates. The exasperated Cain thereupon rendered the following evaluation of the incorrigible Negro in a letter to her owner:

as I have commenced the subject I will give you a full history of my Belief of Darkey. to wit I believe her disposition as to temper is as Bad as any in the whole world. I believe she is as unfaithful as any I have Ever Been acquainted with in every respect   I believe she has Been more injury to you in the place where she is than two such negroes would sell for. I do not believe there is any negro on the place But would do Better than she has Ever done since I have been acquainted with her. I have tryed and done all I could to get on with her hopeing that she would mend. but I have Been disappointed in Every instant. I can not hope for the better any longer. [59]

Following the demise of Telfair in 1834, the plantation passed to his two daughters, who apparently became somewhat apprehensive about the treatment accorded their Negroes by the veteran overseer. Cain's promotion of a trusted slave to the rank of driver in the fall of 1840 caused several Negro men to run off, and the overseer was obliged to defend his action in a letter to Miss Mary Telfair. Denying that the driver had been appointed "to lay off tasks & use the whip" or "for the purpose of indulging myself," Cain explained that "the extension of the plantation and increase of hands has placed it beyound my power to render all the attention in *person*, that my judgement dictates absolutely necessary." The "Retreat" slave force was divided into three separate gangs, continued the manager, "and so soon as I am absent from either they are subject to quarrel & fight, or to idle time, or beat and abuse the mules, and when called to an account, each negro present when the misconduct took place, will deny all about the same." Therefore, in order to forestall such improver behavior, Cain had deemed it expedient to place in a position of authority "some faithful and trusty hand, whose duty it should be to report to me those in fault." In response to Miss Telfair's admonition that her Negroes should not be treated with severity, the overseer remarked dryly: "I have ever thought my fault on the side of lenity; If they were treated severe as many are I should not be their overseer on any consideration." ⁶⁰ It should be noted that the designation of a Negro driver was an innovation at "Retreat." Cain was apparently able to persuade his superiors of the efficacy of the new system, which the elder Telfair had never seen fit to institute.

No antebellum southern overseer had a more distinguished career than that of Garland D. Harmon. Born in Georgia in 1823, Harmon began his farming career as a petty landowner in Floyd County. In 1847 he sold the 5-acre plot on which he lived and was engaged by Judge Thomas H. Sparks to oversee the latter's large cotton plantation near Cedartown, Georgia. Displaying early an interest in agricultural reform, Harmon took an active part in the proceedings of the Floyd County Agricultural and Mechanical Association, serving with important planters of the community on its committees. His exhibit of farm tools won a prize at the Floyd County Agricultural Fair in 1852. ⁶¹ After nine years in the service of Sparks, the Georgia overseer began to move westward with the expanding frontier of cotton culture. During the years 1856–57 he managed the affairs of a planter near Utica, Mississippi, and the following year he moved to Hinds County where he directed the interests of the noted Mississippi agriculturist Martin W. Philips. Harmon, now much in demand as an overseer, moved on to Louisiana in 1859 and pursued his calling in that state until the outbreak of the Civil War.[62]

A fiery advocate of the southern cause, Harmon enlisted as a private in the 9th Louisiana Infantry on July 7, 1861. [63] He saw action at the first battle of Bull Run and served under "Stonewall" Jackson for two years before being discharged from the Army of Northern Virginia in April, 1863, "on account of 'Surgeon's certificate of disability' for the field." Unable to return home to Louisiana, Harmon traveled to his native Georgia in search of an overseeing position. "My disease is palpitation of the heart, which renders me unfit for heavy marching, but I can manage a plantation as well as ever," declared the veteran overseer.[64]

Harmon managed to secure employment as an overseer at Sand Town on the banks of the Chattahoochee River in Campbell County, but in 1864 he was forced to move again as Sherman swept through the heart of Georgia. Following the war he apparently worked for several years as a tenant farmer in Cobb County, Georgia. "He then moved to Macon County, near Montezuma, where his trail mysteriously ends in 1870." [65]

During the period from 1848 to 1864 Harmon contributed nearly one hundred articles to various agricultural periodicals in the Lower South. In the pages of the *Southern Cultivator,* the *American Cotton Planter,* and other leading cotton belt journals, he assumed the role of unofficial spokesman for the members of his class.[66] He vigorously defended his profession against unfair attacks by the proprietary group and contemptuously repudiated the charge that the overseer was primarily responsible for the ills of southern agriculture. But, at the same time, he recognized the deficiencies in the overseer system and called upon his fellow managers to broaden their outlook, acquire a wider range of knowledge, and set a high standard of conduct for the slaves under their supervision.

Harmon was a persistent and vocal advocate of southern agricultural reform during the last decade of the antebellum period. He mastered the system of horizontal plowing developed by Richard Hardwick in middle Georgia and practiced it on plantations under his management.[67] He was also a prominent advocate of hillside ditching and in 1857 contemplated entering "the business of Hill Side Ditching and Horizontalizing during the coming year." [68] For some reason, Harmon apparently did not follow through with this plan. The Georgia manager also opposed the practice, especially common in the Lower South, of working plantations until their fertility had been depleted and then moving westward to new lands. Writing in the *Southern Cultivator* in July, 1858, he delivered the following plea for soil conservation:

> Oh, let us, for goodness sake, change our system of plantation economy. Let us quit moving. Let the planters of the old cotton growing districts, as I have elsewhere remarked, feel themselves at home. Let them fill up the old gullies—improve the old red hills—prune the old orchard—improve the old homestead—enjoy the society of old friends—visit the old moss-covered church, in whose yard slumbers the remains of long departed friends. Then, and not until then, will the South begin to grow stronger and stronger, and her institutions placed upon an immoveable basis. [69]

Harmon himself carried out a wide range of experiments, recording the results in his contributions to agricultural journals. For example, during his year on Martin W. Philips' "Log Hall" plantation, the energetic overseer experimented with six acres of a new variety of corn and joined his employer in undertaking to determine the breed of hogs best suited to the South. [70] He urged all planters to devote a small portion of land to agricultural experiments each year. In 1858 he proposed that a silver pitcher valued at $100 be awarded to the man who, during the succeeding year, should "make an experiment of the greatest utility to the planting interest of the South," and that a like prize be given to "the writer of the best Essay on the Reclamation of Exhausted Land." He himself pledged $5 toward the purchase of each prize. [71]

Harmon was an exponent of diversified agriculture and economic independence for his beloved South—a position which induced him to embark upon a crusade for southern nationalism near the end of the antebellum period. Thus, in 1860 he urged southern planters to purchase agricultural implements manufactured in the South. The mechanics of the South "can, and will, in a few years, supply the planting States with all their implements of husbandry," predicted Harmon. Specifically, he advised agricultural proprietors to patronize T. C. Brinley of Louisville, Kentucky, whom he termed "the *best* plow maker in the United States of America," and to purchase Prescott's Gin-Feeders, which were manufactured in Memphis, Tennessee.[72]

Following the outbreak of war Harmon strongly denounced those cotton planters who had long contended that it was cheaper to buy meat and provisions than to raise corn and hogs on cotton land. Noting that supplies were being cut off from the South at such commercial centers as Louisville and Cincinnati, he issued the following plea for self-sacrifice and economic independence:

> The long threatened storm has come upon us at last, and the elements are in wild commotion. The thunder which has long muttered in the distance now bellows around us. The 'forests wane and the mountains nod around.' The voice of the cannon shakes the solid ground, and rivers of blood will be spilt. *Planters!* be up and doing. *Feed your people* while they fight your battles. Drop off a few Cotton bales, and raise Corn and pork. Let us strike for independence, for home, for country.[73]

Two years later when the food shortage had become critical in many parts of the South, he asserted that time had demonstrated what he and other agricultural reformers had been preaching for years—the wisdom of rendering the South economically independent of the North and Northwest. Harmon remained optimistic about the prospects for a southern victory if the problem of subsisting the Confederate army could be successfully resolved. "The Yankees are now *whipped*," he declared, "and if the result of this year's agricultural operations proves to them that they can't starve us out—that the plow is as powerful as the sword, they will *acknowledge* their defeat." [74]

Through his frequent contributions to agricultural journals in the Lower South, Harmon earned a reputation with the planting public as an authority on agricultural topics. "Judging from his contributions, I think that there are few more competent than himself to give advice on agricultural subjects," observed a Georgia planter in 1858. [75] A Richmond, Louisiana, proprietor was even more lavish in his praise of Harmon, declaring in 1860 that "Mr. Harmon is a trump not often turned up from the pack of which he is a member, and deserves from his readers some more solid emolument than the empty mede of praise that all are ready to heap upon him. Cannot the old State of Georgia send us a few more men of the same stripe to fill the places of incompetent men, who are receiving salaries of which they

are unworthy, and which would be better paid to better men?" [76]
Like most members of the profession of which he was a recognized spokesman and champion, Harmon nourished a secret dream of landownership. His yearning for such a life is revealed in the following passage, written on the eve of the Civil War:

> When I was overseeing for Judge Sparks, in Georgia, I thought that the lands in Cedar Valley and Vann's Valley, and the lands in Cass County, about Cartersville, was just as fine as I cared to have. Riding along, looking at the plantations and the lands of that country, I have thought many a time, that if I was only so fortunate as to own a place there and about 30 hands, I could make it the *model* place of the South. I have located myself upon several plantations there I could name, and then marked out the 'modus operandi' by which I would proceed to make it *the place*. I have horizontalized it, composted it, subsoiled it, laid off my grass lots and clover lots, arranged my buildings, planted an orchard, set out shade trees, employed a landscape gardener, platted off my vegetable garden, and then, when all was accomplished, entertained my friends, and oh! how near Paradise I thought I should be, if in that condition.[77]

Although he never realized this dream, Garland D. Harmon could well be proud of his outstanding achievements as plantation overseer, agricultural reformer, and southern nationalist. "However, his claim to historical recognition perhaps lies in the fact that he was a landless overseer whose life reflects the more intelligent overseer's viewpoint on the plantation regime—a point of view upon which Southern history has hitherto been all too silent." [78]

8

The Steward

OCCUPYING a position in the plantation hierarchy just above that of the overseer was the steward, a person usually charged with the general oversight of two or more plantations owned by the same planter. Stewards in the Old South may be divided into two general classifications—men who earned their livelihood by serving as agents for members of the planter community, and relatives or friends who performed a like service for absentee proprietors. The following discussion will be restricted primarily to members of the former group, as they alone can be described accurately as professional stewards.

The steward acted as the direct representative of the planter in all matters affecting the operation of the plantations under his cognizance and, if successful, was clearly a man of considerable administrative ability. It was commonly the responsibility of the steward to take orders for plantation supplies, advise his employer of necessary work to be undertaken, supervise the overseers of plantations under his direction, introduce improved methods of planting or managing, and keep the proprietor informed of the progress of plantation affairs. A few specific examples will serve to illustrate the wide range of duties which a steward might be called upon to perform.

William Rhodes, the steward of John Perkins, Jr.'s Somerset estate in northeast Louisiana, was required to administer the financial affairs of the three plantations comprising that estate. In a letter to his employer of January, 1859, Rhodes announced that he had just completed a check of Perkins' accounts with two New Orleans factorage firms and had discovered no discrepancies. He then submitted the following rope and bagging requirements for the coming year:

> We will require, of India bagging, forty four inches wide, *six yards to the bale of cotton*, for say Two Thousand Bales, 12,000 Yards. Should they continue to charge, as they have the present season, 48¢ pr. Bale for substituting rope on evry [sic] bale put up with the Iron hoops *of course* we should tie with *rope* at our *presses*. they do not need any alteration, *worth notice*, for making the change, from *hoops* to *rope*. you must calculate 7 pounds of rope to each bale, or *8 lbs pr. bale* to be sure of enough.

Rhodes, who was about to leave the plantation briefly on business, added that he would depart "so soon as I can See the Overseers, & make some necessary arrangements *with, & for them*, during my temporary absence." [1]

Mississippi steward Richard D. Powell was entrusted in 1857 with the responsibility of buying additional land for his absentee employer, Philip St. George Cocke of Virginia. Accordingly, Powell purchased a tract of two thousand acres on Silver Creek in Yazoo County, Mississippi. Although Cocke held a high opinion of his steward's managerial capability, he concluded that Powell had not proved to be conspicuously successful as a purchaser of land. Following the above purchase, the Virginia proprietor confided to his father, John Hartwell Cocke: "Our friend Powell I find will not do as a land buyer—He looses his balance amongst the land sharks. . . . So far however he has done no harm—and I have gained a measure of his capacity that will be useful to me." [3]

Another Mississippi steward made a tour of the extensive holdings of Natchez proprietor Levin Marshall in 1836 and transmitted a detailed report to his employer. During the course of his tour of inspection, the agent instituted an incentive system on Marshall's "St. Albans" plantation in order to facilitate the completion of the cotton harvest. Details of the plan are contained in the following portion of the agent's report to his superior: "In order to get more gathered if possible I have ordered them put in companies according to their speed   to the highest pickers there is promised a premium say a frock pattern to the females & a hat or roundabout etc to the men. I have had considerable practical experience of the benefits resulting from this method of getting out cotton & have uniformly beat all those who have used the whip." [3] Marshall's steward obviously had a more sagacious understanding of human nature than did many plantation managers of the period.

An important responsibility of the plantation agent was that of supervising and, occasionally, of appointing or changing subordinate functionaries on the units in his charge. Following a visit to one of the Weeks plantations in Louisiana, steward Boyd Smith reported: "I cant get your driver to take sufficient interest in your business and he seems to hang so much towards the negroes   I have punished and broke him for several acts of inexcusable carelessness." [4] William Pearce, steward of George Washington's Mount Vernon estate during the latter's second term as President of the United States, was given the responsibility of engaging new overseers. In a communication to his steward in August, 1794, Washington expressed confidence in Pearce's ability to procure suitable overseers for the farms comprising his estate. "For your own ease and satisfaction," wrote Washington, "I am persuaded you will endeavor to provide men of good character; and such as have the reputation of being industrious, sober, and knowing in the management of Negros, and other concerns of a farm." [5] Washington continued to call upon Pearce for recommendations of reputable overseers even after the latter's retirement from the stewardship of Mount Vernon in 1796. [6]

Unlike the overseer, the steward enjoyed a social position comparable to that occupied by members of the planter class.

Although he was employed upon a salaried basis, the heavy responsibilities entailed in his appointment as the manager of large agricultural interests practically guaranteed his acceptance into respectable society.[7] Usually a man of considerable education, the average steward exhibited those so-called gentlemanly qualities, in which so many overseers were strikingly deficient. Such was the appearance presented by a Mississippi steward, who was described by Olmsted as "a gentleman of good education, generous and poetic in temperament, and possessing a capacity for the enjoyment of nature and a happiness in the bucolic life, unfortunately rare with Americans. I found him a delightful companion, and I have known no man with whose natural tastes and feelings I have felt, on so short acquaintance, a more hearty sympathy."[8]

The lofty social status enjoyed by southern stewards is illustrated by the life of Richard D. Powell, who, during the course of occasional summer visits to his native Virginia, frequently spent a portion of his time at the fashionable Springs in the western part of the state.[9] When Powell's employers, John Hartwell Cocke and Philip St. George Cocke, journeyed southward to inspect their holdings in Alabama and Mississippi, the hospitable steward entertained them on his own plantation near Columbus, Mississippi.[10] On the Louisiana estate of John Perkins, Jr., steward William Rhodes apparently resided in the proprietor's plantation house.[11] Similarly, William Pearce established his residence in the mansion house at Mount Vernon following his arrival on the estate in the fall of 1793.[12] During his term of service at Mount Vernon, Pearce was frequently called upon to entertain distinguished visitors. Such examples indicate clearly that the steward occupied a social position commensurate with the vital function he performed in the plantation organization of the Old South.

The youthful sons of wealthy planters occasionally undertook the management of large estates in order to prepare themselves for later careers as agricultural proprietors. An interesting arrangement of this type was outlined in the diary of the noted Virginia aristocrat Colonel Landon Carter. On April 30, 1770, Billy Beale, "a lad of about 18," was engaged to serve Carter for three years at the rate of £10 per year "in order to be instructed in the stewardship or management of a Virginia estate." Beale's initial assignment was to visit Carter's "lower plantations, and bring me an account from under the hands of the overseers what quantity of grounds they are tending, how far they are advanced in it, what cattle they have lost and what stocks are remaining." [13] It is not clear whether or not other large Virginia proprietors made similar agreements with youthful stewards during the colonial period.

Successful overseers were sometimes rewarded for their competence and initiative by being elevated to positions as stewards. Instances of such promotions have been noted in the preceding chapter with reference to the careers of Johnson G. Giles, Andrew Nicol, Richard Sampson, Thomas Ferguson, and Jordan Myrick. Another overseer who earned an advancement to the rank of steward was Joseph B. Traylor, who managed Philip St. George Cocke's "Belmead" plantation in Powhatan County, Virginia, from 1847 to 1850. In 1851 Traylor was shifted to "Meherrin" plantation in Brunswick County, Virginia, where he was installed as the chief manager of his employer's extensive holdings in that county. [14] Similarly, James M. Stanbrough was elevated to the stewardship of Somerset estate in August, 1859, after having served for more than four years as the overseer of "Homestead" plantation, one of the units comprising the estate. [15]

As might be anticipated, the earnings of plantation agents were considerably higher than those of overseers. For example, during the 1790's overseers on Mount Vernon estate received a maximum salary of £60 per annum, while the steward of the estate was paid about £100. [16] As has been noted previously, overseer wages in Virginia during the nineteenth century rarely exceeded $400 per year. [17] In contrast to this modest figure, Richard Sampson was, by 1810, receiving an annual salary of $1,500 in compensation for his services as the steward of a large James River estate. [18] Such a lucrative stipend was probably uncommon in the Upper South, but the wage differential between steward and overseer was one of considerable magnitude in all staple regions. Records of the vast Hamilton estate, located on the Altamaha River in eastern Georgia, indicate that in 1859 overseers of individual units on the estate were being paid at the rate of $1,500, whereas the steward was drawing an annual salary of $3,500. [19] Census statistics confirm the logical conclusion that the substantial salaries earned by southern stewards enabled them to accumulate significant amounts of real and personal property. This was true even in those counties where the percentage of managerial personnel listing substantial property was especially low.

Largely as a consequence of their general excellence as a group, stewards tended to remain longer in the employment of a single planter than was commonly the case with southern overseers. Instances in which stewards retained their posts for periods of less than five years were rare. The plantation records of North Carolina proprietress Ruth S. Hairston furnish an interesting comparison of the relative length of tenure of stewards and overseers. Although the overseers of Mrs. Hairston's Stokes County plantations were noteworthy for their long terms of service, none equaled the 16-year term of steward Sterling Adams. The differentiation was even more striking on Mrs. Hairston's absentee plantations in Lowndes County, Mississippi. Although records are available only for the period 1852–56, they indicate that during that time no overseer remained more than two years on either of the two Hairston plantations in Lowndes County, whereas steward John M. Witherspoon retained his position for the entire period.[20] The average term of five known stewards of Philip St. George Cocke's extensive holdings in Virginia and Mississippi during the period 1835–65 was at least ten years. The briefest term was that of R. H. Sharp, who served as Cocke's steward in Brunswick County, Virginia, for six years. On the other hand, Richard D. Powell enjoyed a tenure of at least twenty-two years as Cocke's agent, first in Brunswick County and later in Lowndes County, Mississippi.[21]

The general directions issued by plantation owners to their stewards did not differ markedly from those drawn up for the guidance of overseers. Upon his assumption of the stewardship of several Virginia tobacco plantations in 1759, James Semple received the following instructions from his employer, Richard Corbin:

As it will be necessary to say something to you and to suggest to you my thoughts upon the business you have undertaken, I shall endeavor to be particular & circumstantial.

1st.   The care of negroes is the first thing to be recommended that you give me timely notice of their wants that they may be provided with all Necessarys: The Breeding wenches more particularly you must Instruct the Overseers to be Kind and Indulgent to, and not force them when with

Child upon any service or hardship that will be injurious to them & that they have every necessary when in that condition that is needful for them, and the children to be well looked after and to give them every Spring & Fall the Jerusalem Oak seed for a week together & that none of them suffer in time of sickness for want of proper care.

Observe a prudent and watchful conduct over the overseers that they attend their business with diligence, keep the negroes in good order, and enforce obedience by the example of their own industry, which is a more effectual method in every respect of succeeding and making good crops than Hurry & Severity; The ways of industry are constant and regular, not to be in a hurry at one time and do nothing at another, but to be always usefully and steadily employed. A man who carries on business in this manner will be prepared for every incident that happens. He will see what work may be proper at the distance of some time and be gradually & leisurely providing for it, by this foresight he will never be in confusion himself and his business instead of a labor will be a pleasure to him.

2nd.   Next to the care of negroes is the care of stock & supposing the necessary care taken, I shall only here mention the use to be made of them for the improvement of the Tobo Grounds, Let them be constantly and regularly Pend. Let the size of the Pens be 1000 Tobo Hills for 100 Cattle, and so in proportion for a Greater or less Quantity, and the Pens moved once a week. By this practise steadily pursued a convenient quantity of land may be provided at Moss's neck without clearing, and as I intend this seat of land to be a settlement for one of my sons, I would be very sparing of the woods, and that piece of woods that lies on the left hand of the Ferry Road must not be cut down on any account. A proper use of the cattle will answer every purpose of making Tobo without the disturbance too commonly made of the Timber land & as you will see this Estate once a Fortnight, you may easily discover if they have been neglectful of Pening the Cattle and moving the Cowpens.

Take an exact account of all the Negroes & Stocks at each Plantation and send to me; & Tho once a year may be sufficient to take this account yet it will be advisable to see them once a month at least; as such an inspection will fix more closely the overseers' attentions to these points. As complaints have been made by the negroes in respect to their provision of Corn, I must desire you to put that matter under such a Regulation as your own Prudence will dictate to you; The allowance to be Sure is Plentiful and they ought to have their Belly full but care must be taken with this Plenty that no waste is Committed; You must let Hampton know that the care of the Negroes' corn, sending it to mill, always to be provided with meal that every one may have enough & that regularly and at stated times, this is a duty as much incumbent upon him as any other. As the corn at Moss's neck is always ready money it will not be advisable to be at much Expense in raising Hogs: the shattered corn will probably be enough for this purpose. When I receive your Acct of the spare corn At Moss's Neck and Richland which I hope will be from King and Queen Court, I shall give orders to Col. Tucker to send for it.

Let me be acquainted with every incident that happens & Let me have timely notice of everything that is wanted, that it may be provided. To employ the Fall & Winter well is the foundation of a successful Crop in the Summer: You will therefore Animate the overseers to great diligence that their work may be in proper forwardness and not have that to do in the Spring that ought to be done in the Winter: there is Business sufficient for every Season of the year and to prevent the work of one Season from interfering with the work of Another depends upon the care of the overseer.

The time of sowing Tobo seed, the order the Plant Patch ought to be in, & the use of the Wheat Straw I have not touched upon, it being too obvious to be overlooked.

Supposing the Corn new laid & the Tobo ripe for Housing: To cut the Corn Tops and gather the blades in proper time is included under the care of Cattle, their Preservation in the Winter depending Upon Good Fodder. I shall therefore confine myself to Tobo. Tobo hhds should always be provided the 1st week in September; every morning of the month is fit for striking & strip[p]ing; every morning therefore of this month they should strike as much Tobo as they can strip whilst the Dew is upon the Ground, and what they strip in the morning must be stemd in the Evening: this method Constantly practised, the Tobacco will be all prised before Christmas, weigh well, and at least one hhd in Ten gained by finishing the Tobo thus early. You shall never want either for my advice or assistance. These Instructions will hold good for Poplar Neck & Portobacco & perhaps Spotsylvania too.[22]

Like Corbin, most proprietors endeavored to impress upon their stewards the importance of closely supervising and directing the overseers under their jurisdiction. At the outset of William Pearce's administration as steward of Mount Vernon, George Washington dispatched to Pearce a lengthy missive in which he carefully evaluated the character and ability of each overseer on the estate and advised his agent of the "necessity of keeping these Overseers strictly to their duty." Pearce was authorized to discharge, without compensation, any overseer whom he found to be "inattentive to the duties which by the articles of agreement they are bound to perform, or such others as may reasonably be enjoined." [23] "To treat them civilly is no more than what all men are entitled to," counseled Washington, "but, my advice to you is, to keep them at a proper distance; for they will grow upon familiarity, in proportion as you will sink in authority, if you do not." Finally, the proprietor advised Pearce to establish propitious rules and a regular system, which, together "with an inquisitive inspection into, and a proper arrangement of everything on your part, will, though it may give more trouble at first, save a great deal in the end." [24]

As a result of the general competence and relatively high

economic and social status of plantation stewards, their relations with members of the proprietary class were not usually characterized by the friction and animosity which frequently marred relations between overseer and planter. The steward was also accorded far greater independence of action by his employer than was normally the case with the overseer. This freedom of action, which, in many cases, was accentuated by the physical separation of planter and agent, reduced the likelihood of clashes between the two men over routine managerial decisions.

The capable and efficient manner in which William Pearce handled affairs at Mount Vernon during the period 1794–96 soon earned for him the respect and admiration of his employer, and relations between the two men remained cordial throughout Pearce's term of service. Although Washington kept a close hand in the administration of the estate by issuing weekly instructions relating to every conceivable phase of plantation business, Pearce was given a great deal of authority. For example, the latter administered the estate's accounts without any interference from the President and frequently offered suggestions relating to the conduct of agricultural operations, which were later adopted by his employer. As early as July, 1794, Washington expressed complete satisfaction with Pearce's management. "It is but justice to acknowledge to you," penned the President, "that so far as I was able, from the hurt which confined me whilst I was at Mount Vernon, to look into my business, I was well satisfied with your conduct, and I am persuaded I shall have no cause to complain of it in future. Good judgment and experimental knowledge properly exerted, never can when accompanied with integrity and zeal, go wrong.—These qualifications you have the character of possessing, and I place confidence therein." [25]

Upon being informed of Pearce's intention to retire from the management of Mount Vernon at the end of 1796, Washington urged his steward to reconsider his decision and expressed the hope that "your determination is not so fixed but it will be altered." [26] Pearce, however, persisted in his resolve, and on the occasion of his retirement the grateful Washington presented to him the following laudatory certificate:

Mr. William Pearce having Superintended the Farms, and other business appertaining to my estate of Mount Vernon, during my absence as President of the United States for the last three years (ending the 31st of the present month)—It is due to him to declare, and I certify it accordingly, that his conduct during that period has given me entire satisfaction; and that I part with him reluctantly, at his own request, on account of a Rheumatic affection which he thinks would prevent him from giving that attention to my business which from laudable motives he conceives would be necessary.

His industry and zeal to serve me, during the period above mentioned have been conspicuous on all occasions.—His knowledge in Farming, and mode of managing my business in all its relations, have been highly satisfactory to me.—and I have every reason to believe that his conduct in paying and receiving money has been strictly regular and just.—In a word, I have great confidence in his honesty, sobriety, industry and skill; and, consequently, part with him with regret.

> Given under my hand at Philadelphia this 18th day of December 1796.
> G° Washington.[27]

With such a recommendation from the President of the United States, it is unlikely that Pearce experienced any difficulty in securing a new situation.

A particularly illuminating account of relations between owner and steward is contained in the plantation journal of R. R. Barrow, wealthy Louisiana planter. On January 1, 1857, E. A. Knowlton, a native of New York, assumed the stewardship of Barrow's four Terrebonne Parish sugar plantations—"Residence," "Myrtle Grove," "Caillou Grove," and "Point Farm." Knowlton, a man of modest education and apparently a former overseer, continued in the service of his affluent employer for at least four years. Unlike many of his colleagues, Knowlton acquired little property and in 1860 listed personal assets of only $500. [28] On the other hand, his employer owned plantations in at least four parishes and was one of the leading sugar producers in the nation during the last two decades of the antebellum period.[29] After conducting an inventory of Barrow's extensive property in February, 1858, Knowlton estimated the total worth of the Louisiana proprietor at $2,150,000 and remarked dryly that "he is in very good circumstances and with economy he has enough to last him & his family for several years to come." [30]

During Knowlton's initial year of service, differences concerning various aspects of plantation management began to emerge between steward and proprietor. As the year progressed, Knowlton became increasingly concerned with the failure of his employer to proceed with dispatch in making necessary repairs to the sugar house equipment on the estate. On May 13, 1857, the steward noted: "I thought it my duty to name the importance to Mr. B about our repairs. Mr B appeared not to like it and he told me to finish the cabins now commenced and not think of any thing else." When the proprietor had still taken no steps to initiate the needed repairs by mid-July, Knowlton expressed the "fear that we will loose a large proportion of our crop by delay and not having time to do our repairs well." [31] "I cannot see why Mr Barrow delays his repairs," complained the distressed steward on July 13.

During the summer relations between Barrow and his agent were further strained by a difference of opinion concerning the merits of S. F. Graham, the overseer of "Point Farm." Knowlton had been critical of Graham from the outset of the latter's term, and in July, 1857, he declared: "Graham at Point Farm will not do to oversee   he is not enerJetic enough   he is too indulgent with the Negros   Mr B Says he does very well   I cannot See how he thinks so." [32] Finally, after a visit to "Point Farm" in November, Barrow too concluded that Graham was not equal to the responsibilities imposed by his position, and he was replaced at the end of the year. [33]

Knowlton continued, without success, during the summer and early fall to prod his employer to make the necessary repairs to the sugar machinery. On October 11 he evaluated the situation in these terms:

> We have had a very buisy day and we are making every effort to get ready to rool our crop and Should the planters know what we have to do to get ready they would say that Residence & M G crop is lost   We have got to build a Sugar house nearly compleet at Mertle Grove   the Residence Boilers is yet to set   coolers to make &c also at M Grove— and if we do get ready it will astonish me much   that is if we save the two crops—Point Farm is nearly as far behind   At M G would is yet to cut and haul   Mr B says that we must get ready and save our crop at that—if we save our crop I will acknowledge he can do more in less time than any other planter of my knowledge   I think Mr B will loose by delay fully $20,000—

Two days later, the frustrated steward emphasized his displeasure with the delaying tactics of his employer by entering the following comment in the plantation journal:

WE TALK STRONG ABOUT REBUILDING MERTLE GROVE SUGAR HOUSE   I

FEAR MUCH THAT WE SHALL LOOSE MUCH OF OUR CROP BY VERY DEFECTIVE
MACHINERY PARTICULARLY AT MERTLE GROVE & POINT FARM   AT MERTLE
GROVE I FEAR THE BOILERS ARE NOT STRONG ENOUGH AND AT POINT FARM I
FEAR THE STRENGTH OF BOILERS & ALSO THE MILL BUT I HOPE FOR THE
BEST   I WOULD BE MUCH PLEASED IF WE COULD SAVE OUR CROP WITHOUT
ACCIDENT OF IMPORTANCE—I THINK MR B HAS STRONG HOPES TO SAVE HIS
INTIRE CROP, OLD SHELL IS AT POINT FARM REPAIRING THE MILL & ENGINE
AND THE WAY HE IS DOING THE WORK I FEAR THE RESULT.[34]

Barrow finally gave the order to commence work on the "Myrtle
Grove" sugar house on October 17, as Knowlton grumbled that
"Mr B had some design in the delay of repairs of M G sugar
house."

Fearing a killing frost, Knowlton, during the second week of
November, began to urge Barrow to windrow his cane.[35] The
harassed subordinate, at first, was reluctant to approach his
employer on the subject for fear that he would "ridicule the
Idea—as he does most every thing I suggest of late." [36] Knowlton's fears proved well-founded, for, when he finally summoned
the courage to suggest that Barrow windrow the crop, the latter
replied that "I wished to ruin his crop—he said their was no
sense in windrowing cane this warm wether." [37] The experienced steward's judgment was vindicated when all the cane froze
on the morning of November 20.

As the grinding season progressed, Knowlton became more
convinced than ever of the deleterious effect produced by his
employer's delay in processing the crop. Shortly before Christmas he remarked: "Every days grinding convinces me more
that we have managed badly this year in delaying so long   we
should have commenced grinding on the 10th or 15th of October
and then we should have winrowed our cane, Say to commence
on the 10th of November or 15th at latest." Mismanagement
of the crop, concluded Knowlton, had cost the owner "many
thousand dollars . . . this year." [38] Notwithstanding the persistent
efforts of his steward to accelerate preparations for the sugar
harvest, Barrow did not hesitate to reprimand the former when
the grinding season extended through Christmas and into the
new year. Early in January, 1858, the headstrong proprietor
directed Knowlton "to write [in the plantation journal] and say
that any man who was grinding & Rooling at this time a year
he considered that such a man is no manager and has no buisness
with a Sugar Plantation and he considered such a man nothing
more than a DAM Jack ass." [39]

Knowlton had the last word concerning the tempestuous year, when, upon the completion of grinding at "Residence" plantation on January 11, 1858, he commented: "There is something wrong in the management of this plantation   we are working 75 hands and onely [sic] made 175 Hogsheads of Sugar   now the question is what is wrong   I answer that we have not more than half cultivated our crop." It would seem from the above account that Knowlton's perception of planting procedures was superior to that of his obstinate employer. Apparently Barrow and his disgruntled steward were able to resolve their differences, for Knowlton retained his post through at least 1860. [40]

Although relative harmony usually prevailed between proprietor and steward, the relations between steward and overseer were considerably less placid. The steward did not ordinarily hold the overseer class in any higher regard than did members of the planter community. This is scarcely surprising, since, in his capacity as the direct representative of the planter, the agent occupied the same position relative to the overseer as did the proprietor. As a consequence, friction developed between steward and overseer for substantially the same reasons that it arose between planter and overseer. In a conversation with one visitor, the manager of a large absentee cotton estate in the Lower South described "the great majority" of overseers as "passionate, careless, inefficient men, generally intemperate, and totally unfitted for the duties of the position." [41] This view was doubtless shared by a great many plantation agents.

Discord between steward and overseer frequently resulted in the dismissal of the latter. The inability of overseer N. B. Holland to get along harmoniously with E. A. Knowlton precipitated the overseer's departure from R. R. Barrow's "Residence" plantation just two weeks after his arrival. The circumstances of Holland's exodus from the plantation are revealed in the following entry in Barrow's plantation journal: "Mr N.B. Holland declines overseeing Residence any longer and took his departure for Donaldson   he leaves because he does not like Mr Knowlton. Mr. K thinks the loss of his services will not be seriously felt by the Plant[ation]." [42]

In like manner, friction between steward Richard D. Powell and L. L. Singleton, overseer of John Hartwell Cocke's "Hopewell" plantation in Greene County, Alabama, resulted in Singleton's removal from the plantation at the end of 1855. The nature of the disagreement between Powell and Singleton is not revealed in the records, but a hint of trouble is reflected in the latter's remark to Cocke in July, 1855, that he was sorry that Powell "could not make it convenient" to stop at "Hopewell" on his annual trip northward to Virginia.⁴² While the steward was in Virginia, he communicated to Cocke his desire to remove Singleton from the overseership at the end of the year. Powell, however, did not want the responsibility of informing the unfortunate overseer of his impending discharge and, therefore, advised his employer to "write to Singleton the last of Sept. that you requested me last winter to employ another man for the next year. . . . I think it best for him to learn this from you & let me see him after he Knows it." ⁴³ The proprietor acceded to his agent's request, and Singleton departed at the end of the year. Happily, Powell was highly pleased with Singleton's successor, J. Walter Carter, who remained at "Hopewell" for a term of three years.

Powell, who served for more than thirty years as manager of the Cocke family interests in Virginia and later in the Lower South, was one of the most distinguished plantation agents in the Old South.⁴⁴ Born about 1800 in Brunswick County, Virginia, Powell commenced his career as a steward while still in his twenties. In 1828 he was serving as agent for the Brunswick County estate of John T. Bowdoin. From at least 1835 until 1844 Powell managed the Brunswick estate of Philip St. George Cocke. Shortly thereafter he moved to Mississippi, where, during the period from at least 1855 to 1866, he exercised an agency over the Mississippi plantations of Philip St. George Cocke and the Alabama holdings of the latter's father, John Hartwell Cocke.

Upon his removal to Mississippi, Powell purchased a tract of land in Lowndes County, situated six miles from Columbus and only five miles from the plantations of the younger Cocke. The ambitious steward acquired a number of slaves in addition to his tract of land and soon became comfortably fixed. By 1860 he owned twenty-one slaves, and his total estate was valued at $42,000. ⁴⁵ Well-educated, intelligent, and deeply religious, Powell moved easily in the circles of polite society. As has been noted previously, he made occasional trips to Virginia, where he visited friends and relatives in Brunswick County and frequented the

fashionable resort communities in the western part of the state."
The agent's son, Richard D. Powell, Jr., studied medicine and
in 1856 established a practice in his native Brunswick County.
John H. Cocke served as his benefactor, paying his expenses at
medical school and setting him up as a practicing physician.
The following letter from the younger Powell to Cocke defines
the relationship between the two men shortly after the former
had entered upon his chosen profession. Powell had requested
that Cocke provide him with a sulky in order to make his
country practice more comfortable. This request provoked the
wrath of his benefactor, who criticized him sharply for seeking
such an extravagant conveyance. Powell responded with the
following:

Brunswick co. Va august 8th/56

Genl Cocke
    Dear Sir   The medicines have been received and the selection entirely
satisfactory, and for which as heretofore for favors, I feel extremely
thankful.
    You were mistaken in supposing I wished a costly outfit. all I desired
was a respectable conveyance   I am however willing to do the best I
can. If you prefer my being a pedestrian practitioner of medicine I will do
it for your gratification   I have no right to be displeased at any thing
you may suggest, but on the other hand have every reason to be thankful.
You saw ambition struggling against poverty, and in accordance with the
generous impulses of a noble soul, came to its rescue. Your heart melted
in compassion at the sight of youthful aspiration struggling against destitution and kneeling on the armor of christian benevolence you gallantly
proffered assistance, and I consider it my duty to repay your kindness by
a willing submission to your decrees. I feel sad when I think of my
situation, but am determined to do the best I can. I hope you are well
and will be pleased to hear from you when convenient.

Your Young Friend
R.D. POWELL[48]

The elder Powell's nephew, Smith Powell, served as overseer of
Cocke's Alabama plantations from the beginning of 1860 until
his departure for military service shortly after the outbreak of
the Civil War. He returned to "Hopewell" after the war and
resumed his duties as overseer.

    Richard Powell largely shared the religious and moral views
of his employer, John H. Cocke.[49] IIis letters to the latter frequently contained such pious pronouncements as the following:
"I feel thankful to learn you have a good hope, that the Col.

[Philip St. G. Cocke?] is looking to his soul's interest, more earnestly. May God's Grace be sufficient for him to triumph over temptations & possess victory over Sin. & may we all meet at last in Heaven is my poor prayer for Christ's Sake." [50]

Since Powell resided at some distance from the Cocke plantations in Greene County, Alabama, he necessarily exercised only a general oversight over those holdings. He made periodic trips to the plantations, at intervals of one to two months, and dispatched detailed reports to his employer, outlining the progress of agricultural operations on the absentee units. Shortly after J. Walter Carter became the overseer of "Hopewell," Powell visited that plantation and, prior to his departure, wrote John H. Cocke clarifying his own managerial role as follows:

. . . I leave here Monday morning 21st inst. with the perfect understanding that Mr Carter is to write to me if any thing turns up with the servants, & I will Come down immediately, & Settle up Matters in full with them. Mr Carter speaks kindly & acts kindly toward them & I see they begin to feel it, but *it is important* for them *to Know I am ready* to *see them if necessary*. . . . It is very important that these servants have some one to respect, & fear besides Mr Carter, to get on at all, & particularly in your absence, after a life of freedom for 10 or 15 years, when you were absent." [51]

The wily steward later saved overseer Carter from an embarrassing attempt by the "Hopewell" slaves to discredit him in the eyes of his superiors.[52]

Powell continued to conduct his stewardship of the Cocke interests in the Lower South with unexceptionable ability and faithfulness until after the Civil War. Following the death of Philip Cocke in 1861, the latter's Mississippi estate was left entirely in the capable hands of the veteran steward. At the conclusion of hostilities, Powell expressed the desire to terminate his agency of the Mississippi property. He offered to join the sons of the deceased owner in managing the estate, with all proceeds to be divided as follows: one-half to the executors of the estate and the other half to the managing farmers. In the event that no member of the Cocke family elected to move to Mississippi, Powell announced his readiness to assume the entire management of the estate in return for one-half of the net profits.[53] Finally, in January, 1866, Philip St. George Cocke, Jr., set out for Columbus, Mississippi, to "become associated with

Mr Powell in the management of the places" in Lowndes County." Thus, Richard D. Powell, one of the truly outstanding plantation agents in the Old South, viewed the dawn of a New South from his familiar position as the manager of a large agricultural establishment.

9

Conclusion

ALTHOUGH his cardinal position in the plantation regime of the Old South has been acknowledged by most observers, the overseer has heretofore been subjected to rather harsh treatment by many authorities in the field of southern history. He has usually been portrayed as an uncouth, uneducated, dissolute slave driver, whose twin delights consisted of abusing the Negroes in his charge and sabotaging the progressive goals of his employer. The myth of the general ineptness of the overseer class was created by members of the planter community and has been perpetuated unwittingly by writers whose chief insight into the character of the overseer has been gained through the eyes of his employer. Most of the available information which bears upon the management of southern plantations is contained in diaries and journals authored by members of the proprietary group and in the accounts of travelers whose principal contacts were with persons of the same group. Moreover, many researchers have erred in their evaluation of the data included in contemporary plantation records. It does not require a spectacular imagination to discern that instances of mismanagement were more likely to be recorded by disenchanted proprietors than were examples of good management. As one writer has sagely remarked: "It is in the nature of man to remember and record the extreme in human conduct rather than the mean."[1]

One important factor which contributed to the unsavory reputation of southern overseers was the existence in the Lower South of a large floating population of amateur overseers, whose general lack of competence provoked a storm of abuse from cotton belt planters. The members of this group moved from one plantation to another, offering their services at lower rates than those demanded by more experienced managers. Articulate representatives of the better class of overseers recognized the pernicious effect which the activities of such incompetents had upon the managerial profession as a whole, and they sought in vain to dissuade proprietors from engaging such ill-qualified men to manage their agricultural enterprises. Primary responsibility for the perpetuation of this inept group must therefore be assigned to those planters who continued to employ such operatives simply because they could be engaged for a few dollars less than could more experienced and better qualified members of the overseeing profession. Unfortunately, many secondary writers have equated the entire class of southern overseers with this group of ill-paid, inexperienced, unqualified wanderers, thereby producing a stereotyped image of the southern overseer which does not accord with the facts.

Although the common image of the plantation overseer has been considerably distorted, it is true that a number of factors militated against the establishment and perpetuation of a more satisfactory class of overseers. In the first place, the task of directing slave labor was distasteful to many and was held in social disrepute by a large segment of the general public. As a result, the overseer was relegated to a status in southern society far beneath that of the planter and even below that of the small independent farmer. With few exceptions, members of the proprietary class failed to accord their overseers the respect to which their responsible position entitled them and did little to encourage them to take pride in their profession. Moreover, many planters imposed demands upon their subordinates which few men could reasonably be expected to meet. Few plantation owners really appreciated the difficulties faced by those who directed their agricultural enterprises. Another factor which lessened the attractiveness of the occupation was the social isolation which overseers were obliged to endure. Shunned by his employer, forbidden to fraternize with the slaves, discouraged from entertaining company, and obliged by the nature of his arduous duties to remain constantly at his post, the overseer lived in a virtual social vacuum. His situation might almost be likened to that of a prisoner in solitary confinement.

Inadequate pay, coupled with brevity and uncertainty of tenure, were other disadvantages which tended to discourage ambitious young Southerners from entering the overseeing profession. Although overseers received more substantial incomes than did most other white operatives on southern plantations, their compensation was not commensurate with the broad responsibilities which they were called upon to shoulder. There is little doubt that the more attractive economic opportunities afforded by other occupations seduced many competent young agriculturists away from the overseeing profession. Similarly, the disposition of many proprietors to change overseers frequently, no matter what degree of ability the latter had displayed, and the inclination to hire a less capable overseer if he would agree to work for lower wages than the incumbent, were other practices which retarded the development of a more distinguished group of managers.

The lack of opportunity for advancement within the overseeing profession induced many of the best-qualified managerial functionaries to seek employment in other occupations. Although an overseer might graduate from the management of a small plantation to the overseership of a larger estate, his pay was not usually increased sufficiently to compensate him for the added duties and responsibilities of his new post. A few overseers were elevated to positions as stewards, but the opportunities for such a promotion were extremely limited. The only real chance for advancement lay *outside* the overseeing profession.

Thus, the most ambitious managers aspired to positions as independent farmers and small slaveholders, thereby impeding the formation of a corps of topflight, professional overseers. Such a conclusion is confirmed by statistics derived from the state census returns, which reveal that about four-fifths of those engaged in the business of overseeing in 1860 were below the age of forty.

Finally, the propensity of plantation owners to bombard their overseers with a constant stream of complaints and criticism engendered an atmosphere of discouragement and low morale among those who followed the overseer calling. The average planter was not noted for his penetrating discernment of the difficulties faced by the man who directed the labor of his slaves and supervised the cultivation of his land. No matter how zealously an overseer endeavored to fulfill the wishes of his employer, the latter usually found some point upon which to criticize him. In the light of such circumstances, it is little wonder that an air of frustration and discouragement pervaded the overseer group.

Those within the overseeing profession were confronted by additional difficulties which proceeded from the very nature of their position in the plantation establishment. The overseer was pulled in two incompatible directions by the concurrent planter emphases upon production of a large staple crop, on the one hand, and upon the care of Negroes, livestock, and farm implements and buildings on the other. His plight was rendered even more difficult by the failure of the planter class to reach a general unanimity of opinion on this subject. An overseer might manage the interests of a proprietor who regarded the size of the crop as paramount and then find himself, in the following year, with an owner who placed primary emphasis upon long-range agricultural considerations. The fact that few overseers remained in one situation long enough to decipher the personality of their employer added to the magnitude of their predicament.

Another problem engendered by the nature of the overseer system concerned the division of managerial responsibility between planter and overseer and the consequent degree to which the activities of the latter should be subjected to supervision by the owner. Understandably, few proprietors displayed much willingness to entrust to hired subordinates complete authority over agricultural enterprises which frequently represented investments amounting to many thousands of dollars. On the other hand, the overseer argued with considerable logic that he should be given control of routine matters associated with the operation of the plantation if he were to be held accountable for the results. It is difficult to discern how this fundamental conflict between planter and overseer could have been resolved with mutual satisfaction to both principals.

In assessing the personal character and managerial acumen of southern overseers, three important factors must be considered: (1) the size of the plantation; (2) the place of residence of the owner (whether an absentee or resident proprietor); and (3) the geographical area in which the plantation was situated. There is little doubt that the best overseers tended to secure employment with the largest and most affluent proprietors. The management of a large agricultural establishment with its concomitant slave force clearly necessitated the employment of an experienced and capable man. Moreover, upper-class planters were able to pay salaries which were sufficiently high to attract the most talented managers. In like manner, the added responsibilities and higher pay associated with the management of absentee properties usually resulted in the procurement of able overseers for those units. In addition, the greater freedom of action accorded to overseers of absentee plantations appealed to ambitious and self-reliant managers and rendered such a post more desirable than a situation on a resident plantation of comparable size.

One of the most important facts revealed by this study is the significant differentiation in overseer characteristics among the various staple regions. As a group, overseers in the rice and sugar districts were superior to those in any other staple area. It required men of considerable ability, experience, and judgment to manage the intricate and complicated operations associated with the production of rice and sugar and to control the large slave gangs which predominated in those regions. In addition, the higher salaries offered by affluent rice and sugar planters attracted more competent managerial personnel. The demand for overseers of superior ability was probably greatest on the South Carolina-Georgia rice coast, where unhealthy climatic conditions induced many proprietors to leave the direction of their agricultural affairs in the hands of hired subordinates during the crucial planting and harvesting period from mid-May until mid-November. Consequently, the overseer became the most important single element in the managerial hierarchy of the rice belt.

The more settled nature of society along the Atlantic seaboard had the effect of producing a more stable and permanent group of overseers than that which developed in the newer slave states of the Southwest. Overseers in the tobacco and rice areas tended to be slightly older than their counterparts in the Lower South, and a substantially greater percentage were married and owned some property. Another important consequence of the social stability which prevailed in the older slave states was the tendency for overseers in those regions to continue in the service of a single employer for longer periods than was generally the case with those who directed planting enterprises in the Southwest.

Overseers in the Lower South were frequently subjected to greater pressures by their employers, and this too tended to promote a rapid turnover of slave managers in that region. Plantation owners in the seaboard slave states were, in general, well-established and financially secure. In many instances they had inherited their land and slaves and, as a result, were not oppressed by financial worries. Moreover, opportunities for the expansion of planting operations were not present in the same degree as they were in the Gulf states. On the other hand, many of the enterprising men who had acquired plantations in the fertile cotton and sugar states of the Southwest had not yet made their fortunes. Consequently, intense pressure was brought to bear upon overseers in those areas to produce large staple crops. The overseer of a cotton plantation in the Lower South was given one year—if he were lucky—in order to prove his ability. If he did not harvest a bountiful crop during his initial year of service, he was likely to find himself looking for a new position the following year.

Happily, the lot of the steward was considerably more agreeable than that of the average overseer. Usually a man of conspicuous administrative ability, substantial education, and acceptable background, the steward enjoyed a social position comparable to that occupied by members of the planter class. The latter accorded him the respect to which his responsible role in the plantation hierarchy entitled him, and they usually compensated him adequately for his important services. Largely as a result of their general excellence as a group, southern stewards retained their positions for longer periods than was usually the case with their managerial subordinates. Most stewards remained in the employment of a single proprietor for at least five to ten years. As the direct representative of the planter, the steward more frequently came into conflict with the, overseers under his jurisdiction than with his employer. Indeed, his relations with the overseer group were strikingly similar to those which characterized the association between planter and overseer. On the whole, southern plantation agents performed their duties in a competent and efficient manner and, as a consequence, escaped the deluge of criticism which was showered upon the heads of plantation overseers.

Ironically, it was the planter class—the group most disposed to crucify the overseer—which was primarily responsible for many of the flaws which did exist in the managerial system. It was the planter who refused to pay just and adequate wages, who failed to accord his overseer the respect to which his responsible position entitled him, who constantly and capriciously changed managers, who persisted in the practice of hiring ill-qualified operatives merely because they could be secured for lower rates, and who contributed to the low morale of the overseer group by his irresponsible criticism.

Despite his deficiencies, the overseer remained a key figure in the plantation-slavery establishment until the end of the antebellum period. He was, in fact, an indispensable agent in the commercial agricultural system which flourished in the Old South. The over-all success of the overseer system is conclusively demonstrated by the following developments: (1) the consolidation and expansion of the plantation-slavery organization during the decades immediately preceding the Civil War; (2) the retention, despite frequent complaints, of the overseer system by the overwhelming majority of those proprietors whose agricultural units were sufficiently large to justify the employment of such an agent; and (3) the storm of planter protests which greeted the efforts of Confederate authorities to draft overseers into military service during the Civil War.

In the final analysis, the conclusion seems warranted that, within the limitations imposed by their background and by the vast responsibilities with which they were burdened, the majority of southern overseers performed their duties with commendable energy, efficiency, and competence.

Notes

Introduction

1 John Spencer Bassett, *The Southern Plantation Overseer as Revealed in His Letters* (Northampton, Mass.: Southworth Press, 1925), 1; hereinafter cited as Bassett, *Plantation Overseer.*

2 James Benson Sellers, *Slavery in Alabama* (University, Ala.: University of Alabama Press, 1950), 44.

3 Kenneth Milton Stampp, *The Peculiar Institution: Slavery in the Ante-Bellum South* (New York: Alfred A. Knopf, 1956), 40.

4 Basil Hall, *Travels in North America, in the Years 1827 and 1828* (3rd. ed.; Edinburgh: Printed for Robert Cadell, 1830), III, 192.

5 Martin W. Philips, *American Cotton Planter,* V (November, 1857), 349.

6 Carl Bridenbaugh, *Myths and Realities: Societies of the Colonial South* (Baton Rouge: Louisiana State University Press, 1952), 63.

7   George Dangerfield, *The Era of Good Feelings* (New York: Harcourt, Brace, 1952), 214.

8   Lewis Cecil Gray, *History of Agriculture in the Southern United States to 1860* (Washington: Carnegie Institution of Washington, 1933), I, 557.

9   *Ibid.*, I, 502.

10   Ralph Betts Flanders, *Plantation Slavery in Georgia* (Chapel Hill: University of North Carolina Press, 1933), 115, 141.

11   Ulrich Bonnell Phillips, *Life and Labor in the Old South* (Boston: Little, Brown, 1929), 310.

12   Frank Lawrence Owsley, *Plain Folk of the Old South* (Baton Rouge: Louisiana State University Press, 1949), 153.

Chapter 1

1   Gray, *History of Agriculture*, I, 501.

2   Heloise H. Cruzat (trans.), "Agreement Between Louis Cezard (Cesaire) Le Breton, and Jean Baptiste Goudeau as Overseer on His Plantation, 1744," *Louisiana Historical Quarterly*, IX (October, 1926), 590–92.

3   Thomas Jefferson Wertenbaker, *Patrician and Plebeian in Virginia* (Charlottesville: The Michie Company, 1910), 134.

4   Gray, *History of Agriculture*, I, 407–408.

5   *Ibid.*, II, 647.

6   Weymouth T. Jordan, *Hugh Davis and His Alabama Plantation* (University, Ala.: University of Alabama Press, 1948), 71–72.

7   James Calvin Bonner, "The Plantation Overseer and Southern Nationalism as Revealed in the Career of Garland D. Harmon," *Agricultural History*, XIX (January, 1945), 1; Ulrich Bonnell Phillips, *American Negro Slavery* (New York: D. Appleton and Company, 1918), 282–83; John Hebron Moore, *Agriculture in Ante-Bellum Mississippi* (New York: Bookman Associates, 1958), 164.

8   Bonner, "The Plantation Overseer and Southern Nationalism," 1; Sellers, *Slavery in Alabama*, 44.

9   Fortescue Cuming, *Sketches of a Tour to the Western Country, 1807–1809* (Cleveland: The Arthur H. Clark Company, 1904), 328. Vol. IV of Reuben Gold Thwaites (ed.), *Early Western Travels, 1748–1846.*

10   Frederick Law Olmsted, *A Journey in the Seaboard Slave States* (New York: G.P. Putnam's Sons, 1904), II, 121.

11   Hall, *Travels in North America*, III, 193.

12   A. De Puy Van Buren, *Jottings of a Year's Sojourn in the South* (Battle Creek, Mich.: Review and Herald Print, 1859), 151.

13   *Ibid.*

14   Frederick Law Olmsted, *A Journey in the Back Country* (New York: Mason Brothers, 1860), 176.

15   Joseph Holt Ingraham, *The Southwest* (New York: Harper and Brothers, 1835), I, 237.

16   William Howard Russell, *My Diary North and South* (Boston: T. O. H. P. Burnham, 1863), 262.

17   *Ibid.*, 277.

18   This figure is cited by the following authorities: Stampp, *The Peculiar Institution*, 38; Charles Sackett Sydnor, *Slavery in Mississippi* (New York: D. Appleton-Century, 1933), 67; Thomas Battle Carroll, *Historical Sketches of Oktibbeha County, Mississippi* (Gulfport, Miss.: The Dixie

Press, 1931), 86; James Glen, "A Description of South Carolina Containing Many Curious and Interesting Particulars Relating to the Civil, Natural and Commercial History of that Colony," in B. R. Carroll (ed.), *Historical Collections of South Carolina* (New York: Harper and Brothers, 1836), II, 202.

19 James H. Hammond to Edmund Ruffin, September 26, 1847, in Edmund Ruffin Papers and Books, Southern Historical Collection, University of North Carolina, Chapel Hill.

20 Sydnor, *Slavery in Mississippi*, 68; Olmsted, *Back Country*, 81.

21 Olmsted, *Back Country*, 72–73, 80.

22 Theodora Britton Marshall and Gladys Crail Evans (eds.), "Plantation Report from the Papers of Levin R. Marshall, of 'Richmond,' Natchez, Mississippi," *Journal of Mississippi History*, III (January, 1941), 46–47.

23 Ruthven Farm Journal (MS in Edmund Ruffin Papers and Books), 1843–47.

24 United States Census Office, *Seventh Census of the United States: 1850* (Washington: Robert Armstrong, 1853), lxxiv–lxxv; United States Census Office, *Eighth Census of the United States: 1860. Population* (Washington: The Government Printing Office, 1864), 670–71.

25 Gray, *History of Agriculture*, I, 529.

26 *Ibid.*, I, 498–99.

27 United States Census Office, *Eighth Census of the United States: 1860. Agriculture* (Washington: The Government Printing Office, 1864), 248; hereinafter cited as *Eighth Census, Agriculture*.

28 *Ibid.*, 247.

29 *Median* slaveholdings are to be distinguished from *average* slaveholdings. The median figure indicates that approximately one-half of the slaves in a given geographical area were in units larger than that number.

30 Gray, *History of Agriculture*, I, 531–32, 534. See also Paul S. Taylor, "Plantation Laborer Before the Civil War," *Agricultural History*, XXVIII (January, 1954), 3.

31 John Berkley Grimball Diary (MS in Southern Historical Collection, University of North Carolina, Chapel Hill), January 1, February 20, 1856. Ham was managing plantations for Doctor George Morris, Mrs. Wayne, Mr. Brisbane, Heyward Manigault, and Grimball.

32 James Harold Easterby (ed.), *The South Carolina Rice Plantation as Revealed in the Papers of Robert F. W. Allston* (Chicago: University of Chicago Press, 1945), 25, 27.

33 Agreement between Richard J. Arnold and A. M. Sanford, December 30, 1827, in Arnold-Screven Papers, Southern Historical Collection, University of North Carolina, Chapel Hill.

34 Phillips, *American Negro Slavery*, 229.

35 Dorothy Seay Magoffin, "A Georgia Planter and His Plantations, 1837–1861," *North Carolina Historical Review*, XV (October, 1938), 362, 365, 369.

36 Magnolia Plantation Journals (MSS in Henry Clay Warmoth Papers and Books, Southern Historical Collection, University of North Carolina, Chapel Hill), 1856–62.

37 Maunsel White to William H. Haynes, September 6, 1847, Maunsel White Lettercopy Book, in Maunsel White Papers and Books, Southern Historical Collection, University of North Carolina, Chapel Hill.

38 Manigault Plantation Records (MSS in Southern Historical Collection, University of North Carolina, Chapel Hill), III.

39 Ulrich Bonnell Phillips (ed.), *Plantation and Frontier, 1649-1863* (Cleveland: The Arthur H. Clark Company, 1909), I, 336-37.

40 Hammond to Ruffin, September 26, 1847, Edmund Ruffin Papers and Books.

41 R. R. Barrow Residence Journal (MS in Southern Historical Collection, University of North Carolina, Chapel Hill), May 19, 1858.

42 V. Alton Moody, "Slavery on Louisiana Sugar Plantations," *Louisiana Historical Quarterly*, VII (April, 1924), 209; Joe Gray Taylor, *Negro Slavery in Louisiana* (Baton Rouge: Louisiana Historical Association, 1963), 214.

43 Olmsted, *Seaboard Slave States*, II, 67.

44 Ellis Merton Coulter, *Thomas Spalding of Sapelo* (Baton Rouge: Louisiana State University Press, 1940), 85-86.

45 Olmsted, *Seaboard Slave States*, I, 49.

46 William Proctor Gould Diaries (Typescript in Alabama Department of Archives and History, Montgomery), December 31, 1854; January 2, 5, 1855.

47 Edwin Adams Davis, *Plantation Life in the Florida Parishes of Louisiana, 1836-1846, as Reflected in the Diary of Bennet H. Barrow* (New York: Columbia University Press, 1943), 89-90, 99-100.

48 Hammond to Ruffin, August 7, 1845; March 26, 1847, Edmund Ruffin Papers and Books.

49 Alexander James Lawton Diary (MS in Southern Historical Collection, University of North Carolina, Chapel Hill).

50 Wendell Holmes Stephenson, "A Quarter-Century of a Mississippi Plantation: Eli J. Capell of 'Pleasant Hill,'" *Mississippi Valley Historical Review*, XXIII (December, 1936), 357, 362, 369, 374.

51 Rachel O'Connor to Mrs. Mary C. Weeks, September 4, 1840, in Weeks Hall Memorial Collection, Louisiana State University Department of Archives, Baton Rouge.

52 J. H. Bernard, "The Importance of Grass Crops—Unsuccessful Experiments," *Farmers' Register*, V (July, 1837), 172-73.

53 *Ibid.*, 173.

54 Edmund Ruffin, "Incidents of My Life" (MS in Edmund Ruffin Papers and Books), II, 227-28.

55 Dennis Murphree, "Hurricane and Brierfield, the Davis Plantations," *Journal of Mississippi History*, IX (April, 1947), 102; Lane Carter Kendall, "John McDonogh—Slave-Owner," *Louisiana Historical Quarterly*, XVI (January, 1933), 131.

56 Edwin A. Davis, *Plantation Life in Louisiana*, 156.

57 James C. Darby, "On Planting and Managing a Rice Crop," *Southern Agriculturist*, II (June, 1829), 249.

58 Mount Airy Plantation Books (Microfilm copy in Southern Historical Collection, University of North Carolina, Chapel Hill), III.

59 Bennett Harrison Wall, "Ebenezer Pettigrew, An Economic Study of an Ante-Bellum Planter" (Ph.D. dissertation, University of North Carolina, 1946), 202.

60 Phillips, *American Negro Slavery*, 438.

61 Annie Lee West Stahl, "The Free Negro in Ante-Bellum Louisiana," *Louisiana Historical Quarterly*, XXV (April, 1942), 391.

Chapter 2

1 Phillips, *Life and Labor in the Old South*, 307.

2 Edmund W. Hubard, "On the Manner and Time of Employing Overseers," *Farmers' Register*, III (April, 1836), 715.

3 R. H. Carnal to Lewis Thompson, September 23, 1857, in Lewis Thompson Papers, Southern Historical Collection, University of North Carolina, Chapel Hill.

4 Francis Terry Leak Diary (MS in Southern Historical Collection, University of North Carolina, Chapel Hill), October 17, 1854.

5 Easterby (ed.), *The South Carolina Rice Plantation*, 262.

6 John Mitchell to Lewis Thompson, July 9, 1860, Lewis Thompson Papers.

7 Albert L. Boyett to Lewis Thompson, October 12, 1858, Lewis Thompson Papers.

8 Phillips, *American Negro Slavery*, 229, quoting the Virginia *Gazette*, October 22, 1767.

9 Peter Wilson Hairston Papers (MSS in Southern Historical Collection, University of North Carolina, Chapel Hill), XIX.

10 George Washington to William Pearce, December 18, 1793, in Moncure Daniel Conway (ed.), *George Washington and Mount Vernon* ("Long Island Historical Society Memoirs," IV [Brooklyn: Long Island Historical Society, 1889]), 14.

11 Agreement between John Ewing Colhoun and Thomas Gravestock, February 28, 1793, in John Ewing Colhoun Papers, Southern Historical Collection, University of North Carolina, Chapel Hill.

12 Agreement between Nathaniel Friend and John Berry, n.d., in White Hill Plantation Books, III, Southern Historical Collection, University of North Carolina, Chapel Hill.

13 R. R. Barrow Residence Journal (Southern Historical Collection), November 2, 1857.

14 Deer Range Plantation Journal (MS in Maunsel White Papers and Books), January 19, 1861.

15 E. E. McCollam Diary and Plantation Record (MS in Andrew McCollam Papers, Southern Historical Collection, University of North Carolina, Chapel Hill), December 16, 1846; January 11, 1847.

16 Leak Diary (Southern Historical Collection), January 13, 1857.

17 Phillips (ed.), *Plantation and Frontier*, I, 124–26.

18 Hairston Papers (Southern Historical Collection).

19 Agreement between Robert Hairston and Creed T. Rowland, November 2, 1836, in Hairston Papers, XIX.

20 Leak Diary (Southern Historical Collection), November 15, 1845, and *passim*.

21 Joseph Carlyle Sitterson, "Hired Labor on Sugar Plantations of the Ante-Bellum South," *Journal of Southern History*, XIV (May, 1948), 198.

22 Hopeton Plantation Account Book, 1826–1852; Hopeton Plantation Journal, 1839–1854 (MSS in James Hamilton Couper Plantation Records, Southern Historical Collection, University of North Carolina, Chapel Hill).

23 Evan Hall Plantation Account Books (Microfilm copy in Southern Historical Collection, University of North Carolina, Chapel Hill).

24 Hairston Papers (Southern Historical Collection).

25 Pierre Phanor Prudhomme Records and Papers (MSS in Southern Historical Collection, University of North Carolina, Chapel Hill).

26 William C. Thompson to Lewis Thompson, January 18, 1858, Lewis Thompson Papers.

27 Computed from data contained in letter from William C. Thompson to Lewis Thompson, January 26, 1862, Lewis Thompson Papers.

28   Bremo Recess and Bremo Journal (Microfilm copy in Cocke Papers, Southern Historical Collection, University of North Carolina, Chapel Hill), 1827–43.

29   John Hebron Moore (ed.), "Two Documents Relating to Plantation Overseers of the Vicksburg Region, 1831–1832," *Journal of Mississippi History*, XVI (January, 1954), 32.

30   Sitterson, "Hired Labor on Sugar Plantations of the Ante-Bellum South," 198.

31   Walter Wade Plantation Diaries (Typescript in Mississippi Department of Archives and History, Jackson), II.

32   Leak Diary (Southern Historical Collection), November 15, 1845; November 1, 1854; December 14, 1858; November 12, 1861.

33   *Ibid.*, September 5, 1860.

34   Grimball Diary (Southern Historical Collection), December 12, 1853; January 7, 1856; January 1, 1861.

35   *Ibid.*, March 1, 1841.

36   Hairston Papers (Southern Historical Collection), XIV.

37   Phillips, *Life and Labor in the Old South*, 226.

38   Computed from Bremo Recess and Bremo Journal (Cocke Papers), 1827–43.

39   John Ewing Colhoun Papers (MSS in Southern Historical Collection), June 20, 1794.

40   Agreement between Robert Hairston and William Wilson, November 28, 1833, in Hairston Papers.

41   Phillips, *American Negro Slavery*, 281.

42   Bremo Recess and Bremo Journal (Cocke Papers), 1827–43. Mention is made of an Alabama overseer receiving payment by crop shares in the 1850's in Sellers, *Slavery in Alabama*, 53.

43   Grimball Diary (Southern Historical Collection), November 21, 1834.

44   Mount Airy Plantation Books (Southern Historical Collection), III.

45   John Taylor of Caroline, *Arator* (3rd ed.; Baltimore: J. Robinson, 1817), 49.

46   Olmsted, *Back Country*, 60.

47   C. T. Botts, *Southern Planter*, III (October, 1843), 234.

48   Randolph Harrison, "On the Importance of Farmers Giving Personal Attention and Labor to Their Farms," *Farmers' Register*, IV (May, 1836), 1–2.

49   *Southern Planter*, III (October, 1843), 234.

50   Colhoun Papers (Southern Historical Collection), January 16, 1798.

51   Computed from Killona Plantation Journals (MSS in Mississippi Department of Archives and History, Jackson), I.

52   Orville Walters Taylor, *Negro Slavery in Arkansas* (Durham: Duke University Press, 1958), 88. Taylor lists the average hiring prices for men, women, and youths in each slave state in 1860. For the average rates in Georgia during the period 1800–60, see Flanders, *Plantation Slavery in Georgia*, 195.

53   Account Book of John L. Wilkins (MS in Wilkins Papers, Southern Historical Collection, University of North Carolina, Chapel Hill), 1790–1849.

54   Bremo Recess and Bremo Journal (Cocke Papers), January 1, 1827; Hairston Papers (Southern Historical Collection), XIX, January 5, 1839.

55   Wall, "Ebenezer Pettigrew," 204, 206.

56   Maunsel White to John Denson, July 20, 1845, Maunsel White Letter-copy Book, in Maunsel White Papers and Books.

57   Jordan, *Hugh Davis and His Alabama Plantation*, 79.
58   Phillips, *Life and Labor in the Old South*, 277.
59   Sitterson, "Hired Labor on Sugar Plantations of the Ante-Bellum South," 200.
60   Velasco Plantation Journal (MS in Maunsel White Papers and Books), May 17, 1859.
61   Joseph Carlyle Sitterson, "Magnolia Plantation, 1852–1862: A Decade of a Louisiana Sugar Estate," *Mississippi Valley Historical Review*, XXV (September, 1938), 201–202.
62   Velasco Plantation Journal (Maunsel White Papers and Books), April 13, 1859; Bayside Plantation Records (MSS in Southern Historical Collection, University of North Carolina, Chapel Hill), I, May 10, 1852.
63   Frances Anne Kemble, *Journal of a Residence on a Georgian Plantation in 1838–1839* (London: Longman, Green, Longman, Roberts, and Green, 1863), 26.
64   John Carmichael Jenkins Plantation Diary (Typescript in John C. Jenkins and Family Papers, Louisiana State University Department of Archives, Baton Rouge), December 8, 11, 26–27, 1848.
65   Captain John Nevitt Journal (MS in Southern Historical Collection, University of North Carolina, Chapel Hill), 1826–32.
66   Jordan, *Hugh Davis and His Alabama Plantation*, 59–73, 152, 159–60.
67   See pages 125–26 of this book.
68   Stampp, *The Peculiar Institution*, 39.
69   Sitterson, "Hired Labor on Sugar Plantations of the Ante-Bellum South," 196.
70   Mount Airy Plantation Books (Southern Historical Collection), III.
71   Computed from Hairston Papers (Southern Historical Collection), XIX.
72   Gray, *History of Agriculture*, I, 486.
73   Orville W. Taylor, *Negro Slavery in Arkansas*, 106.
74   Gray, *History of Agriculture*, I, 501–502.
75   David Doar, "Rice and Rice Planting in the South Carolina Low Country," in E. Milby Burton (ed.), *Contributions from the Charleston Museum* (Charleston: Charleston Museum, 1910–55), VIII, 37.
76   Easterby (ed.), *The South Carolina Rice Plantation*, 27.
77   Deer Range Plantation Journal (Maunsel White Papers and Books), January 20, March 19, 26, 1861.
78   Martin W. Philips, *American Cotton Planter*, II (July, 1854), 208.
79   Albert Virgil House (ed.), *Planter Management and Capitalism in Ante-Bellum Georgia: The Journal of Hugh Fraser Grant, Ricegrower* (New York: Columbia University Press, 1954), 107; hereinafter cited as House (ed.), *Planter Management in Georgia*.
80   Felix Flugel (ed.), "Pages from a Journal of a Voyage Down the Mississippi to New Orleans in 1817," *Louisiana Historical Quarterly*, VII (July, 1924), 440.
81   Thomas W. Thompson to Lewis Thompson, April 8, 1856, Lewis Thompson Papers.
82   William H. Hollwell to Lewis Thompson, August 20, 1860, Lewis Thompson Papers.
83   Wall, "Ebenezer Pettigrew," 198.
84   Walter Wade Plantation Diaries (Mississippi Department of Archives), February 19–20, March 6, July 1, 1846.
85   See page 5 of this book.
86   Wall, "Ebenezer Pettigrew," 217.

87   Holden Garthur Evans Diary (Typescript in Mississippi Department of Archives and History, Jackson), June 11, 1858; January 27, 1859.
88   *Carolina Planter*, I (1844-45), 25–30, quoted in Gray, *History of Agriculture*, I, 503.
89   *Southern Agriculturist*, II (November, 1829), 521.
90   Lewis Thompson to Thomas W. Thompson, December 31, 1858, Lewis Thompson Papers.
91   Jordan, *Hugh Davis and His Alabama Plantation*, 50.
92   Francis Taylor Diary (Typescript in Southern Historical Collection, University of North Carolina, Chapel Hill), July 6, 1787, and *passim.*
93   David Gavin Diary (MS in Southern Historical Collection, University of North Carolina, Chapel Hill), May 7, 1856; December 8, 1858.
94   Jenkins Plantation Diary (John C. Jenkins and Family Papers), May 1, 3, 1847.
95   Eliza L. Magruder Diary (MS in Louisiana State University Department of Archives, Baton Rouge).
96   Reeve Lewis to Alonzo Snyder, December 2, 1861, in Alonzo Snyder Papers, Louisiana State University Department of Archives, Baton Rouge.
97   Bassett, *Plantation Overseer*, 169; Roger Wallace Shugg, *Origins of Class Struggle in Louisiana: A Social History of White Farmers and Laborers During Slavery and After, 1840-1875* (Baton Rouge: Louisiana State University Press, 1939), 28.
98   Francis Garvin Davenport (ed.), "Judge Sharkey Papers," *Mississippi Valley Historical Review*, XX (June, 1933), 76.
99   Rules and Regulations for the Government of Waterloo, Southdown, and Hollywood Plantations, in William J. Minor Plantation Diaries (MSS in William J. Minor and Family Papers, Louisiana State University Department of Archives, Baton Rouge), XXXIII (1861-65), XXXIV (1861-68). Also quoted in Joseph Carlyle Sitterson, *Sugar Country: The Cane Sugar Industry in the South, 1753-1950* (Lexington: University of Kentucky Press, 1953), 57-60.
100   Moore Rawls to Lewis Thompson, May 9, 1858, Lewis Thompson Papers.
101   Doro Plantation Account Book (MS in Charles Clark and Family Papers, Mississippi Department of Archives and History, Jackson), XI, April 14, 1861.
102   Owsley, *Plain Folk of the Old South*, 134.
103   Olmsted, *Back Country*, 161.
104   Prior to 1850, census returns did not give the occupations of those listed.
105   This account is based upon data in the John G. Traylor Diary (Typescript in Alabama Department of Archives and History, Montgomery), 1834–47.
106   White Hill Plantation Books (Microfilm copy in Southern Historical Collection), VI, December 13, 1858.
107   *Ibid.*, V, December 31, 1848, and *passim.*
108   MS census returns, 1860 (National Archives, Washington, D.C.), Prince George County, Virginia.
109   Avery Family Papers (MSS in Southern Historical Collection, University of North Carolina, Chapel Hill), III.
110   Sellers, *Slavery in Alabama*, 50, quoting James Asbury Tait, "Memoranda and Observations," 1855 (MS in private possession), 91–92.
111   Moore, *Agriculture in Ante-Bellum Mississippi*, 67, 102.
112   Flanders, *Plantation Slavery in Georgia*, 140.

113   Grimball Diary (Southern Historical Collection), April 20, 1853.
114   Gavin Diary (Southern Historical Collection), January 18, 1858.
115   House (ed.), *Planter Management in Georgia*, 214, 307.
116   MS census returns, 1860 (National Archives, Washington, D.C.), Glynn County, Georgia.
117   Sellers, *Slavery in Alabama*, 48, quoting Preston Brown to S. D. Cabaniss, April 15, 1859, in Cabaniss Papers, University of Alabama Library, Tuscaloosa.
118   John Henninger Reagan, *Memoirs, with Special Reference to Secession and the Civil War*, ed. Walter Flavius McCaleb (New York: The Neale Publishing Company, 1906), 24–26.
119   *Ibid.*, 26.
120   "John Henninger Reagan," in Allen Johnson and Dumas Malone (eds.), *Dictionary of American Biography* (New York: Charles Scribner's Sons, 1928–37), XV, 432–34.

   Chapter 3
1   Tabulated from *Eighth Census, Agriculture*, 23 and *passim*.
2   Computed from MS census returns, 1860 (National Archives, Washington, D.C.), Prince George County, Virginia, Schedule 1 (Vol. XXII), Schedule 2 (Vol. VI); Richmond County, Virginia, Schedule 1 (Vol. XXIII), Schedule 2 (Vol. VI); Northampton County, North Carolina, Schedule 1 (Vol. XII), Schedule 2 (Vol. III); Stokes County, North Carolina, Schedule 1 (Vol. XV), Schedule 2 (Vol. IV).
3   Computed by averaging the results for each county. The final result differs slightly from that which would be obtained by taking the average of all overseers listed, without regard to county boundaries. This disparity is explained by the variation in number of overseers listed in different counties.
4   Computed from MS census returns, 1860 (National Archives, Washington, D.C.), Beaufort District, South Carolina, Schedule 1 (Vol. II), Schedule 2 (Vol. II); Charleston District, South Carolina, Schedule 1 (Vol. II), Schedule 2 (Vol. II); Colleton District, South Carolina, Schedule 1 (Vol. III), Schedule 2 (Vol. III); Georgetown District, South Carolina, Schedule 1 (Vol. IV), Schedule 2 (Vol. IV).
5   Computed from MS census returns, 1860 (National Archives, Washington, D.C.), Ascension Parish, Louisiana, Schedule 1 (Vol. I), Schedule 2 (Vol. I); Plaquemines Parish, Louisiana, Schedule 1 (Vol. IV), Schedule 2 (Vol. III); St. Mary Parish, Louisiana, Schedule 1 (Vol. X), Schedule 2 (Vol. IV); Terrebonne Parish, Louisiana, Schedule 1 (Vol. X), Schedule 2 (Vol. IV).
6   Computed from MS census returns, 1860 (National Archives, Washington, D.C.), Hinds County, Mississippi, Schedule 1 (Vol. III), Schedule 2 (Vol. II); Lowndes County, Mississippi, Schedule 1 (Vol. V), Schedule 2 (Vol. III); Yazoo County, Mississippi, Schedule 1 (Vol. IX), Schedule 2 (Vol. V); Natchitoches Parish, Louisiana, Schedule 1 (Vol. IV), Schedule 2 (Vol. III).
7   *American Cotton Planter*, XII (June, 1858), 197.
8   Owsley, *Plain Folk of the Old South*, 146.
9   See page 22 of this book.
10   Gray, *History of Agriculture*, I, 480.

Chapter 4
1 Moody, "Slavery on Louisiana Sugar Plantations," 209.
2 Andrew Flynn Plantation Book (Microfilm copy in Southern Historical Collection, University of North Carolina, Chapel Hill), 1840.
3 Other outstanding, detailed sets of instructions include the following:
(1) "Rules for Overseers," *Farmers' Register*, VIII (April, 1840), 230–31;
(2) Rules and Directions for Alexander Telfair's "Thorn Island" Plantation, in Phillips (ed.), *Plantation and Frontier*, I, 126–29; (3) Rules on
the Rice Estate of P. C. Weston, in Phillips (ed.), *Plantation and Frontier*,
I, 116–22; also printed in *De Bow's Review*, XXII (January, 1857), 38–44;
(4) Rules and Regulations for the Government of the William J. Minor
Plantations, in Minor Plantation Diaries (William J. Minor and Family
Papers), XXXIII (1861–65), XXXIV (1861–68); and (5) John Hartwell
Cocke, "Standing Rules for the Government of Slaves on a Virginia
Plantation," in Cocke Papers (Southern Historical Collection).
4 Thomas Affleck, "The Duties of an Overseer," in *Cotton Plantation
Record and Account Book* (7th ed.; New Orleans: B. M. Norman, 1857);
also printed in *De Bow's Review*, XVIII (March, 1855), 345.
5 See pages 121–23 of this book.
6 Phillips (ed.), *Plantation and Frontier*, I, 116.
7 Maunsel White to James N. Bracewell, May 17, 1848, Maunsel White
Lettercopy Book, in Maunsel White Papers and Books; italics by author.
8 *De Bow's Review*, X (June, 1851), 626.
9 Rules and Regulations for the Government of the William J. Minor
Plantations, in Minor Plantation Diaries (William J. Minor and Family
Papers), XXXIII (1861–65), XXXIV (1861–68).
10 Thomas Affleck, in *Southern Cultivator*, XIII (March, 1855), 75–76.
11 Phillips, *American Negro Slavery*, 280.
12 Cornelius Oliver Cathey, *Agricultural Developments in North Carolina, 1783–1860* (Chapel Hill: University of North Carolina Press, 1956),
59.
13 *Plantation and Farm Instruction, Regulation, Record, Inventory and
Account Book* (Richmond: J. W. Randolph, 1852), 4. Also printed in *De
Bow's Review*, XVIII (March, 1855), 339–40.
14 Phillips (ed.), *Plantation and Frontier*, I, 128.
15 John Hartwell Cocke, "Standing Rules for the Government of Slaves
on a Virginia Plantation," in Cocke Papers (Southern Historical Collection).
16 Phillips (ed.), *Plantation and Frontier*, I, 122.
17 Moore (ed.), "Two Documents Relating to Plantation Overseers of
the Vicksburg Region," 35, quoting Joseph Johnson to George Comer, December 23, 1831, in Benjamin L. C. Wailes Collection, Mississippi Department of Archives and History, Jackson.
18 Phillips, *Life and Labor in the Old South*, 325.
19 *De Bow's Review*, XXI (September, 1856), 278.
20 Hill Carter, "On the Management of Negroes; Addressed to the
Farmers and Overseers of Virginia," *Farmers' Register*, I (February,
1834), 565.
21 Kemble, *Journal of a Residence on a Georgian Plantation*, 253. For
a critical appraisal of Miss Kemble's narrative, see Margaret Davis Cate,
"Mistakes in Fanny Kemble's Georgia Journal," *Georgia Historical Quarterly*, XLIV (March, 1960).
22 Russell, *My Diary North and South*, 274.

23   Rachel O'Connor to Mrs. Mary C. Weeks, June 4, 1832; O'Connor to David Weeks, July 8, 1832, Weeks Hall Collection.
24   O'Connor to David Weeks, November 6, 1832, Weeks Hall Collection.
25   *Ibid.,* October 23, 1833.
26   *Ibid.,* November 20, 1833.
27   O'Connor to A. T. Conrad, April 12, 1835, Weeks Hall Collection.
28   Phillips, *Life and Labor in the Old South,* 282.
29   Phillips, *American Negro Slavery,* 273-74.
30   John A. Calhoun, "Management of Slaves," *De Bow's Review,* XVIII (June, 1855), 715. Also printed in *Southern Cultivator,* IV (August, 1846), 113.
31   Bassett, *Plantation Overseer,* 274.
32   Stampp, *The Peculiar Institution,* 183.
33   Olmsted, *Back Country,* 82.
34   *Ibid.,* 87.
35   H. M. Seale Diary (MS in Louisiana State University Department of Archives, Baton Rouge), August 8, 1853.
36   Russell, *My Diary North and South,* 275.
37   Flanders, *Plantation Slavery in Georgia,* 266.
38   Moody, "Slavery on Louisiana Sugar Plantations," 210.
39   Wall, "Ebenezer Pettigrew," 184.
40   Chase C. Mooney, *Slavery in Tennessee* (Bloomington: University of Indiana Press, 1957), 161, quoting Lucius Polk to William Polk, May 8, 1827, in Polk-Brown-Ewell Collection, University of North Carolina, Chapel Hill.
41   Richard D. Powell to John Hartwell Cocke, August 14, 1857, Cocke Papers.
42   Bayside Plantation Records (Southern Historical Collection), II, April 3, 1862.
43   William Butler's Observations on Rice Culture (Microfilm copy in Southern Historical Collection, University of North Carolina, Chapel Hill), 1786.
44   Phillips, *American Negro Slavery,* 259.
45   *Ibid.,* 247.
46   Olmsted, *Seaboard Slave States,* II, 64, 112.
47   Easterby (ed.), *The South Carolina Rice Plantation,* 346.
48   Phillips (ed.), *Plantation and Frontier,* I, 117.
49   *Ibid.,* I, 126.
50   Easterby (ed.), *The South Carolina Rice Plantation,* 346.
51   John Hartwell Cocke, "Standing Rules for the Government of Slaves on a Virginia Plantation," in Cocke Papers (Southern Historical Collection).
52   Phillips (ed.), *Plantation and Frontier,* I, 129.
53   *Farmers' Register,* IV (June, 1836), 115.
54   *Ibid.*
55   R. R. Barrow Residence Journal (Southern Historical Collection), April 21, 1858.
56   *Farmers' Register,* VIII (April, 1840), 231.
57   Wall, "Ebenezer Pettigrew," 116-18, 208-209.
58   Olmsted, *Seaboard Slave States,* II, 45-46.
59   *Ibid.*
60   John and Keating S. Ball Books (MSS in Southern Historical Collection, University of North Carolina, Chapel Hill), II.
61   Slave Lists for Rotterdam, Copenhagen, and Hamburg Plantations,

in Heyward-Ferguson Papers and Books (Microfilm copy in Southern Historical Collection, University of North Carolina, Chapel Hill), 1850–61.

62 Slave Lists for Gowrie Plantation, in Manigault Plantation Records (Southern Historical Collection), 1833–61.

63 R. R. Barrow Residence Journal (Southern Historical Collection), July 10, 1857; February 28, 1858; March 12, 1858.

64 Alice Pemble White, "The Plantation Experience of Joseph and Lavinia Erwin, 1807–1836," *Louisiana Historical Quarterly*, XXVII (April, 1944), 393.

65 Valcour Aime, *Plantation Diary* (New Orleans: Clark and Hofeline, 1878), 170.

66 Magnolia Plantation Journals (Henry Clay Warmoth Papers and Books), October 4, 1860.

67 Washington to Pearce, March 22, 1795, in Conway (ed.), *George Washington and Mount Vernon*, 175–76.

68 James R. Sparkman, "Description of Life Among the Slaves, 1858," in Easterby (ed.), *The South Carolina Rice Plantation*, 349.

69 *Plantation and Farm Instruction, Regulation, Record, Inventory and Account Book*, 11.

70 Rawls to Lewis Thompson, October 10, 1857, Lewis Thompson Papers.

71 Rawls to Lewis Thompson, October 28, 1860, Lewis Thompson Papers.

72 Jesse L. Ward to Jacob Bieller, August 23, 1835, Alonzo Snyder Papers.

73 William Dosite Postell, *The Health of Slaves on Southern Plantations* (Baton Rouge: Louisiana State University Press, 1951), 105.

74 *Ibid.*, quoting D. Warren Brickell, "Epidemic Typhoid Pneumonia Amongst Negroes," *New Orleans Medical News and Hospital Gazette*, II (1856), 546.

75 William D. Postell, *Health of Slaves*, 164.

76 Jonas Smith to John B. Lamar, August 25, 1852, in Phillips (ed.), *Plantation and Frontier*, I, 310.

77 Smith to Lamar, October 5, 1852, in Phillips (ed.), *Plantation and Frontier*, I, 311.

78 Washington to Pearce, March 22, 1795, in Conway (ed.), *George Washington and Mount Vernon*, 175. See also Phillips, *American Negro Slavery*, 285.

79 Olmsted, *Back Country*, 79.

80 Rawls to Lewis Thompson, July 27, 1857, Lewis Thompson Papers.

81 Wall, "Ebenezer Pettigrew," 116, quoting Doctrine W. Davenport to Ebenezer Pettigrew, June 12, 1836.

82 Deer Range Plantation Journal (Maunsel White Papers and Books), August 16, 1860.

83 Doro Plantation Account Book (Charles Clark and Family Papers), VIII, September 30, 1853.

84 Seale Diary (Louisiana State University Department of Archives), May 30, 1853.

85 Josiah Smith, Jr., to George Austin, January 31, 1774, in Josiah Smith, Jr., Lettercopy Book, Southern Historical Collection, University of North Carolina, Chapel Hill.

86 George Marsh to John Craig Marsh, August 25, 1845, Avery Family Papers.

87 Phillips, *Life and Labor in the Old South*, 208.

88 Phillips, *American Negro Slavery*, 303, quoting I. E. H. Harvey to H. C. Flournoy, April 16, 1837.

89   Archibald Hyman to Thomas W. Thompson, June 30, 1860, Lewis Thompson Papers.
90   Andrew McCollam Papers (Southern Historical Collection), VII, March 31, 1856.
91   William Taylor Diary (MS in Louisiana State University Department of Archives, Baton Rouge), December 19, 1841.
92   Manigault Plantation Records (Southern Historical Collection), III.
93   Sellers, *Slavery in Alabama*, 286-87; Joe G. Taylor, *Negro Slavery in Louisiana*, 189.
94   Olmsted, *Back Country*, 48.
95   Edwin A. Davis, *Plantation Life in Louisiana*, 370. For other examples of the utilization of dogs in tracking runaway slaves, see Magruder Diary (Louisiana State University Department of Archives), December 14, 1854; May 31, June 3, 1857; Walter Wade Plantation Diaries (Mississippi Department of Archives), August 5, 1851; February 8-9, March 14, 22, 1854.
96   Olmsted, *Back Country*, 88.
97   Velasco Plantation Journal (Maunsel White Papers and Books), September 25, 1860.
98   Phillips (ed.), *Plantation and Frontier*, I, 321.
99   Franklin A. Hudson Diary (MS in Southern Historical Collection, University of North Carolina, Chapel Hill), June 11, 1855, and *passim*.
100   Edwin A. Davis, *Plantation Life in Louisiana*, 112.
101   Rules and Regulations for the Government of the William J. Minor Plantations, in Minor Plantation Diaries (William J. Minor and Family Papers), XXXIII (1861-65), XXXIV (1861-68).
102   Doro Plantation Account Book (Charles Clark and Family Papers), IX, marginal notation in section entitled "Duties of an Overseer."
103   Phillips (ed.), *Plantation and Frontier*, I, 118.
104   Olmsted, *Seaboard Slave States*, II, 68.
105   Russell, *My Diary North and South*, 263.
106   Magoffin, "A Georgia Planter and His Plantations," 374.
107   Phillips (ed.), *Plantation and Frontier*, I, 126.
108   William R. Elley Plantation Record Book (MS in Mississippi Department of Archives and History, Jackson).
109   *Ibid.*, December 7, 1855.
110   Washington to Pearce, May 10, 1795, in Conway (ed.), *George Washington and Mount Vernon*, 184.
111   J. E. Taliaferro to Governor John J. Pettus, August 21, 1860, in Governor's Records, Ser. E, Vol. XLIX, Mississippi Department of Archives and History, Jackson. The author is indebted to Robert W. Dubay, a graduate student at the University of Southern Mississippi, for calling his attention to this item.
112   Charles Sackett Sydnor, *A Gentleman of the Old Natchez Region: Benjamin L. C. Wailes* (Durham: Duke University Press, 1938), 112, quoting Wailes Diary, n.d. given, in Duke University Library, Durham; hereinafter cited as Sydnor, *Benjamin L. C. Wailes.*
113   *Ibid.*, 114, quoting Wailes Diary, June 2, 1859.
114   Lewis Carter to John Perkins, Jr., August 4, 1859, in John Perkins Papers, Southern Historical Collection, University of North Carolina, Chapel Hill.
115   James M. Torbert Plantation Diaries (Typescript in Alabama Department of Archives and History, Montgomery), III, January 24, 1857.
116   Phillips, *Life and Labor in the Old South*, 312.

117 Magnolia Plantation Journals (Henry Clay Warmoth Papers and Books), December 18, 1860.
118 R. R. Barrow Residence Journal (Southern Historical Collection), May 3, 9, 1858.
119 Stancil Barwick to John B. Lamar, July 15, 1855, in Phillips (ed.), *Plantation and Frontier*, I, 312-13.
120 Phillips, *American Negro Slavery*, 458.
121 Thomas B. Carroll, *Historical Sketches of Oktibbeha County*, 76.
122 Olmsted, *Back Country*, 83.
123 Charlotte Ann Allston to Robert F. W. Allston, June 8, 1823, in Easterby (ed.), *The South Carolina Rice Plantation*, 60.
124 Concordia Parish Inquest Record (Transcript in unpublished inventory of Concordia Parish prepared by the Historical Records Survey, Louisiana State University Department of Archives, Baton Rouge), July 5, 1857; original in "Ante-Bellum Criminal" case files, Office of Clerk of Court as Recorder, Concordia Parish Courthouse, Vidalia, Louisiana. Also quoted (though cited incorrectly as undated) in Joe G. Taylor, *Negro Slavery in Louisiana*, 202-203.
125 William Jacobs to Mrs. Mary C. Weeks, November 29, 1837, Weeks Hall Collection.
126 *Ibid.*
127 Alexander Franklin Pugh Plantation Diaries (MSS in Louisiana State University Department of Archives, Baton Rouge), November 25, 1861.
128 Aventine Plantation Diary (MS in Mississippi Department of Archives and History, Jackson), September 18, 1859.
129 Gray, *History of Agriculture*, I, 517.
130 Joe G. Taylor, *Negro Slavery in Louisiana*, 205.
131 Orville W. Taylor, *Negro Slavery in Arkansas*, 108, citing Des Arc *Weekly Citizen*, August 24, 1859.
132 S. M. Meek Book (Microfilm copy in Southern Historical Collection, University of North Carolina, Chapel Hill), December 3, 1857.
133 Phillips (ed.), *Plantation and Frontier*, II, 119, quoting *Federal Union*, May 26, 1857.

Chapter 5

1 Carter, "On the Management of Negroes; Addressed to the Farmers and Overseers of Virginia," 565.
2 Contract between Jacob Bieller and overseer Garret P. Rawlings, January 16, 1834, Alonzo Snyder Papers.
3 *Southern Cultivator*, II (June, 1844), 97.
4 Garland D. Harmon, "Overseers and Their Enjoyments," *Southern Cultivator*, XVIII (May, 1860), 151.
5 Rawls to Lewis Thompson, December 24, 1857, Lewis Thompson Papers.
6 Bonner, "The Plantation Overseer and Southern Nationalism," 2, quoting *Southern Cultivator*, XX (1862), 287.
7 Paul S. Taylor, "Plantation Laborer Before the Civil War," 6, quoting *Southern Cultivator*, XX (1862), 136.
8 *Ibid.*
9 Moody, "Slavery on Louisiana Sugar Plantations," 284.
10 Leak Diary (Southern Historical Collection), July 31, 1859.
11 Olmsted, *Back Country*, 65.

12   Daniel Coleman, "A Few Words About Overseers," *Southern Cultivator*, VII (September, 1849), 139–40.
13   Stampp, *The Peculiar Institution*, 39.
14   *Southern Agriculturist*, II (November, 1829), 520–21.
15   Avery Odelle Craven, *Edmund Ruffin, Southerner; A Study in Secession* (New York: D. Appleton and Company, 1932), 19.
16   Phillips, *Life and Labor in the Old South*, 310.
17   Edwin A. Davis, *Plantation Life in Louisiana*, 154.
18   *Southern Cultivator*, IV (July, 1846), 106.
19   *Ibid.*
20   *Ibid.*, VI (September, 1848), 134.
21   *Ibid.*, II (October, 1844), 170.
22   Hammond to Ruffin, August 7, 1845, Edmund Ruffin Papers and Books.
23   *American Agriculturist*, IV (October, 1845), 319.
24   Washington to Pearce, November 23, 1794, in Conway (ed.), *George Washington and Mount Vernon*, 130.
25   Jordan, *Hugh Davis and His Alabama Plantation*, 67.
26   *Ibid.*, 68–69.
27   Torbert Plantation Diaries (Alabama Department of Archives), II, December 1, 1855.
28   *Ibid.*, December 31, 1855.
29   *Ibid.*, January 25, 1856.
30   Franklin L. Riley, "Diary of a Mississippi Planter, January 1, 1840 to April, 1863," in Franklin L. Riley (ed.), *Publications of the Mississippi Historical Society* (Oxford, Miss.: Printed for the Society, 1909), X, 453.
31   *Ibid.*
32   *Ibid.*, 456.
33   Gavin Diary (Southern Historical Collection), February 24, 1859.
34   *Ibid.*, May 3, 1859.
35   *Ibid.*, May 6, 1859.
36   *Ibid.*, June 7, 1859.
37   *Ibid.*, February 28, 1860.
38   Bassett, *Plantation Overseer*, 148.
39   Note appended to agreement between John Ewing Colhoun and John Harman, February 22, 1800, in Colhoun Papers.
40   Hudson Diary (Southern Historical Collection), August 17, 1856.
41   *Ibid.*, November 29, 1856.
42   Orville W. Taylor, *Negro Slavery in Arkansas*, 105.
43   Ruffin, "Incidents of My Life" (Edmund Ruffin Papers and Books), II, 104.
44   Phillips, *Life and Labor in the Old South*, 311.
45   Joseph Carlyle Sitterson, "The William J. Minor Plantations: A Study in Ante-Bellum Absentee Ownership," *Journal of Southern History*, IX (February, 1943), 62.
46   James Allen Plantation Book (Typescript in Mississippi Department of Archives and History, Jackson), April 22, June 21, 1862.
47   Flanders, *Plantation Slavery in Georgia*, 112.
48   Ann E. Eldridge to Alonzo Snyder, October 10, 1858, Alonzo Snyder Papers.
49   John and Keating S. Ball Books (Southern Historical Collection), III.
50   Deer Range Plantation Journal (Maunsel White Papers and Books), March 26, 1861.

51   Maunsel White to Maunsell White, Jr., July 12, 1855, Maunsel White Papers and Books.
52   See pages 76–77 of this book.
53   O'Connor to David Weeks, January 2, February 12, April 2, 1834; O'Connor to Mrs. Mary C. Weeks, July 30, August 12, December 26, 1834, Weeks Hall Collection.
54   O'Connor to Conrad, February 2, 1836, Weeks Hall Collection.
55   Jenkins Plantation Diary (John C. Jenkins and Family Papers), November 1, 1845.
56   *Ibid.*, April 26, 1847.
57   Easterby (ed.), *The South Carolina Rice Plantation*, 27.
58   Magnolia Plantation Journals (Henry Clay Warmoth Papers and Books), September 3, 1862.
59   Torbert Plantation Diaries (Alabama Department of Archives), III, October 3, 1857.
60   Lucille Griffith (ed.), "The Plantation Record Book of Brookdale Farm, Amite County, 1856–57," *Journal of Mississippi History*, VII (January, 1945), 25.
61   *De Bow's Review*, X (June, 1851), 626.
62   Olmsted, *Back Country*, 57.
63   *De Bow's Review*, XXI (August, 1856), 148.
64   *Southern Cultivator*, XII (September, 1854), 270.
65   Carter, "On the Management of Negroes; Addressed to the Farmers and Overseers of Virginia," 565.
66   Martin W. Philips, *American Cotton Planter*, I (December, 1853), 377.
67   *Ibid.*, II (May, 1854), 149–50.
68   Garland D. Harmon, "Overseers, &c.," *American Cotton Planter*, II (July, 1854), 214.
69   Martin W. Philips, "Reply to Mr. Harmon," *American Cotton Planter*, II (September, 1854), 281.
70   *Ibid.*, 282.
71   Garland D. Harmon, "Reply to Dr. Philips," *American Cotton Planter*, II (November, 1854), 347.
72   *Southern Cultivator*, VII (July, 1849), 103.
73   *Ibid.*, VII (September, 1849), 140.
74   Maunsel White to Bracewell, November 13, 1847, Maunsel White Lettercopy Book, in Maunsel White Papers and Books.
75   Maunsel White to Bracewell, December 4, 1847, Maunsel White Lettercopy Book, in Maunsel White Papers and Books.
76   See page 80 of this book.
77   *Farmers' Register*, VIII (April, 1840), 230.
78   *American Cotton Planter*, II (May, 1854), 150.
79   Stampp, *The Peculiar Institution*, 107–108, quoting *Southern Cultivator*, XVIII (1860), 131.
80   Samuel L. Straughan to Robert Carter, September 27, 1787, in Phillips (ed.), *Plantation and Frontier*, I, 324–25.
81   Gabriel L. Ellis to Robert F. W. Allston, September 16, 1838, in Easterby (ed.), *The South Carolina Rice Plantation*, 255. Ellis was the overseer of Allston's "Chicora Wood" plantation. The Mrs. Allston referred to was Mary Allan Allston, a sister-in-law of Robert Allston.
82   Magoffin, "A Georgia Planter and His Plantations," 361.
83   William J. Eve, "Hog Raising in the South," *Southern Cultivator*, XIV (July, 1856), 209.

84   John H. Dent, "Overseers and Their Employers," *American Agriculturist*, IV (December, 1845), 368.
85   *Southern Cultivator*, II (November, 1844), 177.
86   William H. Cook, "Overseers and Plantation Management," *American Cotton Planter*, XII (April, 1858), 113.
87   John Taylor of Caroline, *Arator*, 49.
88   *Southern Cultivator*, II (August, 1844), 123. See also Olmsted, *Back Country*, 59.
89   Cathey, *Agricultural Developments in North Carolina*, 58.
90   R. Butterfield, "Overseers and a Word of Encouragement to Them," *American Cotton Planter*, XIII (July, 1859), 214.
91   *American Cotton Planter*, XII (June, 1858), 197.
92   Hubard, "On the Manner and Time of Employing Overseers," 714.
93   Jordan, *Hugh Davis and His Alabama Plantation*, 59-73.
94   Walter Wade Plantation Diaries (Mississippi Department of Archives), June 23, 1850; December 27, 1853.
95   *Ibid.*, Agreement between Walter Wade and Hiram Reeves, 1849.
96   Martin W. Philips, "Explanatory," *American Cotton Planter*, II (July, 1854), 208.
97   Martin W. Philips, "Domestic Economy—Overseers, &c—A Few Thoughts on the Subject," *Southern Cultivator*, XIV (November, 1856), 339.
98   Ruffin, "Incidents of My Life" (Edmund Ruffin Papers and Books), II, 131.
99   *Southern Cultivator*, XIX (May, 1861), 151.
100 Garland D. Harmon, "Bedding Cotton," *Southern Cultivator*, VIII (April, 1850), 50.
101 See page 39 of this book.
102 Manigault Plantation Records (Southern Historical Collection), IV, February 1, 1857.
103 Phillips, *Life and Labor in the Old South*, 238.
104 Mooney, *Slavery in Tennessee*, 164, quoting Lucius Polk to Mrs. Sarah Polk, September 9, 1839, in Polk-Yeatman Collection, University of North Carolina, Chapel Hill.
105 Milton Baggs, Jr., "Changing Overseers," *Southern Cultivator*, XVIII (July, 1860), 207.
106 *Ibid.*
107 A. T. Goodloe, "Overseers," *Southern Cultivator*, XVIII (September, 1860), 287.
108 *Ibid.*
109 *American Cotton Planter*, II (May, 1854), 150.
110 Olmsted, *Seaboard Slave States*, II, 154-55, quoting *Southern Agriculturist*, IV (1831), 323.
111 *American Cotton Planter*, II (December, 1854), 372.
112 *American Farmer*, VIII (May, 1826), 60.
113 *Farmers' Register*, V (September, 1837), 301-302.
114 Olmsted, *Back Country*, 60.
115 Martin W. Philips, "Overseers, Agents," *American Cotton Planter*, II (November, 1854), 347.
116 Butterfield, "Overseers and a Word of Encouragement to Them," 214.
117 *American Cotton Planter*, V (May, 1857), 134.
118 James Barbour, *American Farmer*, VII (December, 1825), 290-91. See also Paul S. Taylor, "Plantation Laborer Before the Civil War," 5-6.
119 Goodloe, "Overseers," 287.

120 *Ibid.*
121 *Southern Cultivator*, VI (November, 1848), 163.
122 Garland D. Harmon, "Personal Attention," *Southern Cultivator*, VII (May, 1849), 75.
123 *American Cotton Planter*, II (May, 1854), 149.
124 *Ibid.*, 150.
125 *Southern Cultivator*, VII (September, 1849), 140.
126 *Ibid.*
127 John H. Hairston to Robert Hairston, February 13, 1838, Hairston Papers.
128 Coleman, "A Few Words About Overseers," 139.
129 *Southern Cultivator*, XIX (May, 1861), 151.
130 Philips, "Explanatory," 207.
131 Philips, "Overseers, Agents," 347.
132 Calhoun, "Management of Slaves," 716; also printed in *Southern Cultivator*, IV, 113.
133 *Southern Agriculturist*, II (November, 1829), 522.
134 Whitemarsh B. Seabrook, "On the Causes of the General Unsuccessfulness of the Sea-Island Planters," *Southern Agriculturist*, VII (April, 1834), 179.
135 Moore (ed.), "Two Documents Relating to Plantation Overseers of the Vicksburg Region," 32, citing Jefferson Davis to John Robinson, F. S. Hunt, and others, September 12, 1859, in Jackson (Miss.) *Mississippian*, October 5, 1859.
136 *De Bow's Review*, XXVIII (February, 1860), 239.
137 *Southern Agriculturist*, II (January, 1829), 4.
138 *Ibid.*, 5.
139 Dent, "Overseers and Their Employers," 368.
140 Butterfield, "Overseers and a Word of Encouragement to Them," 214.
141 *Ibid.*
142 Garland D. Harmon, "Hints to Overseers," *Southern Cultivator*, VIII (September, 1850), 135.
143 Cook, "Overseers and Plantation Management," 112.
144 *Southern Cultivator*, XVIII (March, 1860), 74.
145 John M. Daniel, *Southern Planter*, VIII (April, 1848), 104.
146 *Soil of the South*, IV (March, 1854), 70–71, cited in Flanders, *Plantation Slavery in Georgia*, 90; Paul Wallace Gates, *The Farmer's Age: Agriculture, 1815–1860* (New York: Holt, Rinehart and Winston, 1960), 347.
147 *American Farmer*, VIII (May, 1826), 60.
148 *Southern Cultivator*, XIII (May, 1855), 158.
149 Sydnor, *Benjamin L. C. Wailes*, 117.

Chapter 6

1 Letter of James B. Heyward, November 12, 1861, Heyward-Ferguson Papers and Books.
2 Charles P. Roland, *Louisiana Sugar Plantations During the American Civil War* (Leiden: E. J. Brill, 1957), 80.
3 Bell Irvin Wiley, *Southern Negroes, 1861–1865* (New Haven: Yale University Press, 1938), 49.
4 Easterby (ed.), *The South Carolina Rice Plantation*, 277.
5 Wiley, *Southern Negroes*, 50.

6   Henry Parnell to John Perkins, Jr., May 12, 1864, John Perkins Papers.
7   *Southern Cultivator,* XXII (January, 1864), 13.
8   Easterby (ed.), *The South Carolina Rice Plantation,* 277–78.
9   *Ibid.,* 26.
10   Dudley Avery to Major General Richard Taylor, June 2, 1864, Avery Family Papers.
11   Hairston Papers (Southern Historical Collection), XX.
12   Agreement between James R. Sparkman and G. V. McMillan, February 16, 1864, in Sparkman Family Papers, Southern Historical Collection, University of North Carolina, Chapel Hill.
13   Newstead Plantation Diary (Microfilm copy in Southern Historical Collection, University of North Carolina, Chapel Hill), August 18, 1861.
14   Doro Plantation Account Book (Charles Clark and Family Papers), XI, December 1, 1861.
15   Sitterson, "The William J. Minor Plantations," 71.
16   Parnell to Perkins, May 12, 1864, John Perkins Papers.
17   Sydnor, *Benjamin L. C. Wailes,* 299, quoting Wailes Diary, March 13, 1862.
18   James Allen Plantation Book (Mississippi Department of Archives), March 20, 1862.
19   William J. Minor to Andrew McCollam, August 30, 1863, Andrew McCollam Papers.
20   Pierre Phanor Prudhomme Records and Papers (Southern Historical Collection), XIII, March 7, 8, 1862.
21   Gavin Diary (Southern Historical Collection), February 9, 1861.
22   Smith Powell to John Hartwell Cocke, December 7, 1865, Cocke Papers.
23   Albert Wood to John Hartwell Cocke, February 13, 1864, Cocke Papers.
24   Phillips, *Life and Labor in the Old South,* 315.
25   Ralph Ancil Wooster, "The Secession Conventions of the Lower South: A Study of Their Membership" (Ph.D. dissertation, University of Texas, 1954), 265. See also the expanded version of this dissertation, *The Secession Conventions of the South* (Princeton: Princeton University Press, 1962), 106, 110.
26   Magnolia Plantation Journals (Henry Clay Warmoth Papers and Books), June 13, 1861; also quoted in Ulrich Bonnell Phillips, "The Central Theme of Southern History," *American Historical Review,* XXXIV (October, 1928), 32; Sitterson, "Magnolia Plantation," 206.
27   Magnolia Plantation Journals (Henry Clay Warmoth Papers and Books), March 4, 1862.
28   *Ibid.,* February 19, 1862.
29   *Ibid.,* April 24, 1862.
30   James Allen Plantation Book (Mississippi Department of Archives), May 15, 1862.
31   *Ibid.,* May 21, 1862.
32   R. D. Powell to J. H. Cocke, December 10, 1863, Cocke Papers.
33   R. D. Powell to J. H. Cocke, May 5, 1864, Cocke Papers.
34   Magnolia Plantation Journals (Henry Clay Warmoth Papers and Books), April 3, 1862.
35   *Ibid.,* April 21, 1862.
36   Wiley, *Southern Negroes,* 127.
37   *Ibid.*

38   Bayside Plantation Records (Southern Historical Collection), II, October 29, 1862.
39   Minor Plantation Diaries (William J. Minor and Family Papers), XXXVI, October 5, 1863. Also cited in Roland, *Louisiana Sugar Plantations*, 81.
40   Minor Plantation Diaries (William J. Minor and Family Papers), XXXVI, October 8, 1863.
41   Jane Minge Friend, "Recollections of Life on White Hill Plantation" (Microfilm copy in White Hill Plantation Books), 40.
42   Peter Wilson Hairston to Fanny Caldwell Hairston, [June] 5, 1861, Hairston Papers.
43   R. D. Powell to J. H. Cocke, January 23, 1864, Cocke Papers.
44   Pugh Plantation Diaries (Louisiana State University Department of Archives), June 26, 1861.
45   Wiley, *Southern Negroes*, 244-45, citing New Orleans *Daily Picayune*, August 6, 1863.
46   Wiley, *Southern Negroes*, 252, citing New Orleans *Daily Picayune*, November 22, 1862; December 19, 1863.
47   Pierre Phanor Prudhomme Records and Papers (Southern Historical Collection), XIII, May 12, 1862.
48   *Ibid.*, XIV, May 5, 1863.
49   Edmund Ruffin, Jr., Plantation Diary (MS in Southern Historical Collection, University of North Carolina, Chapel Hill), May 15, 1862.
50   *Ibid.*, May 26, 1862.
51   *Ibid.*, June 9, 1862.
52   *Ibid.*, January 1, 1866.
53   Fonsylvania Plantation Diary (MS in Mississippi Department of Archives and History, Jackson), May 6, 1863.
54   *Ibid.*, May 25, 1863.
55   *Ibid.*, June 6, 1863.
56   Pugh Plantation Diaries (Louisiana State University Department of Archives), October 27, 1862.
57   *Ibid.*, October 30, 1862.
58   *Ibid.*, November 2, 1862.
59   *Ibid.*, November 20, 1862.
60   Magnolia Plantation Journals (Henry Clay Warmoth Papers and Books), May 14, 1862.
61   *Ibid.*, June 15, 1862.
62   *Ibid.*, August 16, 1862.
63   *Ibid.*, August 25, 1862.
64   *Ibid.*, September 5, 1862.
65   *Ibid.*, October 14, 1862.
66   *Ibid.*, October 18, 1862.
67   *Ibid.*, December 1, 1862.
68   *Ibid.*, December 25, 1862.
69   *Ibid.*, January 25, 1863.
70   Sitterson, "Magnolia Plantation," 209.
71   Sydnor, *Benjamin L. C. Wailes*, 301, quoting Wailes Diary, March 18, 1862.
72   H. B. Shaw to Alonzo Snyder, December 6, 1861, Alonzo Snyder Papers.
73   Sitterson, *Sugar Country*, 217.
74   Paul Everett Postell, "John Hampden Randolph, A Louisiana Planter,"

Louisiana Historical Quarterly, XXV (January, 1942), 198–99. See also Sitterson, *Sugar Country,* 217–18.
75   See page 4 of this book.
76   Roland, *Louisiana Sugar Plantations,* 82.
77   See pages 48, 141–42 of this book.
78   Deer Range Plantation Journal (Maunsel White Papers and Books), April 6, 1869.
79   Wiley, *Southern Negroes,* 245.
80   *Ibid.,* 252.

Chapter 7

1   Cathey, *Agricultural Developments in North Carolina,* 67.
2   Garland D. Harmon, "Yost's Plow and Scraper," *Southern Cultivator,* XIV (December, 1856), 364.
3   Moore, *Agriculture in Ante-Bellum Mississippi,* 184–85.
4   J. Alston Reynolds to Robert F. W. Allston, September 28, 1861, in Easterby (ed.), *The South Carolina Rice Plantation,* 267–68.
5   See page 157 of this book.
6   Hairston Papers (Southern Historical Collection), VIII–XII, XIV–XVI, XX–XXII.
7   MS census returns, 1860 (National Archives, Washington, D.C.), Henry County, Virginia.
8   Ruffin, "Incidents of My Life" (Edmund Ruffin Papers and Books), II, 132–33.
9   Hammond to Ruffin, March 11, 1851, Edmund Ruffin Papers and Books.
10   Ruffin, "Incidents of My Life" (Edmund Ruffin Papers and Books), II, 133.
11   Solon Robinson, "Farm of Mr. Bolling, in Virginia," *American Agriculturist,* VIII (August, 1849), 254–55.
12   Andrew Nicol, "Notes on the Sandy Point Estate," *Farmers' Register,* IX (June, 1841), 343.
13   *Ibid.,* IX, 214.
14   Ruffin, "Incidents of My Life" (Edmund Ruffin Papers and Books), II, 133.
15   Edmund Ruffin, "Some Account of the Farming of Richard Sampson, Esq., of Goochland," *Farmers' Register,* V (October, 1837), 373.
16   Phillips, *Life and Labor in the Old South,* 308. See also Gray, *History of Agriculture,* I, 495.
17   Ruffin, "Some Account of the Farming of Richard Sampson, Esq., of Goochland," 364, 371–72. See also Phillips, *Life and Labor in the Old South,* 309.
18   Ruffin, "Some Account of the Farming of Richard Sampson, Esq., of Goochland," 372–73.
19   Phillips, *Life and Labor in the Old South,* 310, quoting *Southern Planter,* XVI (1856), 49.
20   Phillips, *Life and Labor in the Old South,* 307–308.
21   Easterby (ed.), *The South Carolina Rice Plantation,* 25–27.
22   MS census returns, 1860 (National Archives, Washington, D.C.), Georgetown District, South Carolina.
23   Robert F. W. Allston to Benjamin Allston, June 8, 1858, in Easterby (ed.), *The South Carolina Rice Plantation,* 144.

24 Mrs. Robert Allston to Benjamin Allston, April 22, 1866, in Easterby (ed.), *The South Carolina Rice Plantation*, 218.
25 Manigault Plantation Records (Southern Historical Collection), IV, May 3, 1859.
26 *Ibid.*, April 24, 1860.
27 William Capers to Charles Manigault, June 13, 1860, in Phillips (ed.), *Plantation and Frontier*, II, 94.
28 Capers to Charles Manigault, August 5, 1860, in Phillips (ed.), *Plantation and Frontier*, I, 337.
29 Capers to Charles Manigault, October 15, 1860, in Phillips (ed.), *Plantation and Frontier*, I, 338.
30 Manigault Plantation Records (Southern Historical Collection), IV.
31 Phillips, *Life and Labor in the Old South*, 259–60.
32 Kemble, *Journal of a Residence on a Georgian Plantation.*
33 *Ibid.*, 50, 207. See also Roswell King, Jr., "On the Management of the Butler Estate, and the Cultivation of the Sugar Cane," *Southern Agriculturist*, I (December, 1828), 523–24.
34 See page 76 of this book.
35 Kemble, *Journal of a Residence on a Georgian Plantation*, 38 and *passim*.
36 King, "On the Management of the Butler Estate, and the Cultivation of the Sugar Cane," 524.
37 *Ibid.*, 525.
38 Phillips, *Life and Labor in the Old South*, 266.
39 *Ibid.*, 267.
40 Kemble, *Journal of a Residence on a Georgian Plantation*, 90.
41 Roswell King, Jr., Plantation Journal (MS in Louisiana State University Department of Archives, Baton Rouge), October 31, 1838.
42 Roswell King, Jr., Plantation Journal (Louisiana State University Department of Archives). Miss Kemble erroneously states (pp. 123, 265) that King left Butler's Island in 1838 to become a planter in Alabama. The error is repeated by Phillips in *Life and Labor in the Old South*, 261.
43 Roswell King, Jr., Plantation Journal (Louisiana State University Department of Archives), January 12, 17–24, 1841, and *passim*.
44 *Ibid.*, April 14–23, 1843.
45 Professor John A. Scott, who has examined the records of the Butler Estate, indicates in the latest edition of Miss Kemble's *Journal* (New York: Alfred A. Knopf, 1961), 398, that King managed the Butler holdings until at least 1854.
46 The narrative of the career of Jordan Myrick is drawn from "Mr. Jordan Myrick; by a Friend," *Southern Agriculturist*, VII (December, 1834), 636–38.
47 James Hamilton Couper Plantation Records (Southern Historical Collection), IV, 33-35.
48 "Mr. Jordan Myrick; by a Friend," 638.
49 Rawls to Lewis Thompson, October 3, 1858, Lewis Thompson Papers.
50 See page 28 of this book.
51 See pages 115–16 of this book.
52 MS census returns, 1860 (National Archives, Washington, D.C.), Plaquemines Parish, Louisiana.
53 Sitterson, *Sugar Country*, 55.
54 MS census returns, 1860 (National Archives, Washington, D.C.), St. Mary Parish, Louisiana.
55 Bateman was certainly managing the Manning property as early as

1853 and probably assumed direction of the latter's "Point Houmas" and "Riverton" plantation units several years before that date. See Seale Diary (Louisiana State University Department of Archives), January 14, July 25, August 20, 1853.

56 Russell, *My Diary North and South*, 281.

57 MS census returns, 1860 (National Archives, Washington, D.C.), Ascension Parish, Louisiana.

58 Elisha Cain to Alexander Telfair, October 10, 1829, in Phillips (ed.), *Plantation and Frontier*, II, 85. See also Phillips, *American Negro Slavery*, 234-35.

59 Cain to Alexander Telfair, November 4, 1833, in Phillips (ed.), *Plantation and Frontier*, II, 39. See also Phillips, *American Negro Slavery*, 235-36.

60 Cain to Mary Telfair, December 14, 1840, in Phillips (ed.), *Plantation and Frontier*, I, 335-36. See also Phillips, *American Negro Slavery*, 237.

61 Bonner, "The Plantation Overseer and Southern Nationalism," 3.

62 *Ibid.*, 7-8.

63 *Ibid.*, 9.

64 Garland D. Harmon, "The Farmer-Soldier—G. D. Harmon," *Southern Cultivator*, XXI (May-June, 1863), 77.

65 Bonner, "The Plantation Overseer and Southern Nationalism," 10.

66 *Ibid.*

67 *Ibid.*, 3.

68 Garland D. Harmon, "Ditching Hill Side—Mr. Harmon's Terms," *Southern Cultivator*, XV (October, 1857), 298.

69 Garland D. Harmon, "Wearing out Land!—Deterioration and Ruin," *Southern Cultivator*, XVI (July, 1858), 210.

70 Garland D. Harmon, "Corn Cribs and Hogs," *American Cotton Planter*, XII (June, 1858), 181-82.

71 Garland D. Harmon, "Experiments and Essays—A Proposition," *Southern Cultivator*, XVI (April, 1858), 127.

72 Garland D. Harmon, "Agricultural Implements," *Southern Cultivator*, XVIII (February, 1860), 54.

73 Garland D. Harmon, "Supplies Stopped—Let Us Make Our Own," *Southern Cultivator*, XIX (July, 1861), 218.

74 Harmon, "The Farmer-Soldier—G. D. Harmon," 77.

75 John S. Wilson, "Medicine, Land Levels, &c.," *American Cotton Planter*, XII (October, 1858), 310.

76 *Southern Cultivator*, XVIII (July, 1860), 214.

77 Garland D. Harmon, "Mississippi Country—Quality of Land, &c.," *Southern Cultivator*, XIX (April, 1861), 119.

78 Bonner, "The Plantation Overseer and Southern Nationalism," 11.

Chapter 8

1 William Rhodes to John Perkins, Jr., January 27, 1859, John Perkins Papers.

2 Philip St. George Cocke to John Hartwell Cocke, June 21, 1857, Cocke Papers.

3 Marshall and Evans (eds.), "Plantation Report from the Papers of Levin R. Marshall," 53.

4 Boyd Smith to David Weeks, August 20, 1834, Weeks Hall Collection.

5   Washington to Pearce, August 3, 1794, in Conway (ed.), *George Washington and Mount Vernon*, 97.
6   Washington to Pearce, July 17, 1797, in Conway (ed.), *George Washington and Mount Vernon*, 272–73.
7   Moody, "Slavery on Louisiana Sugar Plantations," 208.
8   Olmsted, *Back Country*, 73.
9   Lucy Skipwith to John Hartwell Cocke, September, 1858, Cocke Papers.
10   R. D. Powell to J. H. Cocke, August 10, 1860, Cocke Papers; Diary of Philip St. George Cocke (Microfilm copy in Cocke Papers), January 31, 1847.
11   Rhodes to Perkins, July 14, 1857, John Perkins Papers.
12   Washington to Pearce, October 6, 1793, in Conway (ed.), *George Washington and Mount Vernon*, 6.
13   Phillips (ed.), *Plantation and Frontier*, I, 324.
14   Inventory of Brunswick Estate, in Cocke Papers (Southern Historical Collection), VIII, January 1, 1853.
15   James M. Stanbrough to John Perkins, Jr., August 2, 1859, John Perkins Papers.
16   Conway (ed.), *George Washington and Mount Vernon*, 3, 62, 273.
17   See page 29 of this book.
18   See page 162 of this book.
19   Flanders, *Plantation Slavery in Georgia*, 104.
20   Hairston Papers (Southern Historical Collection).
21   Cocke Papers (Southern Historical Collection), VIII, XVII.
22   Richard Corbin to James Semple, January, 1759, in Phillips (ed.), *Plantation and Frontier*, I, 109–12.
23   See page 23 of this book.
24   Washington to Pearce, December 18, 1793, in Conway (ed.), *George Washington and Mount Vernon*, 13–14.
25   Washington to Pearce, July 13, 1794, in Conway (ed.), *George Washington and Mount Vernon*, 89–90.
26   Washington to Pearce, February 21, 1796, in Conway (ed.), *George Washington and Mount Vernon*, 227.
27   Conway (ed.), *George Washington and Mount Vernon*, 271–72.
28   MS census returns, 1860 (National Archives, Washington, D.C.), Terrebonne Parish, Louisiana.
29   Pierre A. Champomier, *Statement of the Sugar Crop Made in Louisiana, 1844–1861* (New Orleans: Cook, Young and Company, 1845–62).
30   R. R. Barrow Residence Journal (Southern Historical Collection), February 21, 1858.
31   *Ibid.*, July 9, 1857.
32   *Ibid.*, July 31, 1857.
33   *Ibid.*, November 5, 1857.
34   *Ibid.*, October 13, 1857.
35   *Ibid.*, November 10, 1857. Windrowing was a device utilized by sugar planters to protect the cane from damaging frosts. The cane was cut and laid in the field in beds about two feet high, in such a manner that the stalks of each layer were covered by the leaves of the layer above. The danger in windrowing was that cane laid up in windrows would spoil if a freeze were followed by a prolonged spell of warm weather.
36   R. R. Barrow Residence Journal (Southern Historical Collection), November 11, 1857.
37   *Ibid.*, November 13, 1857.

38 *Ibid.*, December 20, 1857.
39 *Ibid.*, January 5, 1858.
40 MS census returns, 1860 (National Archives, Washington, D.C.), Terrebonne Parish, Louisiana.
41 Olmsted, *Back Country*, 81.
42 R. R. Barrow Residence Journal (Southern Historical Collection), November 18, 1857.
43 L. L. Singleton to John Hartwell Cocke, July 27, 1855, Cocke Papers.
44 R. D. Powell to J. H. Cocke, August 4, 1855, Cocke Papers.
45 Unless otherwise noted, the following account of the career of Richard D. Powell is drawn from the vast quantity of data contained in the Cocke Papers.
46 MS census returns, 1860 (National Archives, Washington, D.C.), Lowndes County, Mississippi.
47 See page 181 of this book.
48 R. D. Powell, Jr., to J. H. Cocke, August 8, 1856, Cocke Papers.
49 For an excellent sketch of the elder Cocke, see Clement Eaton, *The Mind of the Old South* (Baton Rouge: Louisiana State University Press, 1964), Chapter 1.
50 R. D. Powell to J. H. Cocke, June 30, 1856, Cocke Papers.
51 R. D. Powell to J. H. Cocke, July 19, 1856, Cocke Papers.
52 See page 80 of this book.
53 R. D. Powell to J. H. Cocke, November 20, 1865, Cocke Papers.
54 Philip St. George Cocke, Jr., to Cary Charles Cocke, January 18, 1866, Cocke Papers.

Chapter 9
1 Orville W. Taylor, *Negro Slavery in Arkansas*, 106.

Bibliography

I PRIMARY SOURCES

A MANUSCRIPT PLANTATION RECORDS

Alabama Department of Archives and History, Montgomery

William Proctor Gould Diaries, 1828–61 (Typescript). 4 volumes. Diaries of William Proctor Gould, public official and proprietor of "Hill of Howth" plantation in Greene County, Alabama.

James M. Torbert Plantation Diaries, 1848–76 (Typescript). 3 volumes. Daybook and journals of a small absentee cotton planter from the community of Society Hill in Macon County, Alabama.

John G. Traylor Diary, 1834–47 (Typescript). 1 volume. Personal diary of a central Alabama overseer who retired from the managerial profession after fifteen years to embark upon a new career as a small, independent, slaveholding farmer.

229

Louisiana State University Department of Archives, Baton Rouge

Concordia Parish Inquest Record, July 5, 1857 (Transcript in unpublished inventory of Concordia Parish prepared by the Historical Records Survey). 4 items. Principal item is the "voluntary statement" by overseer Albert Foster delivered at a coroner's inquest into the fatal shooting on June 30, 1857, of the slave Samuel, belonging to the estate of Paul Smith, on "Forest Home" plantation in Concordia Parish, Louisiana. The original record is in the "Ante-Bellum Criminal" case files, Office of Clerk of Court as Recorder, Concordia Parish Courthouse, Vidalia, Louisiana.

John C. Jenkins and Family Papers, 1840–1900 (Typescript). 89 items, including 13 volumes. Major portion of the collection is the plantation diary (12 volumes) of Dr. John Carmichael Jenkins, wealthy cotton planter, experimental agriculturist and horticulturist, and proprietor of "Elgin" plantation near Natchez, Mississippi.

Roswell King, Jr., Plantation Journal, 1838–45. 1 volume. Journal of the celebrated manager of the Butler Estate near Darien, Georgia. King was operating two farms of his own and serving as agent for the Butler interests during the period covered by the journal.

Eliza L. Magruder Diary, 1846–57. 2 volumes. Diary of Eliza Lloyd Magruder, who resided on "Locust Grove" plantation in Adams County, Mississippi. Chiefly remarkable for depicting the high social status of overseer John Ireland.

William J. Minor and Family Papers, 1748–1898. 410 items, including 37 volumes. Plantation records, early Natchez banking papers, and personal correspondence of the Stephen, William J., and Henry Minor families of Natchez, Mississippi. William J. Minor's plantation diaries contain a wealth of information concerning the management of his three sugar plantations in Louisiana.

Pre Aux Cleres Plantation Record Books, 1852–54. 2 volumes. Contain brief entries relating to the operation of a Natchitoches Parish, Louisiana, cotton plantation owned by J. H. McKnight.

Alexander Franklin Pugh Plantation Diaries, 1850–65. 7 volumes. Memorandum book and plantation diaries of a wealthy sugar planter who had an interest in five plantations on Bayou Lafourche, Louisiana. Remaining volumes of the Diary, which covers period 1853–79, are in University of Texas library.

H. M. Seale Diary, 1853–57. 1 volume. Plantation diary of the manager of Houmas, a giant sugar estate located in Ascension Parish, Louisiana, and owned by Colonel John S. Preston, son-in-law of General Wade Hampton of South Carolina.

Alonzo Snyder Papers, 1779–1887. 3,534 items, including 6 volumes. Business, official, and personal papers of Alonzo Snyder, cotton planter, judge, and Louisiana state senator. Many of the early papers concern Jacob Bieller, a Concordia Parish cotton planter, and his son Joseph, a planter and merchant of Catahoula Parish.

William Taylor Diary, 1838–42. 1 volume. Plantation diary of William

Taylor, cousin of General Zachary Taylor and proprietor of two sugar plantations in Pointe Coupee Parish, Louisiana. Weeks Hall Memorial Collection, 1782–1894. 10,115 items, including 15 volumes. Personal and business papers of the Weeks and related Conrad, Moore, and Gibson families of New Iberia and South Louisiana. Collection contains a wealth of information relating to the management of the Weeks and Moore plantations.

Mississippi Department of Archives and History, Jackson

James Allen Plantation Book, 1860–65 (Typescript). 1 volume. Plantation journal of James Allen, cotton planter and proprietor of "Nanechehaw" plantation in Warren County, Mississippi.

Aventine Plantation Diary, 1857–60. 1 volume. Plantation journal of an absentee cotton plantation owned by Thomas R. Shields and located near Natchez, Mississippi.

Charles Clark and Family Papers, 1810–92. 239 items, including 24 volumes. Personal and business papers and plantation records of Charles Clark, Mississippi Delta cotton planter. Clark served as a brigadier general in the Confederate Army and was elected governor of Mississippi in 1863.

William R. Elley Plantation Record Book, 1855–56. 1 volume. Contains irregular daily entries relating to operations on a cotton plantation in Washington County, Mississippi.

Holden Garthur Evans Diary, 1854–68 (Typescript). 1 volume. Personal diary of Dr. Holden Garthur Evans, physician and proprietor of a small cotton plantation located about ten miles south of Jackson, Mississippi.

Fonsylvania Plantation Diary, 1863. 1 volume. Diary of Alfred Quine, overseer of "Fonsylvania," an absentee cotton plantation owned by the widow of Benjamin L. C. Wailes and located near Vicksburg. Gives excellent account of the disruption of planting operations during the military campaign against Vicksburg.

Killona Plantation Journals, 1836–44. 2 volumes. Account book and cotton book kept by Jordan Bailey, overseer of an absentee cotton plantation owned by William S. Archer and located near Tchula, Mississippi.

Walter Wade Plantation Diaries, 1834–54 (Typescript). 2 volumes. Contain extensive data relating to the management of "Ross Wood," a cotton plantation in Jefferson County, Mississippi.

Southern Historical Collection,
University of North Carolina, Chapel Hill

Arnold–Screven Papers, 1779–1922. 2,400 items, including 22 volumes. Papers of Georgia rice planters James Proctor Screven, John Screven, and Richard J. Arnold. Includes a number of detailed overseer contracts.

Avery Family Papers, 1796–1916. 1,003 items, including 8 volumes. Primarily the business and personal papers of Daniel Dudley Avery, wealthy Louisiana judge and sugar planter.

John and Keating S. Ball Books, 1779–1884. 10 volumes. Plantation records of John Ball (1760–1817), John Ball, Jr., (1782–1834), and Keating S.

Ball (1818–91) relating to "Comingtee" and other Cooper River rice plantations.

William J. Ball Books, 1804–90 (Microfilm copy). 3 volumes. Plantation records of seven Cooper River rice plantations owned by members of the Ball family.

R. R. Barrow Residence Journal, 1857–58. 1 volume. Daily record of activities on the "Residence" plantation of R. R. Barrow, wealthy Terrebonne Parish sugar planter. Gives excellent insight into the relationship between steward E. A. Knowlton and his employer.

Bayside Plantation Records, 1846–66. 2 volumes. Daily record of affairs on F. D. Richardson's Bayou Teche sugar plantation.

Brownrigg Papers, 1771–1929. 303 items, including 4 volumes. Papers of a planter family with holdings in North Carolina and Mississippi.

John Bullock Papers, 1760–1882. 800 items, including 6 volumes. Correspondence of the Bullock, Hamilton, and Coleman families relating to lands and plantations in Granville County, North Carolina, and Lowndes County, Mississippi.

William Butler's Observations on Rice Culture, 1786 (Microfilm copy). 2 items. Two papers on rice culture in the Santee River region of South Carolina.

Cocke Papers, 1804–83 (Microfilm copy). 798 items, including 22 volumes. Correspondence, plantation books, and diaries of the Cocke family, one of the most distinguished planting families in the Old South. Bulk of data concerns the planting operations in Virginia, Alabama, and Mississippi of John Hartwell Cocke and his son, Philip St. George Cocke.

John Ewing Colhoun Papers, 1774–1850. 250 items. Primarily the papers of John Ewing Colhoun, wealthy rice and indigo planter of Charleston District, South Carolina.

James Hamilton Couper Plantation Records, 1818–54. 4 volumes. Financial accounts and plantation records of a wealthy Glynn County, Georgia, planter, who was noted for his progressive agricultural achievements. Couper employed an exceptionally able group of overseers.

Edwin Edmunds Account Book, 1838–92. 1 volume. Ledger and other accounts of Edmunds, the proprietor of "Rotherwood," a tobacco plantation located near Farmville, Virginia.

Evan Hall Plantation Account Books, 1772–1835 (Microfilm copy). 1 volume. Primarily the financial accounts of Henry McCall, who later became one of the largest sugar producers in Louisiana.

Andrew Flynn Plantation Book, 1840 (Microfilm copy). 1 volume. Plantation book of Flynn's "Green Valley" plantation located in northwestern Mississippi.

John Edwin Fripp Papers and Books, 1804–1924. 1 folder and 8 volumes. Records and diary of John Edwin Fripp, a small cotton and rice planter of Beaufort District, South Carolina.

David Gavin Diary, 1855–74. 1 volume. Diary of a small Colleton District, South Carolina, planter.

John Berkley Grimball Diary, 1832–83. 17 volumes. Gives excellent account of operations on the Grimball plantations in Colleton District, South

Carolina. Contains vast amount of information on Grimball's overseers over a period of more than thirty years.

Peter Wilson Hairston Papers, 1773–1886. 539 items, including 22 volumes. Papers of several generations of the Hairston family covering planting operations in Virginia, North Carolina, and Mississippi over a period of more than a century. Material relates chiefly to the business and planting affairs of Major Peter Hairston (1752–1832), Ruth Stovall Hairston, and Peter Wilson Hairston (1819–86).

Heyward Family Papers Addition, 1802 (Typescript). 2 items. Two tracts on the water culture of rice by Nathaniel Heyward of South Carolina.

Heyward–Ferguson Papers and Books, 1806–1923 (Microfilm copy). 216 items, including 10 volumes. Primarily the plantation books and letters of James B. Heyward, wealthy South Carolina rice planter and son of Nathaniel Heyward.

Heyward–Ferguson Papers Addition, 1810–40 (Typescript). 4 items. One item is a letter from Thomas Pinckney to John Champneys, President of the Agricultural Society of South Carolina, describing an experiment in the water culture of rice conducted by Pinckney in 1810.

Franklin A. Hudson Diary, 1852-59. 7 volumes. Diary of Franklin Hudson, proprietor of "Blythewood" plantation located on Bayou Goula in Iberville Parish, Louisiana.

Alexander James Lawton Diary, 1810–40. 2 volumes. Record of planting operations conducted on Black Swamp in Beaufort District, South Carolina, by a small rice planter.

Francis Terry Leak Diary, 1839–62. 5 volumes. Plantation record and accounts of Colonel Francis Terry Leak, a progressive Mississippi cotton planter.

Andrew McCollam Papers, 1795–1935. 2,835 items, including 15 volumes. Papers and books of the wealthy McCollam family of Louisiana. Contains data relating to two sugar plantations operated by Andrew McCollam during the two decades preceding the Civil War.

Manigault Plantation Records, 1833–87. 5 volumes. Detailed records relating to the Savannah River rice plantations of Charles and Louis Manigault.

S. M. Meek Book, 1835–58 (Microfilm copy). 1 volume. Journal of S. M. Meek, Jr., a lawyer from Columbus, Mississippi.

Mount Airy Plantation Books, 1805–60 (Microfilm copy). 3 volumes. Records of a large grain estate located in Richmond County, Virginia, and owned by the Tayloe family.

Captain John Nevitt Journal, 1826–32. 1 volume. Journal of Nevitt's "Clermont" cotton plantation located in Adams County, Mississippi. Plantation characterized by a fantastic turnover in overseers during this period.

Newstead Plantation Diary, 1857–82 (Microfilm copy). 1 volume. Record of operations on a Washington County, Mississippi, cotton plantation owned by F. A. Metcalfe.

John Perkins Papers, 1822–85. 550 items. Papers of John Perkins, Jr., prominent Louisiana lawyer, officeholder, and cotton planter. Contains data on the management of Perkins' vast Somerset estate located in northeastern Louisiana.

Pierre Phanor Prudhomme Records and Papers, 1804–1940. 19 folders and 26 volumes. Plantation books and papers of Pierre Phanor Prudhomme, prosperous cotton planter of Ile Brevelle, Natchitoches Parish, Louisiana.

Quitman Papers, 1784–1913. 2,362 items, including 62 volumes. Papers and correspondence relating to the prominent Quitman family of Mississippi.

Edmund Ruffin Papers and Books, 1823–93. 1,400 items, including 6 volumes. Collection includes scattered material relating to the farming operations of the famous Virginia agricultural reformer and two of his sons, Edmund, Jr., and Julian C. Ruffin. It also includes a series of fifty letters from James H. Hammond to Ruffin, in which the former bares his critical attitude toward overseers.

Edmund Ruffin, Jr., Plantation Diary, 1851–73. 1 volume. Diary gives details of farming operations at "Beechwood" plantation in Prince George County, Virginia, during period 1851–62 and at "Marlbourne" plantation in Hanover County, Virginia, during the years 1866–73.

William Henry Sims Diary and Papers, 1857–65 (Microfilm copy). 3 items. One item contains Mrs. Serena Upson's instructions to the overseer of her Mississippi cotton plantation in 1857.

Josiah Smith, Jr., Lettercopy Book, 1771–84. 1 volume. Copies of letters written by Smith, a Charleston merchant and agent for English landowner George Austin. A number of the letters relate to the management of two absentee rice plantations owned by Austin and located near Charleston, South Carolina.

William Ruffin Smith Papers, 1772–1886. 68 items, including 4 volumes. Collection includes a series of letters from Howell Adams, overseer of a small absentee cotton plantation in Lowndes County, Mississippi, to Smith, who was acting as executor of the estate of Charles Shields, a former resident of Scotland Neck, North Carolina.

William E. Sparkman Plantation Record, 1844–66. 1 volume. Plantation record book of William Sparkman, proprietor of two rice plantations located on Black River in Georgetown District, South Carolina.

Sparkman Family Papers, 1811–1904. 300 items, including 9 volumes. Primarily the papers of James R. Sparkman, a prominent physician and rice planter of Georgetown District, South Carolina.

Francis Taylor Diary, 1786–99 (Typescript). 1 volume. Diary of Francis Taylor of Orange County, Virginia. Includes observations on the management of Taylor's small "Midland" plantation.

Lewis Thompson Papers, 1717–1894. 2,800 items, including 8 volumes. Principally the business, legal, and personal papers of Lewis Thompson (1808–67), a native of Bertie County, North Carolina. Collection contains scattered data on Thompson's farming operations in North Carolina and detailed information relating to the management of his absentee sugar plantation in Rapides Parish, Louisiana.

Henry Clay Warmoth Papers and Books, 1798–1931. 120 folders and 82 volumes. Includes journals of "Magnolia" plantation, a large Plaquemines Parish sugar estate owned by Effingham Lawrence. The "Magnolia" journal runs from October, 1856, to January, 1863, and contains one of the most complete accounts in existence of plantation operations in the Old South.

Westover Plantation Journal, 1858–64 (Microfilm copy). 1 volume. Journal of the famous Westover estate, located on the James River about twenty miles east of Richmond, Virginia. John A. Selden, the proprietor during the period covered by the journal, did not utilize an overseer.

Maunsel White Papers and Books, 1802–1912. 91 items, including 10 volumes. Business correspondence, family letters, and plantation records of Maunsel White (1783–1863) and his son, Maunsell White, Jr. Collection contains extensive information on the elder White's "Deer Range" sugar plantation and on several absentee cotton plantations located in Plaquemines and Pointe Coupee parishes, Louisiana

White Hill Plantation Books, 1817–60 (Microfilm copy). 6 volumes. Journal of agricultural operations on Charles Friend's "White Hill" plantation located two miles east of Petersburg in Prince George County, Virginia.

Charles Whitmore Diary, 1834–64 (Microfilm copy). 1 volume. Plantation diary of the owner of a small cotton plantation located near Natchez, Mississippi.

Wilkins Papers, 1782–1864. 204 items, including 8 volumes. Letters, plantation records, and accounts of the Wilkins family of Brunswick County, Virginia, and Northampton County, North Carolina. Bulk of agricultural data concerns the Northampton County farming operations of Edmund Wilkins (1796–1867).

John Sherman Woodcock Account Book, 1787–1809. 1 volume. Accounts of John Sherman Woodcock of Frederick County, Virginia, relating to his affairs in the northern neck of Virginia as planter, lawyer, guardian of orphans, executor of estates, and attorney for prominent persons of the area.

Wyche-Otey Papers, 1824–1936. 32 folders and 27 volumes. Correspondence relating to the Otey family of Meridianville, Alabama. Contains series of letters from the overseers of William M. Otey's absentee cotton plantation in Yazoo County, Mississippi.

B MANUSCRIPT CENSUS RETURNS (Eighth Census of the United States, 1860, in National Archives, Washington, D.C.)

Ascension Parish, Louisiana, Schedule 1 (Vol. I), Schedule 2 (Vol. I).

Beaufort District, South Carolina, Schedule 1 (Vol. II), Schedule 2 (Vol. II).

Charleston District, South Carolina, Schedule 1 (Vol. II), Schedule 2 (Vol. II).

Colleton District, South Carolina, Schedule 1 (Vol. III), Schedule 2 (Vol. III).

Georgetown District, South Carolina, Schedule 1 (Vol. IV), Schedule 2 (Vol. IV).

Glynn County, Georgia, Schedule 1 (Vol. VII), Schedule 2 (Vol. III).

Hinds County, Mississippi, Schedule 1 (Vol. III), Schedule 2 (Vol. II).

Lowndes County, Mississippi, Schedule 1 (Vol. V), Schedule 2 (Vol. III).

Natchitoches Parish, Louisiana, Schedule 1 (Vol. IV), Schedule 2 (Vol. III).
Northampton County, North Carolina, Schedule 1 (Vol. XII), Schedule 2 (Vol. III).
Plaquemines Parish, Louisiana, Schedule 1 (Vol. IV), Schedule 2 (Vol. III).
Prince George County, Virginia, Schedule 1 (Vol. XXII), Schedule 2 (Vol. VI).
Richmond County, Virginia, Schedule 1 (Vol. XXIII), Schedule 2 (Vol. VI).
St. Mary Parish, Louisiana, Schedule 1 (Vol. X), Schedule 2 (Vol. IV).
Stokes County, North Carolina, Schedule 1 (Vol. XV), Schedule 2 (Vol. IV).
Terrebonne Parish, Louisiana, Schedule 1 (Vol. X), Schedule 2 (Vol. IV).
Yazoo County, Mississippi, Schedule 1 (Vol. IX), Schedule 2 (Vol. V).

C GOVERNMENT DOCUMENTS

United States Bureau of the Census. *Heads of Families at the First Census of the United States Taken in the Year 1790: South Carolina.* Washington: The Government Printing Office, 1908.
United States Census Office. *Compendium . . . of the Sixth Census of the United States: 1840.* Washington: Thomas Allen, 1841.
United States Census Office. *Seventh Census of the United States: 1850.* Washington: Robert Armstrong, 1853.
United States Census Office. *Eighth Census of the United States: 1860. Agriculture.* Washington: The Government Printing Office, 1864.
United States Census Office. *Eighth Census of the United States: 1860. Population.* Washington: The Government Printing Office, 1864.

D NEWSPAPERS AND AGRICULTURAL PERIODICALS

American Agriculturist. 50 volumes. New York, 1842–91.
American Cotton Planter. 9 volumes. Montgomery, Ala., 1853–61. Combined with the *Soil of the South*, 1857–61.
American Farmer. 78 volumes. Baltimore, Washington, 1819–97.
Columbus (Miss.) *Democrat*, 1834–57.
De Bow's Review. 43 volumes. New Orleans, 1846–80.
Farmers' Register. 11 volumes. Shellbanks, Petersburg, Va., 1833–43.
Kosciusko (Miss.) *Chronicle*, 1850–66.
Mississippi Democrat, 1858–61. (Columbus, Miss.).
Southern Agriculturist. 19 volumes. Charleston, S. C., 1828–46.
Southern Cultivator. 93 volumes. Augusta, Athens, Atlanta, 1843–1935.
Southern Planter. 100 volumes. Richmond, 1841–1939.

E PUBLISHED JOURNALS AND LETTERS, COLLECTED SOURCES

Aime, Valcour. *Plantation Diary of the Late Mr. Valcour Aime, Formerly Proprietor of the Plantation Known as the St. James Sugar Refinery.* New Orleans: Clark and Hofeline, 1878.

Bassett, John Spencer. *The Southern Plantation Overseer as Revealed in His Letters*. Northampton, Mass.: Southworth Press, 1925.

Carroll, Bartholomew Rivers (ed.). *Historical Collections of South Carolina*. 2 vols. New York: Harper and Brothers, 1836.

Conway, Moncure Daniel (ed.). *George Washington and Mount Vernon*. Vol. IV of *Long Island Historical Society Memoirs*. Brooklyn: Long Island Historical Society, 1889.

Cruzat, Heloise H. (trans.). "Agreement Between Louis Cezard (Cesaire) Le Breton, and Jean Baptiste Goudeau as Overseer on His Plantation, 1744," *Louisiana Historical Quarterly*, IX (October, 1926), 590–92.

Davenport, Francis Garvin (ed.). "Judge Sharkey Papers," *Mississippi Valley Historical Review*, XX (June, 1933), 76–77.

Davis, Edwin Adams. *Plantation Life in the Florida Parishes of Louisiana, 1836–1846, as Reflected in the Diary of Bennet H. Barrow*. New York: Columbia University Press, 1943.

Easterby, James Harold (ed.). *The South Carolina Rice Plantation as Revealed in the Papers of Robert F. W. Allston*. Chicago: University of Chicago Press, 1945.

Flugel, Felix (ed.). "Pages from a Journal of a Voyage Down the Mississippi to New Orleans in 1817," *Louisiana Historical Quarterly*, VII (July, 1924), 414–40.

Griffith, Lucille (ed.). "The Plantation Record Book of Brookdale Farm, Amite County, 1856–57," *Journal of Mississippi History*, VII (January, 1945), 23–31.

House, Albert Virgil (ed.). *Planter Management and Capitalism in Ante-Bellum Georgia: The Journal of Hugh Fraser Grant, Ricegrower*. New York: Columbia University Press, 1954.

"Izard–Laurens Correspondence," *South Carolina Historical and Genealogical Magazine*, XXII (January, April, July, 1921), 1–11, 39–52, 73–88.

Marshall, Theodora Britton, and Gladys Crail Evans (eds.). "Plantation Report from the Papers of Levin R. Marshall, of 'Richmond,' Natchez, Mississippi," *Journal of Mississippi History*, III (January, 1941), 45–55.

Moore, John Hebron (ed.). "Two Documents Relating to Plantation Overseers of the Vicksburg Region, 1831–1832," *Journal of Mississippi History*, XVI (January, 1954), 31–36.

Phillips, Ulrich Bonnell (ed.). *Plantation and Frontier, 1649–1863*. Cleveland: The Arthur H. Clark Company, 1909. Volumes I and II of John R. Commons, *et al.* (eds.). *A Documentary History of American Industrial Society*. 11 vols.

Riley, Franklin Lafayette. "Diary of a Mississippi Planter, January 1, 1840 to April, 1863," in Franklin L. Riley (ed.), *Publications of the Mississippi Historical Society*, Oxford, Miss., 1909. X, 305–481.

F   TRAVEL ACCOUNTS, MEMOIRS

Cuming, Fortescue. *Sketches of a Tour to the Western Country, 1807–1809*. Cleveland: The Arthur H. Clark Company, 1904. Volume IV of Reuben Gold Thwaites (ed.). *Early Western Travels, 1748–1846*. 32 vols.

Fulkerson, Horace Smith. *Random Recollections of Early Days in Mississippi.* Vicksburg: Vicksburg Printing and Publishing Company, 1885.

Hall, Basil. *Travels in North America, in the Years 1827 and 1828.* 3 vols. 3rd ed. Edinburgh: Printed for Robert Cadell, 1830.

Ingraham, Joseph Holt. *The Southwest.* 2 vols. New York: Harper and Brothers, 1835.

Kemble, Frances Anne. *Journal of a Residence on a Georgian Plantation in 1838-1839.* London: Longman, Green, Longman, Roberts, and Green, 1863.

Olmsted, Frederick Law. *A Journey in the Back Country.* New York: Mason Brothers, 1860.

Olmsted, Frederick Law. *A Journey in the Seaboard Slave States.* 2 vols. New York: G. P. Putnam's Sons, 1904.

Reagan, John Henninger. *Memoirs, With Special Reference to Secession and the Civil War.* Ed. Walter Flavius McCaleb. New York: The Neale Publishing Company, 1906.

Russell, William Howard. *My Diary North and South.* Boston: T. O. H. P. Burnham, 1863.

Van Buren, A. De Puy. *Jottings of a Year's Sojourn in the South.* Battle Creek, Mich.: Review and Herald Print, 1859.

G MISCELLANEOUS WORKS

Champomier, Pierre A. *Statement of the Sugar Crop Made in Louisiana, 1844-1861.* New Orleans: Cook, Young and Company, 1845-62.

Cotton Plantation Record and Account Book. 7th ed. New Orleans: B. M. Norman, 1857.

Plantation and Farm Instruction, Regulation, Record, Inventory and Account Book. Richmond: J. W. Randolph, 1852.

Taylor, John of Caroline. *Arator; Being a Series of Agricultural Essays, Practical and Political.* 3rd ed. Baltimore: J. Robinson, 1817.

II SECONDARY SOURCES

A MONOGRAPHS AND SPECIAL STUDIES

Aptheker, Herbert. *American Negro Slave Revolts.* New York: Columbia University Press, 1943.

Bridenbaugh, Carl. *Myths and Realities: Societies of the Colonial South.* Baton Rouge: Louisiana State University Press, 1952.

Carroll, Thomas Battle. *Historical Sketches of Oktibbeha County (Mississippi).* Gulfport, Miss.: The Dixie Press, 1931.

Cathey, Cornelius Oliver. *Agricultural Developments in North Carolina, 1783-1860.* Chapel Hill: University of North Carolina Press, 1956.

Coulter, Ellis Merton. *Thomas Spalding of Sapelo.* Baton Rouge: Louisiana State University Press, 1940.

Craven, Avery Odelle. *Edmund Ruffin Southerner: A Study in Secession.* New York: D. Appleton and Company, 1932.

————. *The Growth of Southern Nationalism, 1848-1861.* Baton Rouge: Louisiana State University Press, 1953.

Dangerfield, George. *The Era of Good Feelings*. New York: Harcourt, 1952.

Davis, Charles Shepard. *The Cotton Kingdom in Alabama*. Montgomery: Alabama State Department of Archives and History, 1939.

Doar, David. "Rice and Rice Planting in the South Carolina Low Country," in E. Milby Burton (ed.), *Contributions from the Charleston Museum*, No. 8. Charleston: Charleston Museum, 1936, pp. 7–42.

Eaton, Clement. *The Mind of the Old South*. Baton Rouge: Louisiana State University Press, 1964.

Flanders, Ralph Betts. *Plantation Slavery in Georgia*. Chapel Hill: University of North Carolina Press, 1933.

Gates, Paul Wallace. *The Farmer's Age: Agriculture, 1815–1860*. New York: Holt, Rinehart and Winston, 1960.

Genovese, Eugene D. *The Political Economy of Slavery: Studies in the Economy and Society of the Slave South*. New York: Pantheon Books, 1965.

Gray, Lewis Cecil. *History of Agriculture in the Southern United States to 1860*. 2 vols. Washington: Carnegie Institution of Washington, 1933.

James, Marquis. *The Life of Andrew Jackson*. 2 vols. New York: The Bobbs-Merrill Company, 1937.

Jordan, Weymouth T. *Hugh Davis and His Alabama Plantation*. University, Ala.: University of Alabama Press, 1948.

Mooney, Chase C. *Slavery in Tennessee*. Bloomington: University of Indiana Press, 1957.

Moore, John Hebron. *Agriculture in Ante-Bellum Mississippi*. New York: Bookman Associates, 1958.

Owsley, Frank Lawrence. *Plain Folk of the Old South*. Baton Rouge: Louisiana State University Press, 1949.

Phillips, Ulrich Bonnell. *American Negro Slavery*. New York: D. Appleton and Company, 1918.

————. *Life and Labor in the Old South*. Boston: Little, Brown, 1929.

Postell, William Dosite. *The Health of Slaves on Southern Plantations*. Baton Rouge: Louisiana State University Press, 1951.

"Reagan, John Henninger," in Allen Johnson and Dumas Malone (eds.), Dictionary of American Biography. 21 vols. New York: Charles Scribner's Sons, 1928–37. XV, 432–34.

Roland, Charles P. *Louisiana Sugar Plantations During the American Civil War*. Leiden: E. J. Brill, 1957.

Salley, Alexander Samuel, Jr. "The Introduction of Rice Culture into South Carolina," *Bulletins of the Historical Commission of South Carolina*, No. 6. Columbia: The State Company, 1919.

Sellers, James Benson. *Slavery in Alabama*. University, Ala.: University of Alabama Press, 1950.

Shugg, Roger Wallace. *Origins of Class Struggle in Louisiana: A Social History of White Farmers and Laborers During Slavery and After, 1840–1875*. Baton Rouge: Louisiana State University Press, 1939.

Sitterson, Joseph Carlyle. "Lewis Thompson, A Carolinian and His Louisiana Plantation, 1848–1888: A Study in Absentee Ownership," Chapter 2 in Fletcher M. Green (ed.), *Essays in Southern History*. Chapel Hill: University of North Carolina Press, 1949.

————. *Sugar Country: The Cane Sugar Industry in the South, 1753–1950.* Lexington: University of Kentucky Press, 1953.

Smith, Abbot Emerson. *Colonists in Bondage: White Servitude and Convict Labor in America, 1607–1776.* Chapel Hill: University of North Carolina Press, 1947.

Stampp, Kenneth Milton. *The Peculiar Institution: Slavery in the Ante-Bellum South.* New York: Alfred A. Knopf, 1956.

Sydnor, Charles Sackett. *The Development of Southern Sectionalism, 1819–1848.* Baton Rouge: Louisiana State University Press, 1948.

————. *A Gentleman of the Old Natchez Region: Benjamin L. C. Wailes.* Durham: Duke University Press, 1938.

————. *Slavery in Mississippi.* New York: D. Appleton-Century Company, 1933.

Taylor, Joe Gray. *Negro Slavery in Louisiana.* Baton Rouge: Louisiana Historical Association, 1963.

Taylor, Orville Walters. *Negro Slavery in Arkansas.* Durham: Duke University Press, 1958.

Wertenbaker, Thomas Jefferson. *Patrician and Plebeian in Virginia.* Charlottesville: The Michie Company, 1910.

Wiley, Bell Irvin. *Southern Negroes, 1861–1865.* New Haven: Yale University Press, 1938.

Wooster, Ralph Ancil. *The Secession Conventions of the South.* Princeton: Princeton University Press, 1962.

B PERIODICAL ARTICLES

Anderson, John Q. "Dr. James Green Carson, Ante-Bellum Planter of Mississippi and Louisiana," *Journal of Mississippi History,* XVIII (October, 1956), 243–67.

Bonner, James Calvin. "The Plantation Overseer and Southern Nationalism as Revealed in the Career of Garland D. Harmon," *Agricultural History,* XIX (January, 1945), 1–11.

Calhoun, Robert Dabney. "The John Perkins Family of Northeast Louisiana," *Louisiana Historical Quarterly,* XIX (January, 1936), 70–88.

Craven, Avery Odelle. "Poor Whites and Negroes in the Ante-Bellum South," *Journal of Negro History,* XV (January, 1930), 14–25.

Genovese, Eugene D. "The Significance of the Slave Plantation for Southern Economic Development," *Journal of Southern History,* XXVIII (November, 1962), 422–37.

Kendall, Lane Carter. "John McDonogh—Slave Owner," *Louisiana Historical Quarterly,* XV (October, 1932), 646–54; XVI (January, 1933), 125–134.

Lander, Ernest McPherson, Jr. "Ante-Bellum Milling in South Carolina," *South Carolina Historical and Genealogical Magazine,* LII (1951), 125–32.

Magoffin, Dorothy Seay. "A Georgia Planter and His Plantations, 1837–1861," *North Carolina Historical Review,* XV (October, 1938), 354–77.

Moody, V. Alton. "Slavery on Louisiana Sugar Plantations," *Louisiana Historical Quarterly,* VII (April, 1924), 191–301.

Murphree, Dennis. "Hurricane and Brierfield, the Davis Plantations," *Journal of Mississippi History*, IX (April, 1947), 98–107.

Phillips, Ulrich Bonnell. "The Central Theme of Southern History," *American Historical Review*, XXXIV (October, 1928), 30–43.

Postell, Paul Everett. "John Hampden Randolph, A Louisiana Planter," *Louisiana Historical Quarterly*, XXV (January, 1942), 149–223.

Scarborough, William Kauffman. "The Southern Plantation Overseer: A Re-evaluation," *Agricultural History*, XXXVIII (January, 1964), 13–20.

Seal, Albert Garrel. "John Carmichael Jenkins—Scientific Planter of the Natchez District," *Journal of Mississippi History*, I (January, 1939), 14–28.

Sitterson, Joseph Carlyle. "Hired Labor on Sugar Plantations of the Ante-Bellum South," *Journal of Southern History*, XIV (May, 1948), 192–205.

―――――. "The McCollams: A Planter Family of the Old and New South," *Journal of Southern History*, VI (August, 1940), 347–67.

―――――. "Magnolia Plantation, 1852–1862: A Decade of a Louisiana Sugar Estate," *Mississippi Valley Historical Review*, XXV (September, 1938), 197–210.

―――――. "The William J. Minor Plantations: A Study in Ante-Bellum Absentee Ownership," *Journal of Southern History*, IX (February, 1943), 59–74.

Stahl, Annie Lee West. "The Free Negro in Ante-Bellum Louisiana," *Louisiana Historical Quarterly*, XXV (April, 1942), 301–96.

Stephenson, Wendell Holmes. "A Quarter-Century of a Mississippi Plantation: Eli J. Capell of 'Pleasant Hill,'" *Mississippi Valley Historical Review*, XXIII (December, 1936), 355–74.

Taylor, Paul S. "Plantation Laborer Before the Civil War," *Agricultural History*, XXVIII (January, 1954), 1–21.

Warren, Harris Gaylord. "People and Occupations in Port Gibson, 1860," *Journal of Mississippi History*, X (April, 1948), 104–15.

―――――. "Population Elements of Claiborne County, 1820–1860," *Journal of Mississippi History*, IX (April, 1947), 75–87.

White, Alice Pemble. "The Plantation Experience of Joseph and Lavinia Erwin, 1807–1836," *Louisiana Historical Quarterly*, XXVII (April, 1944), 343–478.

C UNPUBLISHED DOCTORAL DISSERTATIONS

Bonner, James Calvin. "Agricultural Reform in the Georgia Piedmont, 1820–1860." Unpublished Ph.D. dissertation, University of North Carolina, 1943.

Wall, Bennett Harrison. "Ebenezer Pettigrew, An Economic Study of an Ante-Bellum Planter." Unpublished Ph.D. dissertation, University of North Carolina, 1946.

Wooster, Ralph Ancil. "The Secession Conventions of the Lower South: A Study of Their Membership." Unpublished Ph.D. dissertation, University of Texas, 1954.

Index

Absentee estates: overseer wages on, 27, 31; overseer tenure on, 39–40, 183; in Terrebonne Parish, La., 61; status of overseers on, 72–74, 199; miscegenation on, 75–76, 167; overseer brutality on, 95, 97; owners of, inquire about overseer conduct, 119–20; staple production emphasized by owners of, 123; responsibilities of stewards on, 179

Acklen, Joseph A. S., planter, 77, 104

Adams, John Quincy, 129

Adams, Nathaniel B., overseer, 58

Adams, Sterling, steward, 56, 183

Affleck, Thomas, agricultural reformer, 70, 72, 123

Agricultural education: as means of elevating overseer class, 130, 134

Agricultural implements: invented by overseers, 159; manufactured in South, 175–76

Agricultural periodicals: dissemination of, to overseers, 135–36; G. D. Harmon's contributions to, 174

Agricultural proprietors. *See* Planters

Agricultural reformers: criticize overseers, 6; oppose bonus agreements, 30; activities of, 49, 173–77 *passim;* oppose concentration on staple production, 123

Agricultural societies: in South Carolina, 44, 105, 122, 134, 169; in Alabama, 78, 134; in Virginia, 129; in Georgia, 173

Aiken, William, planter, 29, 164
Alabama: number of large slaveholders in, 11–12; median slaveholdings in, 12; hired slaves in, 35; agricultural societies in, 78, 134; cruelty toward slaves in, 96; impact of Civil War on plantation system in, 147, 149; management of Cocke family holdings in, 181, 191–93
Albemarle County (Va.) Agricultural Society of, 129
Allen, James, planter, 143, 146
Allston, Benjamin, planter, 141, 163, 164
Allston, Robert Francis Withers, planter: praises overseers, 22, 163; slave discipline on plantations of, 98, 121; leaves legacies for overseers, 115; seeks exemption for overseer, 140–41; mentioned, 12, 41, 159, 164
Amelia County, Va., 152
American Agriculturist, 122
American Cotton Planter, 117, 127, 128, 174
American Farmer, 136
Amite County, Miss., 17, 116
Anderson, Alexander J., overseer, 58
Anderson, John J., overseer, 58
Andrew, Negro driver: eulogized by overseer, 83
Arkansas: lynching of Negro in, 100; mentioned, 25, 27, 31, 112
Ascension Parish, La.: visited by W. H. Russell, 8, 79, 171; median slaveholdings in, 12, 52; sugar production in, 53; analysis of overseers in, 59–61; mentioned, 28
Assistant overseers. *See* Suboverseers
Austin, George, planter, 89
Avant, Daniel P., overseer, 98
Avery, Daniel Dudley, planter, 48, 157
Avery, Dudley, planter: seeks exemption for overseer, 141–42

Bachemin, R., overseer and sugar maker, 41
Backland plantation, 95
Baggs, Milton, Jr., planter, 125–26
Bailey, Jordan, overseer, 34
Ball, John, Jr., planter, 85, 114
Barbour, James, planter: defends overseers, 129
Barbour County (Ala.) Agricultural Society of, 78, 134
Barnes, J. J., overseer, 107
Barrow, Bennet H., planter: castigates

overseers, 16, 106; on Negroes, 18; uses dogs to track runaways, 92; dresses slave offender in women's clothes, 93
Barrow, R. R., planter: plantation journal of, 14, 83; engages overseer on trial, 24; slave mortality rate on plantations of, 85; fines overseer for striking slave, 96; and conflict with steward, 187–90; total estate of, 187
Barwick, Stancil, overseer, 97
Bateman, W. W., overseer: large estate of, 61, 172; career of, 171–72, 224–25n55
Bayou Congo, La., 149
Bayou Lafourche, La.: impact of Civil War upon, 149, 152, 156; mentioned, 24
Bayside plantation, 81, 147
Beale, Billy, steward, 181
Beaufort District, S. C.: rice production in, 53; analysis of overseers in, 57–58; mentioned, 17
Beaver Bend plantation, 5
Beech Island Farmers' Club of South Carolina, 122
Beechwood plantation, 150, 152, 160
Belflowers, Jesse, overseer: left legacy by employer, 115; career of, 163–64
Belgrade plantation, 19, 43
Belmead plantation, 182
Bennett, John W., overseer, 124
Bermuda plantation, 28, 144, 149–50
Bernard, J. H., planter, 17
Berry, John, overseer, 24
Black Belt: in Alabama, 5, 35
Blythewood plantation, 156
Boineau, Michael, overseer, 34
Bolling, Robert B., planter: Sandy Point estate of, 161–62
Bolling, William, planter, 125
Bonarva plantation, 43
Bond, Joseph, planter, 113, 136
Bonneau's Ferry plantation, 34
Bonus agreements: with overseers, 30–31
Botts, C. T., editor, 33
Bowdoin, John T., planter, 191
Bracewell, James N., overseer, 119
Bremo estate, 29, 32
Brickell, D. Warren, physician, 86–87
Brinley, T. C., plowmaker, 175
Brookdale plantation, 116
Brown, Lucius, overseer: slays former employer, 113

Brown, Preston, overseer: urged to seek legislative seat, 50
Brown, Stephen, overseer, 89
Brunswick County, Va., 169, 182, 183, 191, 192
Bryan County, Ga., 13
Buckingham County, Va., 21
Burke County, Ga., 103
Burnlea plantation: overseer of, assassinated, 113–14
Burnside, John, planter, 8, 61, 76
Burnsville, Ala., 117, 131
Bustian, Little, overseer, 108–109
Butler, John, planter, 166, 169
Butler, Major Pierce, planter: founds Georgia estate
Butler, Pierce Mease, planter, 38, 166
Butler, William, planter: on rice culture, 81
Butler's Island plantation: Fanny Kemble visits, 38; miscegenation on, 76; management of, 166–69
Butler Springs, Ala.: as summer resort, 48
Butterfield, R., physician: on overseer wages, 123; on overseer responsibilities, 128; on improvement of overseer class, 135

Caillou Grove plantation, 187
Cain, Elisha, overseer: career of, 172–73
Calhoun, John A., planter: on overseer attitude toward slaves, 78; on evils of overseer system, 134
Campbell County, Ga., 174
Camp Branch plantation, 31, 159
Capell, Eli J., planter, 17
Capers, William, overseer: whips runaway, 92; career of, 164–66
Carolina Planter, 44
Carpenters: become overseers, 22, 24, 42, 143; wages of, 36; mentioned, 38
Carrol, Jackson, overseer, 23
Carter, Hill, planter: on slave management, 75; on need for harmony between planter and overseer, 102; on obedience of overseer to planter, 117
Carter, J. Walter, overseer, 80, 191, 193
Carter, Landon, planter, 181
Carter, Lewis, overseer, 95, 96
Carter, Robert, planter: pays in crop shares, 31; accused of interfering with slaves, 120–21

Champion, overseer for Martin W. Philips, 109
Chapman, Ewing, overseer, 143, 148
Charles City County, Va., 161
Charleston, S. C., 89, 165, 169
Charleston District, S. C.: rice production in, 53; analysis of overseers in, 57–58
Chicora Wood plantation, 163, 218n81
Chisolm, A. R., planter, 58
Cholera: among slaves, 84, 85, 86
Christmas, Dick, planter: feuds with neighboring overseer, 113–14
Civil War: misbehavior of overseers during, 113, 148; docility of slaves during, 138; impact of, upon plantation system, 138–39, 143, 146–57 passim; shortage of overseers during, 139, 142–43; exemption of overseers during, 139–42, 144; patriotism of overseers during, 144–46, 174, 176; requisition of slaves during, 146–47; Negro insubordination during, 150, 152–55; shortage of liquid capital during, 156
Claiborne County, Miss., 159
Clarendon District, S. C., 142
Clark, Charles, planter: limits slave punishments, 93
Clark, Stephen F., overseer, 25
Clary, overseer for F. A. Metcalfe, 142
Clement, M. W., overseer: serves as tax collector, 49
Clermont plantation, 38
Cloud, Noah B., agricultural reformer, 123
Cobb County, Ga., 174
Cocke, John Hartwell, planter: pays in crop shares, 32; on slave management, 74, 82; stewardship of R. D. Powell on plantations of, 80, 191, 193; patriotism of overseers for, 144; impact of Civil War on plantations of, 147, 149; conflict between steward and overseer on plantation of, 190–91; as benefactor of steward's son, 192; mentioned, 29, 179, 181
Cocke, Philip St. George, planter: and relations with steward R. D. Powell, 179, 181, 191; promotes overseer to post as steward, 182; tenure of stewards on plantations of, 183; death of, 193
Cocke, Philip St. George, Jr., planter, 193
Coleman, Daniel, overseer, 105, 133
Colhoun, John Ewing, planter, 23, 32, 34, 112

Colleton District, S. C.: former overseer elected sheriff of, 49; rice production in, 53; analysis of overseers in, 57–58; volunteer company organized in, 144; mentioned, 12, 44
Columbia, S. C., 131, 134
Columbia *South Carolinian*, 33, 128
Columbus, Miss., 100, 181, 191, 193
Comingtee plantation: infant mortality rate on, 85
Commission merchant. *See* Factor
Concordia Parish, La.: median slaveholdings in, 12; cholera epidemic in, 86; inquest into slave death in, 98–99; misbehavior of overseers in, during Civil War, 156
Concord plantation, 119
Confederacy: posts in held by John H. Reagan, 50; exemption of overseers by, 139–42; prayer for success of, 145; requisition of slaves by, 146–47
Confederate Conscription Act, 139–40
Conscription: of overseers, opposed by planters, 139–42, 201; payment of substitutes to avoid, 142
Cook, Elijah, overseer, 49
Cook, William H., overseer, 122, 135
Cooleemee Hill plantation, 28, 148
Cooper, G. T., overseer, 14
Cooper River, S. C., 163, 169
Coopers: wages of, 36; become overseers, 42
Copenhagen plantation, 85
Corbin, Richard, planter, 183–85
Cotton: plantations, number of, 10; culture, 16, 80; reputation of overseer based on production of, 30, 121–23, 134; volume of production, 53; planter emphasis on production of, 71, 116, 121–23, 134, 200; ordered burned, 113, 139, 156; baling of, 179; incentive system for picking, 180
Cotton Plantation Record and Account Book: overseer duties outlined in, 70
Couper, James Hamilton, planter, 27, 49–50, 168, 169
Couper, William Audley, overseer, 27
Covington, Levin, planter, 89
Cowikee Creek, Ala., 135
Crimes: committed by overseers, 45, 95, 99, 113, 149; incidence of, by slaves, 98; committed by slaves, 98, 100–101, 149; legal penalties for, 100; commit-

ted by planters, 113-14. *See also* Murder
Crop shares: payment of overseers by, 26, 31–32; criticism of, 33–34; support for, 34; during Civil War, 156–57; mentioned, 4
Croxton, C., overseer, 32
Cruelty: toward slaves, by overseers, 78–79, 94–97, 112, 121
Cumbea, Major W., overseer, 48
Cuming, Fortescue, English traveler: criticizes overseers, 7
Curry, John H., overseer, 21

Dabney, Thomas S., planter, 159
Daley, Robert B., carpenter and overseer, 24
Daniel, John M., editor, 136
Davenport, Doctrine W., overseer, 35, 84, 88
Davidson County, N. C., 159
Davie County, N. C., 28, 148
Davis, Hugh, planter, 5, 39, 108, 124
Davis, Jefferson: use of slave foremen by, 18; favors agricultural schools, 134; proclamation by, 145
Deas, David, planter, 169
De Bow's Review, 116
Decker, T. J., overseer, 153–54
Deer Range plantation: suboverseers on, 13; overseer tenure on, 40; slave discipline on, 88; compassionate treatment accorded overseers of, 114; mentioned, 24, 41, 157
Delaplane, Joseph, overseer: invents plow, 159
Dent, John H., planter, 122, 135
Diseases: among slaves, 71, 84–87
Dismukes, Isaac H., overseer, 112
Dogs: use of, in tracking runaways, 91–92, 215*n*95
Dogue Run farm, 107
Donaldsonville, La., 152, 190
Drivers: used as foremen, 16–18; limits of authority, 18; duties of, 69, 81, 173; relations with overseers, 82–84, 165, 168; administer whippings, 93–94; defied by slaves, 98–99, 165; overseers relegated to status of, 117; punishment of, by stewards, 180; mentioned, 7, 80, 92. *See also* Foremen, Negro
Dunbar, Olivia, planter, 45

East Hermitage plantation, 25, 92, 164–66

Edgefield District, S. C., 136
Elizafield plantation, 42
Ellendale plantation, 91
Ellis, Gabriel L., overseer, 12–13, 121
Ellis County, Texas, 140
England: bailiffs in, 3; status of overseers and stewards in, 132
Erwin, Lavinia, planter, 85
Etheredge, William G., overseer, 96
Evans, Holden, Jr., overseer and farmer, 43
Eve, William J., planter, 122
Evelynton plantation, 150, 152

Factor, 28, 73
Farmers. See Yeoman farmers
Farmers' Register, 21, 34, 160, 161
Farragut, David G.: campaign against New Orleans by, 146, 147
Farran, overseer for John B. Grimball, 32
Farrar, William B., overseer, 46
Fausse River [False River], La., 42
Fayer, John D., overseer: son of physician, 61
Federal Census: reliability of data in, 52–53; free and slave schedules of, 54; mentioned, 51
Federal Union (Milledgeville, Ga.), 101
Ferguson, Thomas, overseer, steward and planter, 163, 182
Flournoy, H. C., planter, 89
Floyd County, Ga., 173
Fluvanna County, Va., 29, 144
Fly, overseer of Burnlea plantation: assassinated by neighboring planter, 113–14
Flynn, Andrew, planter: instructions to overseers of, 68–70
Fonsylvania plantation, 152
Ford, Robert P., overseer, 83
Foremen, Negro: utilization of, 16–19; praised, 17. See also Drivers
Forest Home plantation, 156
Forkland plantation, 18, 32
Fort Donelson, Tenn.: fall of, 146
Fort Jackson, La., 153
Fort St. Philip, La., 153
Foster, Albert, overseer: recounts shooting of slave, 98–99
Friend, Charles, planter, 48, 148
Friend, Nathaniel, planter, 24
Fulcher, James, overseer, 113

Gadsden, Christopher, planter, 163

"Gang System": as method of organizing slave labor, 80–81
Gavin, David, planter, 44, 109, 111, 144
Geiger, Cornelius, suboverseer, 13
Georgetown District, S. C.: median slaveholdings in, 12; rice production in, 53; analysis of overseers in, 57–58, 65; outstanding overseers in, 163, 164; mentioned, 13, 41, 98, 115
Georgia: number of large slaveholders in, 11–12; overseer wages on rice plantations in, 29; former overseers elevated to political posts in, 49; rice production in, 52, 53; murder of overseer in, 101; scarcity of competent overseers in, 106; number of overseers exempted in, 140; rice planting machine invented in, 159; outstanding overseers in, 166–69, 172–77 passim; overseer-steward wage differential in, 182; superior quality of overseers in, 199
Germany, overseer for Rachel O'Connor, 77, 115
Gibbs, overseer for John Burnside, 8
Giles, John S., overseer, 142
Giles, Johnson G., overseer and steward: wages of, 28; receives premiums scaled to production, 31; long tenure of, 157; career of, 159–60; promoted to steward, 182
Gill, J. E., overseer, 91
Glynn County, Ga.: former overseers elected to political office in, 49; rice production in, 52, 53
Goochland County, Va., 162, 163
Goodloe, A. T., planter: opposes annual changing of overseers, 126–27; defends overseers, 130–31
Gowrie plantation: wages of overseers and suboverseers on, 13; cholera epidemics on, 85; management of, by William Capers, 164–66; mentioned, 14 25
Grace, J. B., overseer, 35
Graham, S. F., overseer, 188
Grant, Hugh Fraser, planter, 42
Grant, Ulysses S.: in Virginia campaign, 152
Gravestock, Thomas, overseer, 23
Gray, Lewis, historian: on incidence of overseer employment, 10; on background of Virginia overseers, 41; on

employment of overseers by large planters, 66

Greeley, Horace, 154

Greene County, Ala.: Cocke plantations in, 80, 144, 190, 193

Green Hill, Tenn., 130

Green Valley plantation: regulations governing, 68–70, 71

Greenville County, Va., 35

Grier, Samuel, overseer, 45

Griffin, H. J. F., overseer, 109, 111

Griffin, John, overseer, 29, 31–32

Grimball, John Berkley, planter, 31, 32, 49

Guendalos plantation, 141

Hains, C. R., overseer, 139

Hairston, John H., planter: complains of overseers in Mississippi, 132–33

Hairston, Peter, planter, 25–26, 31

Hairston, Peter Wilson, planter: purchases substitute for overseer, 142; overseer of, misbehaves during Civil War, 148; mentioned, 28, 31, 157, 159–60

Hairston, Robert, planter, 26, 32

Hairston, Ruth Stovall, planter: contract of, with overseer, 23; rotates overseers, 40; overseer-steward tenure differential on plantations of, 183; mentioned, 56

Hall, Basil, English traveler: lauds overseers, 7

Hall, Thomas, planter and agricultural reformer, 49

Hall, William, planter, 22

Ham, Thomas A., overseer, 12

Hamburg plantation, 85

Hamilton estate, 27, 50, 182

Hammond, James H., planter: on ratio of slaves to overseer, 9; on suboverseers, 14; seeks to dispense with overseers, 16; criticizes overseers, 107; on merits of overseer Andrew Nicol, 161

Hanover County, Va., 150

Hardwick, Richard, agricultural reformer: develops system of horizontal plowing, 174

Harman, John, overseer, 112

Harmon, Garland D., overseer: complains of bedevilment by Negroes, 103; on subordination of overseers to planters, 117–18; complains of low wages, 125; denies overseers to blame for soil exhaustion, 131; urges colleagues to raise standards, 135; career of, 173–77

Harvey, I. E. H., overseer, 89–90

Haynes, William H., suboverseer, 13

Henry County, Va., 31, 159–60

Heriot, F. W., planter, 141

Heyward, James B., planter, 85, 139

Highland plantation, 18

Hinds County, Miss.: cotton production in, 53; analysis of overseers in, 62–63; mentioned, 43-173

Hired slaves. See Slaves

Holland, N. B., overseer, 24, 190

Hollwell, William H., yeoman farmer: applies for overseeing position, 42–43

Hollywood plantation, 143, 148

Homestead plantation, 182

Hopeton plantation, 27, 168, 169

Hopewell plantation: slaves attempt to discredit overseer of, 80, 193; overseer of, joins army, 144, 192; conflict between steward and overseer of, 190–91

Houmas estate, 61, 79

Hubard, Edmund W., planter, 21

Hudson, Franklin A., planter, 92, 112

Hyman, Archibald, overseer, 90

Iberville Parish, La., 85, 92, 112, 156

Indigo, 23, 32

Infant mortality: among slaves, 85

Ireland, John, overseer, 45

Issaquena County, Miss.: median slaveholdings in, 12

Jackson, "Stonewall" (Thomas J.), 174

Jacobs, William, overseer, 99–100

James River: plantations on, 16, 161, 162, 182

Jefferson County, Ga., 89, 172

Jefferson County, Miss., 43, 124

Jehossee Island plantation, 30, 164

Jenkins, John Carmichael, planter and physician: builds overseer house, 38; displays warmth toward overseers, 45, 115

Johnson, Joseph, planter, 75

Johnson, Julius A., overseer and planter, 171

Johnston, Albert Sidney, 146

Joly, F., overseer, 112

Kearney, Joseph P., overseer: rises to planter status, 48; military exemption requested for, 141–42; continues overseeing career after Civil War, 157

Kellett, J., suboverseer, 96

Kemble, Frances Anne, actress: describes overseer house, 38; charges overseer with miscegenation, 75–76; marries Pierce Mease Butler, 166; on overseer Roswell King, Jr., 167–68
Kentucky: median slaveholdings in, 12; mentioned, 60, 94
Killona plantation, 34
King, overseer for John Perkins, Jr.: accused of brutality toward slaves, 95, 96
King, James, planter, 58
King, Roswell, Sr., overseer, 167
King, Roswell, Jr., overseer: charged with miscegenation, 76; career of, 166–69
Knowlton, E. A., steward: and friction with overseers, 24, 190; and conflict with employer, 187–90
Kollock, George Jones, planter, 13, 94, 121
Kosciusko (Miss.) *Chronicle*, 101

Lamar, John B., planter, 87, 97
Lawrence, Effingham, planter: employs suboverseers, 13, 96; comments on slave epidemics, 85; shooting of Negro on plantation of, 96; provides home for retired overseer, 115–16, 171; demoralization of Negroes on plantation of, 153–56; mentioned, 145, 146
Laws: requiring use of overseers, 14, 16; protecting overseers, 100; exempting overseers from military service, 139–40; governing supervision of impressed slaves, 147
Lawton, Alexander James, planter, 17
Leak, Francis Terry, planter, 25, 27, 30–31, 104
Leasing: of plantations, 4, 156–57
Leatherwood plantation, 159
Lee, Daniel, agricultural reformer, 123
Leven, slave foreman: eulogized, 17
Liquor: overseer use of, 109, 112
Locust Grove plantation, 45
Lofton, Stephen, overseer, 144
Log Hall plantation, 109, 118, 175
Londerbough, Morris, carpenter, 36
London *Times*, 8
Louisiana: Negroes introduced into, 3; sugar houses in, 8, 103; number of large slaveholders in, 11–12; median slaveholdings in, 12; laws requiring use of overseers in, 14, 16; Negro overseers in, 19; overseer wages in, 29; hired

slaves in, 35; wages of plantation employees in, 36; French ancestry of overseers in, 42; sugar production in, 52, 53; cotton production in, 53; analysis of overseers in, 58–63; slave mortality rate in, 85; cholera epidemics in, 85–86; shooting of runaways in, 91, 98–99; use of dogs to track runaways in, 92; cruelty toward slaves in, 95, 96; laws protecting overseers in, 100; assassination of overseer in, 113–14; praise for overseers in, 115; exemption of overseers in, 141–42; impact of Civil War on plantation system in, 143, 147–56 *passim;* patriotism in, 144, 145–46; secession convention of, 145; outstanding overseers in, 170–72; conflict between planter and steward in, 187–90
Loussade, Raymond, overseer, 24
Lower Bremo plantation, 144
Lowndes County, Miss.: cotton production in, 53; analysis of overseers in, 62–63; poor quality of overseers in, 132–33; tenure of stewards in, 183; Cocke plantations in, 191, 194; mentioned, 26

McCall, Henry, planter, 28
McCants, L. W., overseer: elected sheriff of Colleton District, S. C., 49
McClellan, George B., 150
McCollam, Andrew, planter, 24, 91, 143
McDonogh, John, planter, 18
McMillan, G. V., overseer, 142
Macon County, Ala., 108
Macon County, Ga., 174
Magnolia plantation: suboverseers on, 13, 96, 154; carpenter wages on, 36; slave epidemics on, 85; shooting of slave on, 96; house accorded retired overseer on, 115–16, 171; prayer of overseer on, 145; impact of Civil War upon, 147, 153–56
Manigault, Charles, planter: on suboverseers, 14; slave mortality on plantations of, 85; slave discipline on plantations of, 92, 165; mentioned, 13, 25, 164
Manigault, Louis, planter: on apprehension of runaways, 91; on changing of overseers, 125; evaluates overseer William Capers, 164, 166
Manning, J. L., planter, 61, 171
Marlborough plantation, 13

Marlbourne plantation: slave foreman on, 17–18; flight of Negroes from, during Civil War, 150; destroyed during Civil War, 152
Marshall, Levin, planter, 9, 180
Mason, Grief G., overseer, 28, 148
Massie, William, planter: accuses overseer of brutality, 96; criticizes overseers, 106, 112–13
Matanza plantation, 98
Meherrin plantation, 182
Memphis, Tenn., 68, 113, 176
Mercer, James, planter, 13, 23
Metcalfe, F. A., planter, 142
Metcalfe, James K., overseer, 113
Midland plantation, 44
Milledgeville, Ga., 101
Milliken's Bend, La., 125
Minor, William J., planter: instructions to overseers from, 46, 72, 93; limits slave punishments, 93; dismisses overseer, 113; and overseer problems during Civil War, 143, 148; mentioned, 61
Minty, Charles, overseer and carpenter, 143
Miscegenation: of overseers and slaves, 75–78, 167
Mississippi: as territory, 7; accounts of, by travelers, 7; number of large slaveholders in, 11–12; median slaveholdings in, 12; overseer wages in, 29; cotton production in, 53; illiterates in, 53, 61; analysis of overseers in, 61–63; duties of stewards in, 88, 179, 180; tracking of runaways in, 91–92, 215n95; cruelty toward slaves in, 95; overseers murdered by slaves in, 98, 100–101; praise for overseers in, 115; poor quality of overseers in, 132–33; impact of Civil War on plantation system in, 142–43, 146, 147, 152, 156; agricultural inventions in, 159; career of Garland D. Harmon in, 173–74; management of Cocke family holdings in, 181, 183, 191, 193–94
Mississippi Department of Archives and History: data on overseer wages in, 29
Mississippi River, 9, 42, 141
Mitchell, John, overseer, 22, 66
Montezuma, Ga., 174
Moore, John, planter, 171
Moore, John Hebron, historian: estimates overseer wages in Mississippi, 29
Moreton, John E., overseer, 114

Mount Airy estate, 18, 40
Mount Vernon estate: supervision of overseers on, 23, 180, 185; slaves feign illness on, 88; steward resides in mansion house on, 181; wages of overseers and stewards on, 182; William Pearce's stewardship of, praised, 186
Muddy Creek plantation, 26
Mulattoes: employed as overseers, 19
Mulkey, overseer for Rachel O'Connor, 76–77, 115
Murder: by overseers, 45, 95, 99, 113; incidence of, by slaves, 98; of overseers by slaves, 98, 100–101, 149; of overseers by planters, 113–14
Myers, James, suboverseer, 49–50
Myrick, Jordan, overseer, steward and planter: career of, 169–70; mentioned, 161, 182
Myrtle Grove plantation, 83, 187, 188, 189

Natchez, Miss.: plantations near, 30, 38, 45, 50, 91, 115, 180; mentioned, 47, 49, 123, 128, 135
Natchitoches Parish, La.: cotton production in, 53; analysis of overseers in, 61–63; impact of Civil War upon, 144, 149; mentioned, 28
Negroes: introduced into French Louisiana, 3; capacity for self-government of, 18; as overseers, 19; overseer attitude toward, 45, 78–79, 104, 166, 170–71; "tale-bearing" by, 104, 120, 121. See also Drivers; Foremen, Negro; Slaves
Nevitt, John, planter, 38
New Orleans, La.: free Negro overseers in, 19; in Civil War, 146, 147, 153; mentioned, 48, 86, 114, 134, 179
Newstead plantation, 142
Nicol, Andrew, overseer and steward, 160–62, 182
Nightingale Hall plantation, 141
Nomini Hall plantation, 120
Northampton County, N. C.: cotton production in, 53; analysis of overseers in, 55–56; slave discipline in, 90
North Carolina: number of large slaveholders in, 11–12; contract negotiations in, 20; crop shares in, 31–32; hired slaves in, 35; yeoman farmers seek overseeing positions in, 43; cotton production in, 53; tobacco production in, 53; analysis of overseers in, 55–56; number of overseers exempted in, 140;

impact of Civil War on plantation system in, 148

O'Connor, Rachel, planter, 76-77, 115
Oden, Thomas, overseer, 27, 168
Oktibbeha County, Miss., 98
Olmsted, Frederick Law: characterizes overseers, 7; describes organization of cotton plantation, 9; on severity of overseers, 78-79; praises "task system," 81-82; lauds Mississippi steward, 181; mentioned, 16, 88, 98
Orange Grove plantation, 8
Ossabaw Island, Ga., 13
Overseers: in colonial America, 3-4; three categories of, 5-6; criticized by agricultural reformers and planters, 6; anomalous position of, 6; described by travelers, 7-8, 171-72; incidence of employment, 10; wages of, 13, 27-34, 123-25, 132, 197; statutory provisions relating to, 14, 16, 100, 139-40, 147; dismissal of, 16, 22, 24, 38, 41, 77, 95, 96, 107, 111-14 passim, 143, 144, 148, 190; contract negotiations with, 20-21; mode of hiring, 21-23; praised by planters, 22, 77, 91, 115, 139, 160, 164, 166, 176; termination of contracts with, 23-24, 40, 114, 185; engaged on trial, 24; provisions of contracts with, 25-26, 124; fringe benefits for, 25; bonus agreements with, 30-31; on crop shares, 31-34, 156-57; and conflict with planters, 33-34, 72, 102-37 passim; slaves hired out by, 34-35, 163; wages of, compared with other plantation employees, 35-36; housing of, 36, 38; tenure of, 38-40, 125-27, 129, 197, 200; rotation of, 40; background, 41-43, 56-57, 60, 61-63, 160, 162, 163; migration of, to Lower South, 42, 60, 62-63; social status of, 44-45, 196-97; isolation of, 45-46, 97, 132, 197; attitude toward slaves of, 45, 78-79, 90, 104, 170-71; aspirations of, 46-47, 177, 198; advance to independent farming status by, 47-48, 168; property of, 48, 54-66 passim, 145, 160, 163, 171, 172, 200; advance to planter status by, 48-49, 135, 162, 163, 169, 171; literacy of, 53-66 passim, 71; slaveholdings of, 54-66 passim, 172; age of 55-65 passim, 198, 200; marital status of, 54-65 passim, 200, major responsibilities of,

67-68, 139; instructions to, 68-75, passim, 82, 83-84, 116, 118, 120; restricted as to slave punishment, 69-70, 83-84, 93-94, 120-21; duties of, 67-74, 82, 84-86; status of, on absentee units, 72-74; and miscegenation with slaves, 75-78, 167; punishment of slaves by, 78-79, 83-84, 88-101 passim, 121, 167, 172; cruelty to slaves by, 78-79, 94-97, 112, 121; difficult position of, 79-80, 132; and relations with drivers, 82-84, 165, 168, 173; attacked by slaves, 90, 91, 96, 98-101; complaints by, 103-104, 116-25 passim, 131-32, 170-71; qualities sought in, 104-105, 180; shortcomings of, 105-13 passim; reasons for dismissal of, 112-13; misbehavior of, during Civil War, 113, 148, 156; treated generously by employers, 114-16, 171; division of responsibility between planters and, 116-18, 198-99; defend their occupation, 117, 118, 122, 131-32, 161-62, 174; planters undermine authority of, 120-21; defended by planters, 126-27, 129-31; planters recognize importance of, 127-28; incapacity of, in Lower South, 132-33, 196; shortage of, during Civil War, 139, 142-43; exemption of, during Civil War, 139-42, 144; patriotism of, 144-46, 174, 176; supervise slaves working on fortifications, 147; payment of, during Civil War, 156-57; transition of, to free labor system, 157; inventive genius displayed by, 159; wages of, compared with stewards, 182; and conflict with stewards, 188, 190-91; stereotyped image of, 195, 196
Overseer system: introduced into America, 3; in French Louisiana, 3; suggestions for improvement of, 130-36 passim, 175; planters blamed for deficiencies in, 133-34, 137, 196-98, 201; insoluble maladies afflicting, 137, 198-99; proof of success of, 201
Owsley, Frank Lawrence, historian: on literacy of Southerners, 65-66

Pace, Seneca, overseer, 144
Page, John W., overseer, 30, 43
Parnell, Henry, steward, 140, 143
Patrick, overseer for Rachel O'Connor, 76-77, 115
Pearce, William, steward: receives advice

from George Washington, 88, 185; duties of, 180, 181; lauded by Washington, 186–87

Peebles, Robert R., overseer, 157

Perkins, John, Jr., planter, 95, 140, 143, 179, 181

Petite Anse Island, La., 48, 157

Pettigrew, Charles, planter, 43

Pettigrew, Ebenezer, planter: employs slave foreman, 19; employs sons as overseers, 43; demoralization of slaves on plantation of, 84; mentioned, 35, 88

Pettigrew, William, planter, 43

Pettus, John Jones, Governor of Mississippi, 95

Pharsalia plantation, 112–13

Philips, Martin W., planter and agricultural reformer: prefers southern overseers, 42; and troubles with overseers, 109; on subordination of overseers, 117–18; as agricultural reformer, 123; on overseer pay, 124; on overseer responsibilities, 128; condemns overseers, 131; urges better treatment for overseers, 133–34; employs G. D. Harmon as overseer, 174, 175

Phillips, Ulrich Bonnell, historian: on crop-share system, 32; on incidence of slave crime, 98; on J. A. Randall's fiery prayer, 145

Physicians: criticize owner-overseer tampering with sick slaves, 86–87; paucity of in rural South, 87

Pimlico plantation, 34

Pitman, Harman, overseer, 22, 115

Plantation agents. See Stewards

Plantation books: maintenance of, by overseers, 71–72, 105; value of, 72

Plantation managers. See Overseers; Stewards

Plantations: leasing of, to overseers, 4, 156–57; number of, in various staple regions, 10; simultaneous management of, by single overseer, 12–13; regulations governing, 68–70, 183–85; types of labor organization on, 80–82. See also Absentee estates

Planters: sons of, as overseers, 5, 43, 56, 60, 61; dispraise overseers, 6, 16, 72, 77, 105–13 passim, 117–19, 122, 125, 131, 143, 148, 198; owning more than a hundred slaves, 11–12; dispense with overseers, 16–17; correspondence among, regarding overseers, 21–22, 96; praise

overseers, 22, 77, 91, 115, 139, 160, 164, 166, 176; and contracts with overseers, 23–26, 124; and conflict with overseers, 33–34, 72, 102–37 passim; and social relations with overseers, 44–45; overseers rise to status of, 48–49, 135, 162, 163, 169, 171; categories of, in sugar parishes, 59–60; instructions to overseers by, 68–75 passim, 82, 83–84, 93–94, 116, 118, 120; views of, on slave management, 74–75; 88, 126–27, 139; limit slave punishments, 93–94; rebuke overseers for severity toward Negroes, 96, 97, 121, 173; chastise slaves for insubordination, 100; failure of, to appreciate overseers' problems, 103, 197, 198; treat overseers generously, 114–16, 171; division of responsibility between overseers and, 116–18, 198–99; undermine authority of overseers, 120–21; defend overseers, 126–27, 129–31; change overseers capriciously, 125–27, 197; recognize importance of overseers, 127–28; blamed for deficiencies in overseer system, 133–34, 137, 196–98, 201; protest conscription of overseers, 139–42, 201; sons of, as stewards, 181–82; instructions to stewards by, 183–85; and relations with stewards, 186–90, 200

Plaquemines Parish, La.: hired slaves in, 35; sugar production in, 53; analysis of overseers in, 59–60; impact of Civil War upon, 145–46, 147; mentioned; 13, 24, 52, 92, 115

Pleasant Hill plantation, 17

Pointe Coupee Parish, La., 42

Point Farm: sugar plantation owned by R. R. Barrow, 187, 188, 189

Polk, James Knox: dismisses overseer, 112

Port Royal, Va., 17

Powell, Richard D., steward: estate of, 63; saves overseer from embarrassment, 80; opposes slave requisitions, 147; advises concentration on subsistence crops, 149; purchases land for employer, 179; social status of, 181; long tenure of, 183; seeks ouster of overseer, 190–91; career of, 191–94

Powell, Richard D., Jr., physician, 192

Powell, Smith, overseer, 144, 192

Powhatan County, Va., 182

Prince George County, Va.: grain pro-

duction in, 53; analysis of overseers in, 55; impact of Civil War upon, 150; mentioned, 24
Prince George Parish, S. C., 58
Pringle, James R., planter, 165
Prudhomme, Pierre Phanor, planter, 28, 144, 149
Prudhomme Guard, 144
Pugh, Alexander Franklin, planter: punishes insolent slave, 100; pushes corn production during war, 149; slave insubordination on plantations of, 152; engages overseer on crop shares, 156

Quine, Alfred, overseer, 152

Randall, Joseph Acquilla, overseer: recounts shooting of slave, 96; proffered house after retirement, 116, 171; comments on Civil War, 145–46, 147, 153–54; career of, 171; mentioned, 13, 155, 170
Randolph, Mrs. John Hampden, planter, 156
Rankin County, Miss., 43
Rapides Parish, La.: median slaveholdings in, 12; management of Lewis Thompson's sugar plantation in, 21, 28, 39, 41, 170; sends overseer as delegate to secession convention, 145
Rawls, Moore, overseer: recommends overseer, 21; wages of, 28; complains of isolation, 46; treats ailing slaves, 86; punishes slave for feigning illness, 88; describes duties during rolling season, 103; career of, 170–71
Reagan, John Henninger: brief overseeing career of, 50
Reeves, Hiram, overseer, 30, 124
Reid, Robert R., overseer, 32
Reid, Samuel McDowell, planter, 145
Residence plantation, 24, 83, 187–90 passim
Retreat plantation, 172–73
Reynolds, J. Alston, overseer: invents rice planting machine, 159
Reynolds, J. D., overseer, 40
Rhodes, William, steward, 95, 179, 181
Rice: plantations, number of, 10; area produced in, 52; volume of production, 53; culture, 56, 81, 169; use of "task system" in production of, 81–82; invention of machine for planting, 159
Richardson, F. D., planter, 81, 147

Richmond, La., 176
Richmond County, Va.: grain production in, 53; analysis of overseers in, 55–56; mentioned, 18, 32
Rich Square, N. C., 43
River Place plantation, 38, 115
Robinson, overseer for Francis T. Leak, 22
Roman, Alfred, planter, 8, 94
Ross Wood plantation, 30, 43, 124
Rotterdam plantation, 85
Rowland, Creed T., overseer, 26
Ruffin, Edmund: praises slave foreman, 17–18; dispraises overseers, 106, 124–25; discharges overseers for cruelty, 112; Negroes flee plantation of, 150; praises overseer Andrew Nicol, 160–61; praises farm of Richard Sampson, 163; mentioned, 14
Ruffin, Edmund, Jr., planter, 150, 152
Ruffin, James H., lawyer and planter, 72
Ruffin, Julian C., planter, 9, 18
Ruffin, Thomas, judge and planter, 43, 75
Runaway slaves: punishment of, 70, 92–93, 121; reasons for, 89–90, 100, 172, 173; apprehension of, 90–92
Russell, William Howard, English journalist: describes overseers, 8, 79, 171–72; on miscegenation, 76
Ruthven farm, 9

St. Albans plantation, 180
St. James Parish, La.: cholera epidemic in, 85
St. John the Baptist Parish, La.: slave revolt in, 14
St. Luke Parish, S. C.: analysis of overseers in, 58
St. Mary Parish, La.: outstanding overseers in, 48, 171; sugar production in, 52, 53; analysis of overseers in, 59–61; exemption of overseers in, 141; impact of Civil War upon, 147; mentioned, 81
St. Paul Parish, S. C., 49
St. Simons Island, Ga., 168
Salaries. See Wages
Sampson, Richard, overseer and planter, 162–63, 182
Sandy Point estate, 161
Sanford, A. M., overseer, 13
Santee River, S. C., 83, 165
Santo Domingo: slave revolt in, 170
Sapelo Island, Ga., 16
Savannah River, 14, 164

Seabrook, Whitemarsh B.: on social status of overseers, 44; dispraises overseers, 105–106; favors agricultural schools, 134

Sea Island cotton, 16, 168

Seale, H. M., overseer, 61, 79

Semple, James, steward, 183

Sergeant, James, overseer, 25

Sevier County, Tenn., 50

Sharkey, William Lewis, judge and planter, 46

Sharp, R. H., steward, 183

Shaw, H. B., planter: complains of overseer misbehavior during Civil War, 156

Sherman, William T., 174

Shoe Buckle plantation, 32

Silver Bluff plantation, 107

Singleton, L. L., overseer, 190–91

Sitterson, Joseph Carlyle, historian: estimates overseer wages in Louisiana, 29

Slann's Island plantation, 31, 32, 49

Slave catchers, 91–92

Slaveholders. See Planters

Slaves: number controlled by each overseer, 8–9; areas of greatest concentration, 11–12; median holdings of, 12; hiring of, 34–35; welfare emphasized, 69–70, 71, 85–86, 104, 160, 173, 183–84; medical care of, 69, 84–87; discipline of, 69–70, 74–75, 120–21, 167–68, 173; breeding and rearing, 69, 183–84; limits on punishment of, 70, 93–94, 120–21; miscegenation with overseers, 75–78, 167; punishment of, 78–79, 83–84, 88-101 passim, 121, 167, 172; cruelty toward, by overseers, 78–79, 94–97, 112, 121; attitude of, toward overseers, 79–80, 163; organization of, for agricultural labor, 80–82; mortality rate among, 85; feign illness, 88–89; runaways, 89–93, 100, 121, 167, 172, 173; resistance of, to overseers, 90, 91, 96, 98-101, 149; shooting of, by overseers, 91, 95, 96, 99; minor transgressions of, 94, 98; docility of, during Civil War, 138; requisition of, during Civil War, 146–47, 150; insubordination of, during Civil War, 150, 152–55; suicide of, 165. See also Drivers; Foremen, Negro; Negroes

Smart, William W., overseer: as delegate to Louisiana secession convention, 145

Smith, Boyd, steward, 180

Smith, E. Kirby, 141

Smith, J. C., overseer, 31

Smith, Jonas, overseer, 87

Smith, Josiah, Jr., steward, 89

Snyder, Alonzo, judge: letters to, 114, 156

Soil of the South: copies of, furnished to overseers, 136

Somerset estate, 95, 179, 182

South Carolina: number of large slaveholders in, 11–12; median slaveholdings in, 12; law requiring use of overseers in, 16; overseer wages in, 29; payment by crop shares in, 32; overseer tenure in, 39; background of overseers in, 41, 56–57; agricultural societies in, 44, 105, 122, 134, 169; overseers elected to political offices in, 49; rice production in, 52, 53; analysis of overseers in, 56–58, 65; use of "task system" in, 81–82; scarcity of competent overseers in, 106; legislature of, 134; exemption of overseers in, 139–42; in Civil War, 144; outstanding overseers in, 161, 163–66, 169–70; superior quality of overseers in, 199

Southdown plantation, 143

Southern Agriculturist, 18, 127, 167

Southern Cultivator: articles in, 105, 106, 118, 122, 125, 126, 130, 131–32, 175; distribution to overseers urged, 135; mentioned, 174

Southern nationalism: overseer G. D. Harmon crusades for, 175–76

Southern Planter, 33, 34, 136, 163

South Hampton plantation, 168

South Yadkin plantation, 142, 159

Spalding, Thomas, planter, 16

Sparkman, James R., planter and physician, 86, 141, 142

Sparks, Thomas H., planter and jurist, 173, 177

Springfield plantation, 35

Stampp, Kenneth M., historian: on severity of overseers, 78; on planter dissatisfaction with overseers, 105

Stanbrough, James M., overseer and steward, 182

Stanford, Alexander, overseer, 95

Statutes. See Laws

Stewards: property holdings of, 56, 63, 187, 191; punishment of slaves by, 88, 180; complain of overseer conscription, 140; denounce slave requisitions, 147; former overseers become, 160, 161, 163,

168, 169, 182; duties of, 168–69, 179–80, 182, 186, 193; two categories of, 178; supervision of overseers by, 179, 184–85; management of slaves by, 180, 193; social status of, 181, 191, 200; wages of, compared with overseers, 182; tenure of, 183, 201; instructions to, 183–85; and relations with planters, 186–90, 200; and conflict with overseers, 188, 190–91, 201

Stoke plantation, 85

Stokes County, N. C.: tobacco production in, 53; analysis of overseers in, 55–56; mentioned, 26, 32, 40, 183

Straughan, Samuel L., overseer, 120–21

Stubbs, Archibald, overseer, 43

Suboverseers: discussed, 13–14; dismissed after shooting slave, 96; mentioned, 49, 60, 154, 161

Sugar: plantations, number of, 10; plantations, wages on, 35–36; area produced in, 52; volume of production, 53; harvest, 188–90; windrowing of, 189, 226n35

Sugar houses: scene within described, 8; repairs to equipment in, 188–89; mentioned, 103

Sugar makers: wages of, 36; employed as overseers, 41

Sykes, Jem, slave foreman: lauded by Edmund Ruffin, 17–18

Syphret, Henry G., overseer, 111

Tait, Charles, planter, 35

Tait, James A., planter, 49, 77

Talbot, Benjamin, overseer, 42

Tappan, Arthur, abolitionist, 17

"Task System": as method of organizing slave labor, 80–82

Tayloe, W. H., planter, 18, 32–33, 40

Taylor, Francis, planter, 44

Taylor, John of Caroline: on evils of crop-share system, 33; on wasteful methods of agriculture, 122–23

Taylor, Maj. Gen. Richard, 141, 148

Telfair, Alexander, planter: requires reports from absentee overseers, 74; defines a task, 82; limits slave punishments, 94; mentioned, 172

Telfair, Mary, planter, 173

Tennessee: planters, 80, 125, 126–27, 130; mentioned, 50, 60, 63

Tenure: of overseers, 38–40, 125–27, 197, 200; examples of brevity, 38–39; not

necessarily indicative of competence, 39, 125–26; consequences of brevity, 127, 129; of stewards, 183, 201

Terrebonne Parish, La.: sugar production in, 53; analysis of overseers in, 59–61; shooting of runaway in, 91; overseer problems in, during Civil War, 143, 148; conflict between planter and steward in, 187–90; mentioned, 52

Texas: secession convention in, 50; conscription of overseers in, 140; mentioned, 141

Thibodaux, La., 152

Thompson, Joseph M., overseer, 141

Thompson, Lewis, planter: asked for overseer recommendation, 21; receives overseer applications, 22, 23, 43; employs former railroad overseer, 42; on social status of overseers, 44; mentioned, 28, 39, 41, 46, 86, 88, 170

Thompson, Thomas, planter, 44

Thorn Island plantation, 74, 82, 94

Tobacco: overseer bonuses based on production of, 31; volume of production, 53; abandoned as unprofitable, 162; culture, 184–85

Tone, slave foreman for Eli J. Capell, 17

Torbert, James M., planter, 96, 108–109

Townsend, George, overseer, 25

Traylor, James, farmer, 48

Traylor, John G., overseer: career of, 47–48

Traylor, Joseph B., overseer and steward, 182

Turner, Alexander, overseer, 61

Tuscaloosa, Ala., 47

Twelve Mile Run plantation, 32

Tyler, overseer for John B. Grimball, 31

United Agricultural Society of South Carolina, 44, 105, 134

Upper South: social and economic features of, 54; characteristics of overseers in, 55, 64; migration of overseers from, 60, 62–63; overseer misconduct in, during Civil War, 148

Utica, Miss., 173

Van Buren, A. DePuy, traveler: characterizes overseers, 7–8

Vandivier, T. L., overseer, 94

Velasco plantation, 36, 92

Viamede plantation, 95

Vicksburg, Miss.: during Civil War, 146, 152

Villa plantation, 169

Virginia: number of large slaveholders in, 11–12; median slaveholdings in, 12; slave foremen in, 17–18; resorts in, 17, 18, 181, 192; contract negotiations in, 20–21; payment by crop shares in, 31–32; hired slaves in, 35; overseer tenure in, 39; background of overseers in, 41, 42, 56; prominent families in, 44; grain production in, 53; analysis of overseers in, 55–56; incidence of slave crime in, 98; agricultural societies in, 129; overseers exempted from military service in, 140; overseer attitude toward war in, 144–45; impact of Civil War on plantation system in, 147, 148, 150, 152; outstanding overseers in, 159–63; planters' sons apprenticed as stewards in, 181–82; wages of overseers and stewards in, 182; steward tenure in, 183; instructions to stewards in, 183–85

Virginia Company: introduces overseer system, 3

Virginia Gazette, 23

Wade, Walter, planter and physician, 30, 43, 124

Wages: of suboverseers, 13; of overseers, 13, 27–34, 123–25, 132, 197; proportion received at contract termination, 23; during trial period, 24; and bonus provisions, 30–31; in crop shares, 31–32; of other plantation employees, 36; of stewards, compared with overseers, 182

Wailes, Benjamin L. C., planter and naturalist, 95

Walker, Owen, overseer, 25–26

Walkinshaw, James, overseer, 149

Wallace, L. P., overseer, 145

Ward, Noah A., overseer, 46

Warren County, Miss., 75, 152

Washington, George: on termination of contracts, 23; instructions to absentee overseer from, 73; on health care of slaves, 85–86; on slaves feigning sickness, 88; accuses overseers of brutality toward slaves, 94–95; criticizes overseers, 107; on qualities desired in overseers, 180; counsels steward on supervision of overseers, 185; lauds steward William Pearce, 186–87

Washington County, Miss., 142

Waterloo plantation, 61, 113

Weeks, David, planter: letters to, 76

Weeks, Mrs. Mary C., planter: letters to, 76, 99–100

Welton, Arad, overseer, 35

West Feliciana Parish, La.: tracking of runaways with dogs in, 92

West Indies, 3

Weston, P. C., planter: emphasizes concern for welfare of slaves, 71; on slave discipline, 74–75, 93

White, John, overseer, 5

White, Maunsel, planter: engages overseer on trial, 24; stresses welfare of slaves, 71; shows compassion for overseers, 114; delivers ultimatum to overseer, 119; mentioned, 13, 39–40, 41, 88, 157

White, Maunsell, Jr., planter, 36, 92, 157

White, W. C., overseer, 154

White Hill plantation, 24, 48, 148

Wickham, John, planter, 162

Wilcox County, Ala., 35

Wilkins, John L., planter, 35

Wilson, William, overseer, 32

Witherspoon, John M., steward, 183

Wood, Albert, overseer, 144

Woodland plantation: slave insubordination on, 153

Yalobusha County, Miss., 112

Yazoo County, Miss.: cotton production in, 53; analysis of overseers in, 61–63; mentioned, 179

Yazoo-Mississippi Delta: A. De Puy Van Buren travels through, 7; median slaveholdings in, 12; plantations in, 68, 94, 142

Yeoman farmers: overseers drawn from families of, 41, 42–43, 56, 61, 162, 173; overseers aspire to become, 41; overseers advance to status of, 47–48

Yost, George W. N., overseer: invents plow and cotton scraper, 159